School Library and Media Center Acquisitions Policies and Procedures

School Library and Media Center Acquisitions Policies and Procedures

Edited by Mary M. Taylor

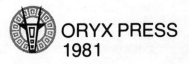

ORYX PRESS
1981

The rare Arabian Oryx is believed to have inspired the myth of the unicorn. This desert antelope became virtually extinct in the early 1960s. At that time several groups of international conservationists arranged to have 9 animals sent to the Phoenix Zoo to be the nucleus of a captive breeding herd. Today the Oryx population is nearing 300 and herds have been returned to reserves in Israel, Jordan, and Oman.

Copyright © 1981 by The Oryx Press
2214 North Central at Encanto
Phoenix, Arizona 85004

Published simultaneously in Canada

Printed and Bound in the United States of America

Library of Congress Cataloging in Publication Data

Main entry under title:

School library and media center acquisitions
    policies and procedures.

    Bibliography: p.
    Includes index.
    1. School libraries—Acquisitions.   2. Instruc-
tional materials centers—Acquisitions.   I. Taylor,
Mary M., 1949–
Z689.S337   025.2'1878   80-23115
ISBN 0-912700-70-X

To my children, Jean and Peter,
and to my partner in
their parenting, Lynne Cocio

Contents

Preface

In 1977, The Oryx Press published a book edited by Elizabeth Futas dealing with acquisitions policies for both academic and public libraries. This book, *Library Acquisition Policies and Procedures*, was designed for library school students, librarians, and publishers as an aid both in understanding the selection process and in developing selection policies.

Because school libraries and media centers differ from academic and public libraries in many ways, it was felt that a book delineating their acquisitions needs would be a valuable tool.

Thus, *School Library and Media Center Acquisitions Policies and Procedures* is designed to examine the acquisitions process in school libraries and media centers. It is intended as an aid in policy development and as a study on how these institutions are handling the selection and ordering process today.

The first and one of the most radical differences between school libraries and other types of libraries relates to nomenclature. School libraries, more than other types of libraries, have been inundated with the multimedia approach to materials collection. Most, if not all, libraries make use of the audiovisual hard- and software now available, but it is in the school setting where the impact has been most felt. In the public and academic sector, centers for all media are still known as libraries, taking their name from the Latin for "book"; in the schools, they are referred to in a variety of terms. We now use the terms "library," "media center," or "learning resource (or resources) center" to refer to what was once the "school library." For the purpose of clarification, the term "library media center" (LMC) will be used in this book to cover this broad spectrum of terms.

Materials for this book were taken from a number of sources. In the spring and fall of 1979, requests for policies were sent to schools and districts throughout the United States. Two hundred thirty-three policies were received; 153 schools and districts reported that they had no policies. Many of these recognized the need for a policy and were either working on them or hoped to in the near future. Fifteen of the policies have been reprinted in full, selected for their representativeness in a number of categories including size, geographic location, and content. In addition, 33 partial policies are reprinted to cover specific areas more fully or some areas not covered in full policies.

Because the policies are primarily designed in broad theoretical terms, a questionnaire was developed and sent out nationally to schools and districts asking specifics on the acquisitions process as practiced by their schools. An analysis of that survey has been included. This is preceded by a brief introduction outlining a literature search undertaken to analyze trends which have impact on the acquisitions process in LMCs.

In addition, ordering instructions from policies, sample forms, and other purchasing aids are included in a section relegated to procedures designed to aid the acquisition of materials.

The policies received and examined make one fact very clear. Policies and procedures for selection of materials differ dramatically from school to school, each fitting a particular set of needs. This collection is designed as a cross section of existing policies. The editor and publisher have applied their best efforts in this collection and have no legal responsibility for any errors and omissions. The full and partial policies in this book have been printed, for the most part, as they were received from the school districts, the only changes made having been for standardization or as normal copy editing procedures.

Acknowledgements

I would like to express my appreciation to those librarians and media specialists who submitted policies and questionnaires, making this book possible.

I would also like to give a special thanks to Carol Suplicki, Sandy Sivertson, Dee Brubaker, and John Davis, who, in their individual ways, have assisted me.

Mary M. Taylor

Introduction

Library media centers (LMCs) apply two distinct categories to their acquisitions process: selection and purchasing. Parts I and II of this book, *Full Policies* and *Partial Policies*, are concerned primarily with the selection process itself—criteria set for the LMC collection. A few of the policies included do give specific details on how to purchase, but in general policies are designed with vague generalities. Part III, *Procedures*, suggests aids for the purchasing of materials after selection. Both policies and procedures are important to a successful acquisitions process.

In 1975, the controversial *Media Programs: District and School* was published. Library media specialists argued for its principles and against its practicality and thought that the book's goals for collection size and staff were unattainable with present budgets and standards. Considered by many to be a utopian document, its general goals are still important to LMCs. *Media Programs* stresses the importance of a policy for selection of materials:

> Formulation of a district media selection policy which guides the selection of materials and equipment is coordinated by the director of the district media program. This policy, developed cooperatively with representation of media staff, administrators, consultants, teachers, students, and other community members, is adopted by the board of education as official district policy.
>
> The media selection policy reflects basic factors influencing the nature and scope of collections, such as curriculum trends, innovations in instruction, research in learning, availability of materials and equipment, the increased sophistication of youth, and the rising expectations of teachers and students. It establishes the objectives of media selection; identifies personnel participating in selection and their roles; enumerates types of materials and equipment to be considered with criteria for their evaluation, as well as criteria for evaluating materials in specific subject areas; and defines procedures followed in selecting materials, including initial selection, reexamination of titles in existing collections, and handling challenged titles.
>
> The selection policy reflects and supports principles of intellectual freedom described in the *Library Bill of Rights*, the *School Library Bill of Rights for School Library Media Center Programs*,

The Students' Right to Read, and other professional statements on intellectual freedom. Procedures for handling questioned materials follow established guidelines and are clearly defined.[1]

In fact, one rarely finds reference to the selection process *without* mention of the acquisitions policy in any of the literature on the subject. Professional librarians and media center specialists are well aware that an acquisitions policy is needed by all libraries and media centers, but many do not have one.

The 2 most frequently cited reasons for failure to have an acquisitions policy are limitations of time and information. No one can deny that writing a policy takes a great deal of time and effort, but it can clarify certain issues for LMC specialists and the public they serve. As money gets tighter and the public becomes more active regarding censorship, the selection policy will become an invaluable tool to the LMC staff.

A number of factors must be considered in the formulation of an acquisitions policy. The first is an evaluation of the population serviced by a particular LMC. For the LMC specialists, this involves a knowledge of the community and the curriculum taught within the school. Most policies state that their basic goal is to meet the needs of all the students, and to do so, this total group must first be identified.

Another factor is an evaluation of current practices used in the selection process. Areas of strength and weakness need to be examined in the context of present purchasing priorities. The externally imposed limits are a third factor. Budgets are fast becoming the major limitation shared by all LMCs, and space limitations are also a critical factor.

LeRoy Merritt stresses the fact that policies and collections will vary because of these factors. He states:

> To use the policy effectively in the selection process and to defend the collection successfully, the staff must have had the experience of thinking through and writing the policy statement.[2]

Thus, the policies included here should be used as examples only. All should be examined in terms of their usefulness to a particular setting.

Most policies are comprised of the following parts: an introduction, including philosophy, goals, and objectives; methods of selection; and methods for reconsideration of materials.

The first section of most policies includes a variety of items. First, it may include a description of the community served, as well as a statement on who is responsible for materials selection. Most policies also include in this section the American Library Association's (ALA) statements concerning intellectual freedom. In this section, one also finds the philosophy, goals, and objectives of the particular LMC.

This is followed by the specifics of the selection process and may include selection aids used in collection development, as well as specific criteria used in the selection process. In some policies this section is very brief, while in others it is both lengthy and detailed.

Because the selection process involves elimination of materials already found in the collection, as well as the acquisition of new materials, most policies include some rationale for their removal. Two reasons are usually cited for removal: the existence of outdated materials and the existence of materials of questioned social value. The practice of "weeding" accomplishes the removal of materials that are outdated, worn-out, or just unused, taking up valuable shelf space. In his book, *Weeding Library Collections*, Slote states:

> It has long been an expressed standard of libraries to weed collections on a regular basis. . . . In spite of the advice, however, it has been observed and reported that too little weeding is being practiced and that library shelves contain quantities of unused and unwanted materials. It is hard to find a practicing librarian who feels that sufficient weeding is being done in his library.[3]

Slote goes on to say that at least 5 percent of the collection should be weeded annually, but few of the schools or districts responding to the questionnaire meet this goal.

The following are the most common reasons for failure to weed effectively:

1. Emphasis on judging collections in terms of numbers of items.
2. Lack of time. Weeding involves pulling not merely material, but cards in the catalog, shelflists and other necessary records.
3. Sacredness of collection. Books are considered by some to be valuable records, necessitating collection.
4. Conflicting criteria on removal practices.

Withdrawal of materials from use is also a result of public pressure, i.e., censorship. Almost without exception, methods for handling the reconsideration of materials of questioned social value were present in all policies, sometimes the *only* statement of any policy.

For LMC specialists, the conflict is First Amendment rights versus public use of public monies. LMC specialists advocate the public's right to know and regularly produce statements such as the *Library Bill of Rights* to stress this issue. Since 1978, numerous incidents of censorship of books and films have more deeply involved school LMCs and professional associations.

This question is particularly difficult in public schools because the LMC is expected to give students exemplary materials, and its users are all minors, still subject to parental control.

The newspapers and literature are full of incidents of censorship taking place in the schools today. Of those schools and districts responding to the questionnaire, over one-third have had materials questioned and have made use of the reconsideration process provided in their policy. According to statistics compiled by ALA's Office for Intellectual Freedom, 90 percent of book banning or censorship incidents take place in schools. Targets are classical as well as modern authors, and even dictionaries have not escaped the ban because they include words that some find objectionable.

The role of parents and their relationships to LMCs are significant:

> Just as parents can complain about the public library giving their minor child something they consider offensive, so do they also have an equal right to complain if the library refuses to provide materials which they consider important to their children. Libraries are educational and social institutions and librarians can get caught while attempting to be all things to all persons.[4]

Indeed, LMC specialists have been advised of the need to perform a delicate balancing act:

> Whatever happens, we must be alert to ensure that our collective intellectual freedom is not abrogated by a few. One individual should not impose her or his opinions on the majority. The majority cannot be allowed to deprive an individual of her or his right to information.[5]

Indications are that the public cry for censorship is going to become even more powerful in the future; it is the responsibility of the LMC specialist to ensure the rights of all the students against what may be a very vocal minority.

Once the selection process has taken place, the LMC specialist can proceed with the purchasing of materials desired. While a few policies stipulate procedures to follow, most do not deal with these specifically.

First, one must decide when to place an order. Daniel Melcher stresses the importance of ordering continuously:

> In too many elementary school libraries, it has long been routine to order annually in the spring and then wait 6 months or more for receipt of the books.[6]

He goes on to say that this practice presents an attitude to publishers and jobbers that LMC specialists don't care when these items are received, and it follows that they are in no hurry to get them to the schools. In response to item 15 on the questionnaire (''Are you required to order materials at or by a specific time?''), most LMC specialists have no specific dates set up for ordering, so materials can be purchased continuously. In some ways, the LMC specialists may have themselves to blame for poor service.

Another decision facing the LMC specialist is whether or not to use a jobber, and, if so, the selection of one. As reflected in both the questionnaires and the literature, ordering is done primarily through jobbers and through periodical subscription services. With the recent closing of a number of medium-sized jobbers, the market is now controlled by the 2 biggest, Baker and Taylor and Brodart. As the number of schools and districts required to get bids for library materials (as is done for other school supplies) grows, the trend toward monopoly will continue because these 2 are often the only jobbers able to make competitive bids.

> It is not pleasant for libraries to face the fact that they are very nearly in the same position (dealing with a monopoly) in dealing with the general book wholesalers, who can, and usually do, establish discounts as they wish, serve or not serve their customers at will, and change any or all policies arbitrarily.[7]

There is concern voiced on many fronts that the near monopoly of these jobbers limits access to publishers, resulting in a reduction of available children's books published each year because of profit limitations. Unlike the adult best-seller, which may sell millions and include paperback and movie rights, the very best of children's books will sell little more than 100,000 copies in hardback. Jobbers who distribute most publishers' output are undoubtedly adding impetus to this drive for profitability.

Suggestions to curb this development and the resulting poor service abound in the literature. Melcher suggests using more than one jobber in order to insure better service. Another suggestion is to order directly through the publisher.

In order to order more frequently and through a variety of sources, forms and purchase orders need to be simplified. With time in short supply to the LMC specialist, forms and procedures used in the acquisitions process need to be examined and cut to an absolute minimum.

Another necessary purchasing decision is whether to buy items pre-processed and cataloged. Individual circumstances will dictate such decisions, but the decision needs to be made based on all the information at hand. As Melcher states:

> All of us get our first lesson in economics in the home. There we grow up feeling that money is money, but time is only time. We tend to put no cash value on time.[8]

This is particularly true of the way many look at the cataloging and processing of new materials. Can the cataloging of materials be a priority for the busy librarian, when the materials can be purchased with catalog cards for an insignificant additional charge per item? Processing may be more cost-efficient in-house if parent or student volunteers are available. A number of districts, which have centralized processing available, responded that they order catalog cards when possible since they have found it to be most cost-effective. If those districts which are set up to provide centralized cataloging don't find it economical, then there is a *real* question of whether the LMC specialist with little access to union catalogs or computer technology can possibly achieve cost-effectiveness.

There is also emphasis in the literature that small libraries and media centers may be wise to join in purchasing materials to qualify for larger discounts. The growing need expressed for networking among school, public, and academic libraries may make such plans more feasible.

The need for an acquisitions policy seems to be the only absolute in the selection and purchasing process for school LMCs. The needs of each school and district can be met only by individual examination and formulation of both policy and procedures. There is every indication that funding is going to continue to be limited, that jobbers are going to become more powerful, possibly resulting in even poorer service, and that the public's clamor for censorship will increase. Trends indicate that the existence of an acquisitions policy and specific procedures for purchasing will become more and more necessary and important to individual school LMCs.

REFERENCES

1. American Association of School Librarians, Association for Educational Communications and Technology, *Media Programs: District and School* (Chicago: American Library Association; Washington, DC: Association for Educational Communications and Technology, 1975), pp. 64–65.
2. LeRoy Charles Merritt, *Book Selection and Intellectual Freedom* (New York: H. W. Wilson Company, 1970), p. 33.
3. Stanley J. Slote, *Weeding Library Collections* (Littleton, CO: Libraries Unlimited, Inc., 1975), p. 3.
4. Regina U. Minudri, "Irresistible Forces and Immovable Objects," *School Library Journal* 26 (4) (December 1979): 39.
5. Ibid.
6. Daniel Melcher, *Melcher on Acquisitions* (Chicago: American Library Association, 1971), p. 5.
7. Audrey B. Eaglen, "Book Distribution: Present Conditions and Implications for the Future," *School Library Journal* 26 (4) (December 1979): 57.
8. Melcher, *Melcher on Acquisitions*, p. 11.

BIBLIOGRAPHY

Bender, David R. "Networking & School Library Media Programs." *School Library Journal* 26 (3) (November 1979): 29–32.
Bonk, Wallace John, and Magrill, Rose Mary. *Building Library Collections*. 5th ed. Metuchen, NJ: Scarecrow Press, Inc., 1979.

Eaglen, Audrey B. "Book Wholesalers: Pros and Cons." *School Library Journal* 25 (2) (October 1978): 116–19.

―――. "More About the Discount Mess." *School Library Journal* 26 (2) (October 1979): 105–08.

―――. "Short Discount Shuffles—What It's All About." *School Library Journal* 25 (9) (May 1979): 30–33.

Futas, Elizabeth, ed. *Library Acquisition Policies and Procedures*. Phoenix, AZ: Oryx Press, 1977.

Katz, Bill, and Gellatly, Peter. *Guide to Magazine and Serial Agents*. New York: R. R. Bowker Company, 1975.

Miller, Marilyn. "How Long, Oh, Lord, Do We Roam in the Wilderness." *School Library Journal* 26 (4) (December 1979): 5–11.

Shapiro, Lillian L. "Celebrations and Condolences: A Time of Reckoning for the School Library." *School Library Journal* 26 (4) (December 1979): 13–18.

―――. "Quality or Popularity? Selection Criteria for YAs." *School Library Journal* 24 (9) (May 1978): 23–27.

Survey

Most of the acquisitions policies received and examined were constructed in broad, theoretical terms, although there were a few which were very explicit and detailed. This is not surprising when one considers that most are designed *only to guide* the school's library media center (LMC) and to give the community a rationale for spending, not to spell out practical day-to-day procedures. It was felt, however, that answers to more practical questions and input from schools having no formal policy would add to the usefulness of this book. To accomplish this, a questionnaire was developed, dealing with explicit detail involved in the acquisitions process. The questionnaire was mailed to 386 schools and school districts.

Questions for the survey came from a number of sources. Those questions asked in *Library Acquisition Policies and Procedures* which were relevant to school LMCs were used. Those requiring it were reworded to apply specifically, and new questions were added. The result was a 4-page questionnaire, divided into 6 parts, sent out in January 1980. The questionnaire was lengthy, but not time-consuming. Despite that, there was one negative response to its length, and there is no way of predicting how many did not respond because of its length.

A total of 157 questionnaires were returned. These came from throughout the United States and from schools and districts of varying sizes. Because the responses were from individual school LMCs and from entire districts, they were divided into these categories when it was felt necessary to clarify certain items and provide more meaningful data. Seventy-four were received from individual schools and 83 were submitted by school districts. As promised, confidentiality has been observed.

POPULATION SERVED

Question 1: If not included in your previous correspondence, please give a description of the population you serve, including the number of students and schools.

In all, questionnaires were returned by schools and districts in 36 states. Many states were represented only once, while a few were represented by more than 10. Large metropolitan school districts and small individual rural schools returned the questionnaire. Individual schools varied in size from 90 to 2,800 students; districts ranged from 269 students in 3 schools to approximately 62,000 students attending 152 schools.

CHART I   Student Population

Number Students	Number Schools	Number Students	Number Districts
2,000 & over	3	50,000 & over	5
1,500–1,999	6	25,000–49,999	5
1,000–1,499	12	10,000–24,999	10
750–999	9	7,500–9,999	9
500–749	4	5,000–7,499	11
250–499	17	2,500–4,999	14
1–249	3	1,000–2,499	18
		1– 999	10

BUDGET

Question 2: What is your budget for LMC materials? Is this based on student population?

Most responses to this question were given in a dollar amount for the school or entire district. There were a small number who responded with the per pupil allotment and, when possible, this was used in combination with the student enrollment to arrive at a total figure.

This figure varied tremendously from questionnaire to questionnaire. Two districts included personnel expenses in this budget figure, and a number included federal funding, as well. The data should be examined with this in mind. Although there are certain indications, no absolutes can be determined.

CHART II   LMC Materials Budget by Number of Schools

Budget	Number of Schools	Budget	Number of Schools
$25,000 & over	1	6,000–6,999	5
20,000–24,999	5	5,000–5,999	9
15,000–19,999	2	4,000–4,999	9
10,000–14,999	8	3,000–3,999	3
9,000– 9,999	4	2,000–2,999	3
8,000– 8,999	5	1,000–1,999	6
7,000– 7,999	9	1– 999	1

MATRIX I LMC Materials Budget by School Size

Number of Students \ Budget	$1–2,499	2,500–4,999	5,000–7,499	7,500–9,999	10,000–19,999	20,000 & over
2,000 & over				2		1
1,500–1,999		1			4	1
1,000–1,499			4	2	2	3
750– 999		1	2	4	3	2
500– 749	2	3	4	3	2	
250– 499	4	8	3	1		
1– 249	1	1	1			

CHART III   LMC Materials Budget by District

Budget	Number of Districts	Budget	Number of Districts
$200,000 & over	5	$30,000- 39,999	4
150,000 - 199,999	3	20,000 - 29,999	2
100,000 - 149,000	2	15,000 - 19,999	5
90,000 - 99,999	2	10,000 - 14,999	6
80,000 - 89,999	2	7,500 - 9,999	5
70,000 - 79,999	4	5,000 - 7,499	7
60,000 - 69,999	3	2,500 - 4,999	4
50,000 - 59,999	5	1 - 2,499	2
40,000 - 49,999	6		

MATRIX II   LMC Materials Budget by District Size

Number of Students \ Budget	$1–4,999	5,000–9,999	10,000–24,999	25,000–49,999	50,000–74,999	75,000–99,999	100,000 & over
50,000 & over						1	1
25,000–49,999					1		3
10,000–24,999		1		2	2	2	1
7,500– 9,999	1			2	2	1	1
5,000– 7,499		1	2	3	2	2	1
2,500– 4,999		3	1	2	3		1
1,000– 2,499	3	3	6	1	1		
1– 999	2	4	2				1

The amount spent per pupil varied tremendously in the survey. A number of schools spend less than $1.00 per student and 2 schools report over $25.00 spent per pupil. Another method used to arrive at a budget amount is to use a percentage of total budget. Although not nearly as common as funding per pupil, it is used by a limited number of schools and districts.

Many of the LMC specialists expressed concern over budget cuts. One specialist's budget was cut in half this year, and another's has been eliminated entirely for next year. As school budgets become tighter, it is apparent that funds will not be as available for LMCs.

Question 3: Are you currently receiving federal funding? If so, how much?

Most of the schools and districts receive some federal funding. Only one school which was nonfunded provided a reason. It stated:

> We have a district coordinator of federal funds and I can't convince him that the library can receive Title IVB funds.

Schools

Twenty-one school LMCs receive no federal funds. Of those who do receive such funds, 6 specify no amount. The remainder report funding, specifying a dollar amount. Most are Elementary and Secondary Education

Act (ESEA) Title IVB, 26 schools naming this source. Other sources listed were ESEA Title IVC and federal grants. The dollar amount of federal monies started at $200.00 and reached its peak at $15,000.

CHART IV   Federal Funding of School LMC Programs

Federal Funds	Number of Schools	Federal Funds	Number of Schools
$10,000 & over	2	$2,000-2,999	11
5,000-9,999	3	1,000-1,999	11
4,000-4,999	6	500 - 999	4
3,000-3,999	7	1- 499	3

Districts

Only 10 of the school districts receive no federal funds. Nine districts reported funds without specifying amounts. The remainder cited dollar amount of federal money going into the budget. Again, almost all receive funding through ESEA Title IVB, although 2 other limited sources of funding were given: ESEA Title I and Title IVC. The amount of funding represented was $550 to $226,605.

CHART V   Federal Funding of District Programs

Federal Funds	Number of Districts	Federal Funds	Number of Districts
$100,000 & over	4	$20,000- 29,999	9
75,000-99,999	2	10,000-19,999	13
50,000-74,999	2	5,000- 9,999	7
40,000-49,999	5	2,500- 4,999	10
30,000-39,999	2	500- 2,499	9

> Question 4: Is federal funding restricted for a certain purpose? If so, what?

About one-third of the LMCs and districts have no restrictions on federal funding. Thirty-seven must meet Title IVB guidelines, and another group spelled these out as guidance (12) and nonconsumable items (3). The remainder of the requirements listed are imposed at the state or district level and become contradictory. Seven schools may use the money for paperbacks while 6 are restricted from this. Almost a third must spend the money on materials only, and half of them divide it between materials and equipment. A small number (9) use the funds for equipment purchase exclusively.

Those LMCs receiving funds from other than ESEA Title IVB are only restricted by the terms of the grant.

Despite the feeling that "our district is very suspicious of federal funds because of strings," the federal funds seem to be given with a minimum of restrictions.

> Question 5: Is your budget categorized by type of material? If so, what is the breakdown, if available by type?

Individual schools and districts supplied similar information. Twenty-three do not classify budget by type, and 124 do so. Two types of categorization used by fewer than 5 of the centers are Dewey decimal classifications or building level. The majority of those having categories are based on type of material and the 120 remaining listed almost as many different categories. On all, books were listed, with supplies, periodicals, and AV materials listed frequently, followed by categories used infrequently: travel, repairs, film rentals, paperbacks, pamphlets, binding, furniture, data processing services, and contract services.

> Question 6: Are there any state minimum levels prescribed for LMC budgeting?

This question elicited contradictory answers. Most respondents reported that there are no state minimums; some said their state had guidelines, but nothing mandated; a number mentioned having to meet North Central Accreditation Standards. Seven schools or districts gave no response and over 20 reported that they did not know. One LMC specialist made the following statement:

> I have been trying to find a copy of state library standards for over a year now and even the state seems dumbfounded as to their standards and can't refer me to the right department for the standards.

Three responded that, although there were standards, they were not enforced. (See Appendix II for names and addresses of state education agencies that can provide this information.)

CHART VI   State Minimums for LMC Budgeting

State	No	Yes	Per Pupil Amount	Guidelines
Alaska	1			
Arizona	1			•
Arkansas	1			
California	1			
Connecticut	1			
Georgia		2	$2.50	
Hawaii	1			
Idaho	1			
Illinois		2		6
Indiana		1		3
Iowa	1			
Kansas	1	1	$6.00	
Kentucky		2	$2.50 Elem. $4.50 Second.	
Louisiana	1			
Massachusetts	1			1
Michigan	2	1		2
Minnesota	2	2		
Mississippi		2	$2.25	
Missouri	1	3	$6.00	
Nebraska		3		
New Hampshire		1		
New Jersey	4			
New York	5	1		1
North Carolina		1		1
Ohio	6	4		1
Oklahoma		1	$5.00	
Oregon	5			
Pennsylvania	3			4
Rhode Island		1		
South Dakota		1	$4.00	
Tennessee		1		
Texas	4	2		2
Virginia		3	$2.50 Elem. $3.50 Second.	
Washington	1	1		
Wisconsin	3	3	$2.75 K $5.50 1–12	
Wyoming	1			

SELECTION

> Question 7: Please list the major reference selection tools used by your LMC in order of preference.

Thirty-one of those schools and districts responding either had no answer to this question or answered "various." Of the 126 remaining questionnaires, 30 selection tools were listed. *Booklist* was cited most frequently, listed on 89 questionnaires. The H. W. Wilson catalogs were used by 73 library media centers and the *School Library Journal* was listed by 70 schools and districts. (See Part III for a list of selection tools.)

CHART VII   Most Frequently Used Selection Tools

Major Tools	Number of LMCs
Booklist	89
Wilson Catalogs	73
School Library Journal	70
Library Journal	27
Previews	17
Wilson Library Bulletin	16
New York Times Book Review	16
Horn Book	14
Elementary School Library Collection	11

> Question 8: What is your selection policy regarding materials for special children—gifted and mentally/physically handicapped?

Most schools and districts have no written or informal policy concerning selection of materials for special children. Many rely on recommendations from teachers and students to ensure meeting this need. A few actively seek out this material and appropriate a certain budget amount or receive funds from special education budgets. Over a quarter of the LMC specialists feel that providing for special students is part of the concept of meeting the needs of all the students. Thus, although policies are not explicit in these areas, a large number of specialists are seeing the need and are attempting to meet it.

Question 9: Are review copies of new or recently published materials available to you on a regular basis? Are you able to attend reviewing sessions with other LMC specialists?

A large number of LMCs do not have access to materials for examination prior to purchase, nor do they attend reviewing sessions, relying mainly on reviews in the various selection tools. Those LMCs and districts holding regular reviewing sessions do so as often as biweekly or as rarely as annually.

Schools

Fifty-three school LMCs stated that they do not have regular access to review materials, while 17 report access to these materials. Forty-seven never attend reviewing sessions, most of these citing their distance from other LMCs as the most common cause. Nineteen do attend regular reviewing sessions.

Districts

For districts, the number having access to review materials and reviewing sessions increased. Thirty-six do not have access to materials, while 42 do. Twenty-three have no regular reviewing sessions, while 21 reported that they do.

Question 10: Is approval required on purchases? If so, whose?

A number of schools and districts reported that approval is required on purchases. The majority stressed that individual purchases were not examined and approved but, rather, the total expenditure was considered. As one librarian stated:

> As long as the allotted money is not overspent and the materials fit special project criteria, my professional judgment is respected.

Schools

Twenty-five school LMCs do not require approval on purchases. When required, approvals by the building principal and the superintendent's office are most frequently used (19). A small number of schools reported that approval is required from such sources as the business office or department heads.

Districts

Eighteen school districts stated that no approval is required prior to purchase. Those districts which responded that approval is necessary cited LMC coordinators (18), superintendent's office (16), building level principals (14), business office (5), and teacher committees (4).

ORDERING

Question 11: Are materials ordered by individual schools or through the district?

Schools

Fifty-seven school LMCs order individually while 15 order through the district; only one reported using both channels.

Districts

As expected, district ordering services are provided far more often in this sampling. Only 28 of the districts reported that orders are sent from individual schools while 42 use the district services. Nine of the districts order both ways.

Question 12: Are the majority of your purchases ordered through a jobber or directly from a publisher? If you use a jobber, which one do you use?

Responses from individual schools and districts were virtually the same. Of all questionnaires returned, only 10 reported that they do not use a jobber. Sixty-four reported ordering both ways, many using the jobber for print and ordering audiovisual materials direct. A small number of schools reported sending orders out for bid to the various jobbers, and as more schools and districts are required to do so, jobbers will be used even more heavily than at present. Fewer than 5 of the schools responded that they were not using a jobber because of poor service.

Baker and Taylor is by far the most commonly used jobber, named by 101 schools and districts; 30 use Brodart; Bound to Stay Bound was mentioned by 11 districts. Over 20 jobbers were named in the questionnaire. (See Part III for a list of names and addresses of jobbers.)

> Question 13: Do you use a magazine subscription service? If so, which one?

Only 6 (4 percent) of all the reporting schools and districts do not subscribe to such services. EBSCO Services is used by 52 (35 percent) of the schools and districts; Moore-Cottrell is used by 31 (21 percent); Faxon is used by 11 (8 percent). A total of 19 subscription agencies were named. (See Part III for a list of names and addresses of magazine subscription services.)

> Question 14: Do you order your materials processed and cataloged? If not, is centralized processing available?

The processing and cataloging of materials is one of the most time-consuming functions of the LMC specialist. Even when a district has facilities set up to process and catalog new materials, it is still costly and time-consuming. As one LMC specialist stated:

> I am the only librarian serving 917 students with no clerical help!! I order all books processed.

Unfortunately, all materials are still not available processed and cataloged, but this number is diminishing rapidly.

Schools

Only one LMC reported having centralized processing. Thirty-three order all materials processed and cataloged; 25 order cards only and process in-house; and 14 catalog and process all materials in-house, many citing delays and cost as primary objections to ordering processed materials.

MATRIX III Processing and Cataloging by School Size

Number of Students	Ordered Cataloged	Ordered, Processed, & Cataloged	In-house Cataloging & Processing	Centralized Cataloging & Processing
2,000 & over	1	1	1	
1,500–1,999	3	3		
1,000–1,499	2	7	2	1
750– 999	4	3	2	
500– 749	7	5	2	
1– 499	7	10	3	

Districts

Nineteen districts report that centralized processing is available and used exclusively. Fourteen indicated that, although centralized processing is available, it is used only when materials cannot be ordered processed, as this is more cost-efficient. Thirty-six order materials fully cataloged and processed, and 16 districts order card kits. Only 10 districts process materials at the building level.

MATRIX IV   Processing and Cataloging by District Size

Number of Students	Ordered Cataloged	Ordered, Processed, & Cataloged	In-house Cataloging & Processing	Centralized Cataliging & Processing
50,000 & over	2	2		3
25,000–49,999	2	1		1
10,000–24,999	1	4	1	2
7,500– 9,999	1	5		3
5,000– 7,499	3	7		3
2,500– 4,999	4	4	2	1
1,000– 2,499	3	6	4	3
1– 999		4	3	1

> Question 15: Are you required to order materials at or by a specific time?

Ninety-six schools and districts had no specific time limit. A large majority had time restrictions of the end of the school year or the end of the schools' fiscal years. Many stated that federal monies do have a time specified. Only one school and 3 districts stipulated an ordering deadline. For most, ordering is an ongoing process throughout the year.

> Question 16: Do you have a formal plan for review of questionable materials? If so, have you had occasion to use it?

Twenty-two (31 percent) of the schools reported that they have no plan, and 49 (69 percent) said they did. Of that number, 29 (59 percent) have never used it and 17 have. Three LMC specialists reported that their principals pull material from the shelves when questioned, never using the plan.

Sixteen (20 percent) school districts have no plan, 64 report that they do. Twenty-five of these have never used it and 39 have—a few, more than 2–3 times a year.

Question 17: How much weeding do you do annually?

Every LMC specialist appeared to approach the art of weeding in a different manner. An approximately equal number stress weeding as either an ongoing or inventory process. A number of schools consistently discard either a percentage of the total collection (.005 percent to 10 percent) or a number equal to about 50 percent of the new books added. Some divide their collections into sections and do a portion ranging from one-third to one-fifth each year. One LMC specialist said she orders heavily in a specified area and then cleans the shelves. A number discard only worn or outdated materials (often to make room for new materials in bulging shelves), and a number also use checkout slips as a guide. A large number do very little weeding (less than 10 books annually), sometimes because the administration objects. Many LMC specialists don't feel they do enough, often citing time as a critical determiner.

The following two responses seem to sum up the controversy:

Very little [weeding], mainly things that become obsolete so fast. Our experience is that things don't move for a while; then they come back in style; an example: *I, Claudius*.

During the past 2 years an emphasis has been put on weeding. My thinking is that the textbooks are evaluated every 5 years and the decision is made at that time to readopt or adopt a new text. Our materials in the library are regarded as an extension of the textbooks and need to be evaluated regularly. Also, with a materials budget (that is very good for this state), the materials begin to fill the shelves very quickly. Our inventory reports begin to read that we are way over minimum standards and yet so many counted as items are so decrepit, so out-of-date, that they are never used and only take up space. The students cannot find the many up-to-date materials for all the place holders that just take up the space.

POLICY

Question 18: If you have a written policy, how often is it reviewed?

Schools

Sixteen LMCs have no policy and 3 had just been written, not yet requiring review. The remaining 49 schools had reviews of the policy annually, irregularly or never. Thirty-one have no provision for review and do so irregularly or not at all. The remainder do regularly review their selection policy, over half of them doing so annually.

Districts

Twelve districts have no selection policy, and 4 more had just written theirs. Again, the length of time between reviews for the remaining 61 districts varies from annually to not at all. Seventeen responded that they review annually, and 18 review irregularly or not at all. The remainder fall somewhere in between, all reviewing at least every 5 years.

CHART X   Schools with Acquisitions Policies

Student Population	Yes	No
2,000 & up	2	1
1,500 - 1,999	5	1
1,000 - 1,499	10	0
750 - 1,000	6	3
500 - 749	8	6
0 - 499	15	3

CHART XI   Districts with Acquisitions Policies

Student Population	Yes	No
50,000 & up	4	1
25,000 - 49,999	5	0
10,000 - 24,999	9	1
7,500 - 9,999	8	1
5,000 - 7,499	9	1
2,500 - 4,999	11	1
1,000 - 2,499	13	4
0 - 999	7	1

> Question 19: Who wrote or is writing your selection policy?

Schools

Twenty-seven of the school LMCs had policies drafted by the LMC specialist. Four of these had faculty approval in addition to board approval. Three LMCs had policies written by the administration, only one of these having LMC input. Five were written by committees, including superintendents (3), principal (4), faculty (3), students (1), and parents (1). Three LMCs had no idea who wrote the policy.

Districts

Twenty-five of the districts had policies written by the LMC specialist or coordinator. Three had policies written by district administration or the superintendent's office. The remainder had policies written by a committee. Twenty-four of these committees were composed of librarians or media personnel exclusively. LMC specialists were included on committees with administrators-superintendents (10), teachers (10), citizens (5), curriculum coordinators (5), principals (4), students (2), and a union representative (1).

While the questionnaires received did not provide enough of a sampling to arrive at conclusions about the acquisitions process, some indications are apparent.

Funding is becoming more difficult to acquire, both from local and federal sources. In addition, inflation has driven up the cost of library materials and equipment. A very limited number of states mandate *any* minimum for LMC spending, and those that do are considering rewriting statutes to eliminate such provisions. Whereas policies were designed to provide the LMC specialist with guidelines for spending, they may become more important as a means to prevent large-scale cuts of the materials budget.

While LMC specialists are fighting budget cuts from administration sources, they are also engaged in a battle against censorship. More and more LMC specialists are using that part of their policy dealing with reconsideration of material.

There is a growing feeling among school LMC personnel that an acquisitions policy is vital to the operation of the center. When the first request for policies was sent out, at least 25 percent of those who had no policy were in the process of writing one. Approximately 10 of the 157 questionnaires reported that their policy had just been written. As budgets get tighter and community members clamor for censorship, an acquisitions policy will become even more vital.

PART I
FULL POLICIES

List of Library Media Centers—Full Policies

Hawaii Public School Libraries, Honolulu, HI 96816

Northern Trails Area Education Agency Media Center, Clear Lake, IA 50428

McAllen Independent School District Learning Resources Centers, McAllen, TX 78501

Fort Wayne Community Schools Media Centers, Fort Wayne, IN 46802

Newton Falls Exempted Village School District Libraries, Newton Falls, OH 44444

Chambersburg Area School District Library Media Centers, Chambersburg, PA 17201

Sonoma Valley Unified School District Library Media Centers, Sonoma, CA 95476

Fairfield Public School Library Resource Centers, Fairfield, CT 06430

Council Bluffs Public Schools Media Centers, Council Bluffs, IA 51501

Oak Lawn Community High School Media Center, Oak Lawn, IL 60453

Cashton Public Schools Instructional Materials Center, Cashton, WI 54619

Mountain Heritage High School Media Center, Yancey County Schools, Burnsville, NC 28714

New York City Public Schools Library Media Centers, Brooklyn, NY 11201

Anchorage School District Library Media Centers, Anchorage, AK 99502

Laredo Independent School District Learning Resources Centers, Laredo, TX 78040

Hawaii Public School Libraries

OBJECTIVES

The primary objective of the school library media center is to implement, enrich and support the educational program of the school. In the area of materials selection, the library media center should provide a wide range of materials on all levels of difficulty, with consideration for diversity of appeal and different points of view. Therefore, the library media center should:

1. Provide materials that will enrich and support the curriculum, taking into consideration the varied interests, abilities, and maturity levels of the students served.

2. Provide materials for teachers and students that will encourage growth in knowledge and that will help to develop literary, cultural and aesthetic appreciation and ethical standards.

3. Provide materials which reflect the ideas and beliefs of religious, social, political, historical, and ethnic groups and their contribution to the American and world heritage and culture, thereby enabling students to develop intellectual integrity in forming judgments.

4. Place principle above personal opinion and reason above prejudice in selection of materials of the highest quality in order to assure a comprehensive collection appropriate for users of the library.

RESPONSIBILITY

The Hawaii State Board of Education is legally responsible for all matters relating to the operation of Hawaii schools. The responsibility for the selection of instructional material is delegated to the professionally

Hawaii State Department of Education, Multimedia Services Branch, Honolulu, HI 96816

trained personnel employed by the school system. Ultimate responsibility for the selection of books and other materials rests with the assistant superintendent of the Office of Instructional Services, who operates within the framework of policies approved by the Board of Education.

The Multimedia Services Branch is responsible for developing and establishing criteria for evaluation and selection of library materials. It will maintain bibliographic tools and establish procedures for selection and coordination of elementary and secondary library materials. Under the direction of this branch, statewide library materials evaluation committees, composed of school level representatives from each district, assist in the evaluation of new titles.

At the school level, the selection of materials involves many people: school administrators, librarians, teachers, and students. Primary responsibility for coordinating the selection of materials and making the recommendations for purchase rests with the school library personnel, subject to the approval of the principal.

CRITERIA

1. General criteria to be considered are:

   a. Needs of individual schools and students.
       - To fill curriculum needs.
       - To provide for a wide range of abilities and interests.
       - To provide for recreational needs.

   b. Needs of school professional staff.

2. Other important considerations:

   a. Accuracy.
   b. Attractive and appropriate format.
   c. Authoritativeness.
   d. Currentness.
   e. Durability.
   f. Freedom from stereotyping, e.g., sexism, racism, etc.
   g. Interest and appeal.
   h. Medium validity.
   i. Presentation of different points of view.
   j. Price.
   k. Quality of the writing/production.
   l. Readability/visual or audio effectiveness.
   m. Relevancy.
   n. Suitable style.
   o. Technical and physical qualities.

CONTROVERSIAL MATERIALS

The material should be consonant with the purposes of the library media center, meet general criteria of quality, and relate to school program needs. Judgment should be based on the total effect of the material and not on the presence of words and phrases or on other visual and aural instances which in themselves might be objectionable.

The Department of Education policy on controversial issues supports the concepts of investigation and objectivity:

1. Student discussion of issues which generate opposing points of view shall be considered a normal part of the learning process in every area of the school program. The depth of the discussion shall be determined by the maturity of the students.
2. Teachers shall refer students to resources reflecting all points of view. Discussions, including contributions made by the teacher or resource person, shall be maintained on an objective, factual basis. Stress shall be placed on learning how to make judgments based on facts.

GIFTS

Gifts should be evaluated by applying the same criteria used for selection of purchased materials.

PROFESSIONAL MATERIALS

These materials need to reflect trends in education, as well as meet general selection criteria.

SERIES

Materials within a series should be considered individually, since they might differ in quality.

SOCIAL CONCERNS

1. Where it is needed for the curriculum, the collection should contain materials which present an objective picture of different problems and life-styles, though they may depict controversial behavior and use frank language.
2. Standard procedures for selection should be used for these materials.

PROCEDURES

Books

1. Most of the books will be selected from the Centralized Processing Center (CPC) order lists. The books on the Juvenile (Elementary) and Young Adult (Secondary) order lists will have undergone examination and review under a statewide book evaluation system involving school and public librarians.

   The school librarians should also refer to reputable, professionally prepared selection aids, such as the H. W. Wilson standard catalogs, and periodicals, such as *Booklist* and *School Library Journal*, for additional assistance.

2. In selecting books, whether it be from CPC order lists or through independent purchase, the librarian should evaluate the existing collection and consult reputable, unbiased, professionally prepared selection aids, staff members from various departments and/or grade levels, and, if available, a committee appointed by the principal to serve in an advisory capacity in the selection of materials.

Nonbook Materials

1. Nonbook materials for school library media centers are evaluated by staff specialists in the Multimedia Services Branch. Approved materials are annotated and listed in *School Library Resources for Children and Teachers of Hawaii: Curriculum-Related Nonbook Materials*.

   School librarians may consult this source as well as reputable, professionally prepared selection aids for additional assistance. They may also consult *Approved Instructional Materials, Book I* and *Book II*, and curriculum guides, compiled by program specialists in the Office of Instructional Services.

2. In selecting nonbook materials, the librarian should evaluate the existing nonbook collection and consult professional selection aids, staff members from various departments and/or grade levels, and, if available, a committee appointed by the principal to serve in an advisory capacity in the selection of materials.

WEEDING

The same thought and care given to selection of materials need to be exercised in weeding the collection so that the collection remains useful to the unique clientele it is meant to serve.

CHALLENGED MATERIALS

Occasional objections to a selection will be made by the public, despite the care taken to select materials for student and teacher use. In such instances, the principles of the freedom to read and professional responsibility of the staff should be defended.

If a complaint is made, the procedures to follow are:

1. Inform the principal about the situation and, if it seems feasible, set up a conference with complainant, principal, librarian, and any other staff member involved in the complaint. In this initial stage, school staff should try to explain to the complainant:

    a. The school's selection procedure, criteria, and qualifications of those persons selecting the material.
    b. The particular place the material occupies in the educational program, its intended educational usefulness, and additional information regarding its use.

    (Note: The vast majority of complaints can be amicably resolved in the first stages. A personal conference can oftentimes solve the problem where a shift into a more formal procedure might inflate the problem.)

2. Should the complainant still not be satisfied, invite the person to file objections in writing and offer to send him/her form No. 70-5, *Hawaii State Library System: Patron Request for Reevaluation of Library Material.* [See Part III for a similar sample form.]

3. Determine whether the material may be sufficiently questionable to warrant its immediate withdrawal pending a decision.

4. Should the situation not be resolved at the school level, the complainant should be referred to the respective district office.

5. Should the complainant not be satisfied with the district superintendent's decision, the matter should be referred to the assistant superintendent of the Office of Instructional Services. The assistant superintendent will request the assistance of the Multimedia Services Branch for study and recommendations. Branch specialists will read, examine, and/or reconsider the material in question and report their findings to the assistant superintendent. The assistant superintendent will then respond to the complainant and try to resolve the matter.

6. Should the complainant insist on taking the matter further, the assistant superintendent will then report to the superintendent, who will present staff recommendations to the Board of Education for a final decision.

Northern Trails Area Education Agency Media Center

RESPONSIBILITY FOR SELECTION OF MATERIALS

1. The Board of Directors is legally responsible for all matters relating to the operation of the Northern Trails Area Education Agency (AEA).

2. The responsibility for the selection of printed and audiovisual materials is delegated to the professionally trained and certificated staff of the AEA and the selection committees.

CRITERIA FOR SELECTION OF MATERIALS

1. The following criteria will be used as they apply:

   a. Materials shall support and be consistent with the general educational goals of the school districts served.

   b. Materials shall be appropriate for the subject area and for the age, emotional development, ability level, and social development of the students for whom the materials are selected.

   c. Materials shall be chosen to foster respect for minority groups, women, and ethnic groups and shall realistically represent our pluralistic society, along with the roles and life-styles open to both men and women in today's world. Materials shall be designed to help students gain an awareness and understanding of the many important contributions made to our civilization by minority groups, ethnic groups, and women.

   Materials shall clarify the multiple historical and contemporary forces with their economic, political, and religious dimensions which have operated to the disadvantage or advantage of women, minority groups, and ethnic groups. These materials shall present and analyze intergroup tension and conflict objectively, placing emphasis upon resolving social and economic problems.

Materials shall be designed to motivate students and staff to examine their own attitudes and behaviors and to comprehend their own duties, responsibilities, rights and privileges as participating citizens in a pluralistic, nonsexist society.

   d. Materials shall be selected for their strengths rather than rejected for their weaknesses.

   e. Biased or slanted materials may be provided to meet specific curriculum objectives.

   f. Physical format and appearance of materials shall be suitable for their intended use.

2. The selection of materials on controversial issues will be directed toward maintaining a balanced collection representing various views.

PROCEDURE IN SELECTION

1. Media:

   a. In selecting materials for purchase for the AEA Media Center, the media specialist will evaluate the existing collection and the curriculum needs and will make recommendations to the selection committee. Committee members will consult reputable professionally prepared selection aids and other appropriate sources.

   b. Recommendations for purchase will be solicited from AEA staff, school media personnel, teachers and administrators in the area.

   c. Gift materials shall be judged, accepted, or rejected by the selection criteria previously outlined.

   d. Selection is an ongoing process which should include the removal of materials no longer appropriate and the replacement of lost and worn materials still of educational value.

REMOVAL OF MATERIALS

Request for the reconsideration, removal, or restriction of materials distributed by the Educational Media Center shall be referred to the local public school district or private school. [See Part III for a similar sample form.] If a local public school district or private school decides that it does not wish to use or wishes to restrict certain materials, it may notify the Educational Media Center in writing and henceforth curtail ordering the item. However, once materials are purchased by the center, they will remain in the collection until every public or private school in the area has notified the center that it has no use for the material in question.

The AEA administrator shall inform the AEA Board of Directors and each local school superintendent of any material that has been restricted for use by any local public school district or private school.

Every citizen in our area who requests access to the materials for the purpose of close scrutiny shall be requested to contact his/her local school to make arrangements for reviewing said material. Should a local school refuse a citizen this cooperation, s/he may view the materials at the Educational Media Center. The fact of the school's refusal to cooperate would be verified by the center's administration before the showing.

INSTRUCTIONS TO THE RECONSIDERATION COMMITTEE

The policy of this school district related to selection of learning materials states that any resident of the district may formally challenge instructional materials used in the district's educational program. This policy allows those persons in the school and the community who are not directly involved in the selection of materials to make their opinions known. The task of the Reconsideration Committee is to provide an open forum for discussion of challenged materials and to make an informed decision on the challenge.

The most critical component of the reconsideration process is the establishment and maintenance of the committee's credibility in the community. For this purpose, the committee is composed primarily of community members. The community should not, therefore, infer that the committee is biased or is obligated to uphold prior professional decisions. For this same reason, a community member will be selected to chair the committee.

The presence on the committee of the school media specialist and the administrative staff member will assure continuity from year to year as well as lend professional knowledge of the selection process. Student members are essential since they are the closest to the student body and will be immediately affected by the decision of the committee.

The reconsideration process, the task of this committee, is just one part of the selection continuum. Material is purchased to meet a need. It is reviewed and examined, if possible, prior to purchase; it is periodically reevaluated through updating, discarding, or reexamination. The committee must be ready to acknowledge that an error in selection may have been made, despite this process. Librarians and school personnel regularly read great numbers of reviews in the selection process, and occasional errors are possible.

In reconsidering challenged materials, the role of the committee, and particularly the chairperson, is to produce a climate for disagreement. However, the committee should begin by finding items of agreement, keeping in mind that the larger the group participating, the greater the amount of information available and, therefore, the greater the number of possible approaches to the problem.

If the complainant chooses, s/he may make an oral presentation to the committee to expand and elaborate on the complaint. The committee will listen to the complainant, to those with special knowledge, and to any other interested persons. In these discussions, the committee should be aware of relevant social pressures which are affecting the situation. Individuals who may try to dominate or impose a decision must not be allowed to do so. Minority viewpoints expressed by groups or individuals must be heard, and observers must be made to feel welcome. It is important that the committee create a calm, nonvolatile environment in which to deal with a potentially volatile situation. To this end, the complainant will be kept continuously informed of the progress of his/her complaint.

The committee will listen to the views of all interested persons before reaching a decision. In deliberating its decision, the committee should remember that the school system must be responsive to the needs, tastes, and opinions of the community it serves. Therefore, the committee must distinguish between broad community sentiment and attempts to impose personal standards. The deliberations should concentrate on the appropriateness of the material. The question to be answered by the committee is, "Is the material appropriate for its designated audience at this time?"

The committee's final decision will be: (1) to remove the challenged material from the total school environment, (2) to take no removal action, or (3) to agree on a limitation of the educational use of the materials. The decision will be reached through secret ballot.

The committee chairperson will instruct the secretary to convey the committee's decision to the office of the superintendent. The decision should detail the rationale on which it was based. A letter will be sent to the complainant outlining the committee's final decision.

McAllen Independent School District Learning Resources Centers

PHILOSOPHY

The Learning Resources Center program broadens the role of the library to assist learners in developing skills to locate, evaluate, synthesize, and use information in solving problems. The McAllen Learning Resources Centers are measuring their service to meet specifications set up by the following professional accrediting agencies as enumerated in their choice of standards:

1. Texas Education Agency.

2. Southern Association of Colleges and Schools.

3. American Association of School Librarians (a division of the American Library Association).

4. Association for Educational Communications and Technology (a division of the National Education Association).

We subscribe in principle to the statements of policy as expressed in the American Association of School Librarians' *Media Programs: District and School* and the American Library Association's *Library Bill of Rights*. [See Appendix I for this current statement.]

RESPONSIBILITIES

The selection of materials for the Learning Resources Centers rests with the professional personnel of each school who are familiar with the courses of study, the methods of teaching, and the maturity and ability of those who will use the materials. Ultimate responsibility for materials in the Learning Resources Centers legally rests with the Board of Trustees.

The building learning resources directors and aides are directly responsible to the building principal. The coordinator of library services has a staff relationship to the principal, learning resources director and aide.

Preparation of the individual building level library budget is a joint responsibility of the building principal and the coordinator of library services. Once the budget has been approved, expenditure of funds becomes primarily the responsibility of the building principal. As the coordinator of library services is the person with the most extensive training in the library specialty and is the only person in a position to see the entire program, s/he must of necessity monitor the expenditure of funds. Once a requisition has been approved by the principal, it will be sent through the coordinator of library services for a countersignature. This procedure will provide a means of insuring that our entire district's program is kept in balance and that budgetary limitations are observed.

GIFTS

Gift materials added to the collection of the Learning Resources Centers must meet the same criteria as the materials selected for purchase. They are accepted with the understanding that, if not suitable, they may be disposed of at the discretion of the learning resources director.

MEMORIALS

It is preferred that the selection of materials for memorial gifts be made by the learning resources director. However, if the group wishing to purchase a memorial would prefer a list of materials for their selection, such a list will be provided by the learning resources director or the coordinator of library services.

No memorial should be set up as a special collection. The center may maintain a memorial book listing all memorial gifts. A designation of the memorial may be made in this book.

FREE LOAN MATERIAL

Nonbook material may be procured for demonstration on a free loan, short- or long-term basis. Such items must contribute to furthering the objectives of the Learning Resources Center and are subject to the same evaluative criteria and selection procedures as those which are reviewed for permanent addition to the collection.

OBJECTIVES

The primary objectives of the school's Learning Resources Center are to implement, enrich, and support the educational program of the school. It is the duty of a center to provide a wide range of materials on all levels of difficulty, with diversity of appeal, and the presentation of different points of view. The responsibilities of the Learning Resources Center are:

1. To provide materials that will enrich and support the curriculum, taking into consideration the varied interests, abilities, and maturity levels of the pupils served.

2. To provide materials that will stimulate growth in factual knowledge, literary appreciation, aesthetic values, and ethical standards.

3. To provide a background of information which will enable pupils to make intelligent judgments in their daily life.

4. To provide materials on opposing sides of controversial issues so that young citizens may develop under guidance the practice of critical analysis of all media.

5. To provide materials representative of the many religious, ethnic, and cultural groups and their contributions to our American heritage.

6. To place principle above personal opinion and reason above prejudice in the selection of materials of the highest quality, in order to assure a comprehensive collection appropriate for the use of the library media center.

CRITERIA FOR BOOKS AND AUDIOVISUAL MATERIALS

The present collection and the school curriculum influence the selection. There are fundamental principles which are used as criteria for selecting material for the Learning Resources Centers:

1. *Authority.* This refers to the qualifications of the people responsible for creating the material (the author, the producer, or publisher) and how capable and prepared they are to have undertaken the project. Information on their background, education, experience, reputation and previous works will supply useful clues. A determination of the nature and repute of research sources used is also useful. If the item under consideration is an adaptation or revision of another work, the extent and nature of the differences should be determined; often these are so slight that a media center that owns the old work may not wish to purchase the revision.

2. *Scope*. Essentially this refers to the overall purpose and coverage of the material. When the breadth and limitation of scope are determined, the work should be compared to others on the same subject to see if it presents a fresh viewpoint or if it displaces, amplifies, or simply repeats existing material in the collection.

3. *Format and technical quality*. The physical makeup of the material should be appropriate to its content. It should meet acceptable production standards and be of sufficient quality to help promote use. Each form of educational material has distinctive physical characteristics.

4. *Authenticity*. The contents should be checked for validity, reliability, and completeness, as well as for the degree of bias or objectivity presented. Recency is also extremely important. The copyright date and imprint date should relate favorably; sometimes they are valid guides to the up-to-dateness of the material. However, the contents will usually have to be examined to make a final and accurate determination of currency.

5. *Treatment and arrangement*. The material should be clearly presented in a well-organized fashion. This involves a logical development and the sequence of the content should flow naturally and easily from one section into another. The material should be well-balanced and place particular stress on the elements of greatest importance. The arrangement should bear a direct relationship to its potential use and be judged by the degree to which it facilitates that use. The style of the presentation, the general comprehension level, and the nature of the concepts being developed must be appropriate, both to the intended audience and to the nature and depth of coverage intended. The material should be developed in light of sound educational principles and make provision for such elements as review and reinforcement. Finally, the work should catch and hold the user's interest and, hopefully, provide stimulation for further learning.

6. *Aesthetic consideration*. The item must be acceptable artistically, with each separate element combining to form an aesthetically pleasant whole. The material should appeal to the imagination, the senses, and the intellect, so that the user's taste and sense of artistic appreciation will be developed.

7. *Price*. The acquisition of any piece of material, particularly expensive ones, must be seen in relation to existing budget limitations. It might be necessary to find out if a satisfactory substitute at a lower price is available. Certainly the initial cost will be weighed against the amount of intended use.

8. *Special features.* The media specialists should try to ascertain the characteristics, if any, that make the item under consideration distinctive or perhaps unique from others of the same type and on the same subject. These might be, for example, an unusual approach to a subject matter, the presence of usage guides, sets of questions and answers, or a list of suggested follow-up activities.

9. *General suitability.* Having evaluated the material in the preceding terms, the media specialists now must view the material in light of the school's existing collection. The appropriateness of the materials to the school's educational objectives and curriculum is an important factor. Questions must be answered as: Is there sufficient need for the item? How many will use it? Is it suited to the particular needs and abilities of those who will use it?

Instructional materials selection shall be a cooperative continuing process in which administrators, teachers, learning resources directors, and students should participate. The learning resources director is guided by standard approved lists and reviewing media. Some of the most useful sources from which to select materials for purchase are:

Books

Books for Secondary School Libraries. 4th ed. Bowker, 1971. Compiled by the Library Committee of the National Association of Independent Schools. Revised periodically. Carefully selected and indexed list, arranged by Dewey Decimal system.

Brown, Lucy Gregor. *Core Media Collections for Secondary Schools.* Bowker, 1975. First listing of its kind, a qualitative selection guide to approximately 2,000 titles of nonprint media. Indexed by both subject and title.

Children's Catalog. 13th ed. Wilson, 1976, and supplements. New edition every 5 years. An annotated listing of titles, intended to include the best books for children.

Gaver, Mary, ed. *The Elementary School Library Collection.* 9th ed. Phases 1-2-3. Brodart, 1974. About 8,000 book titles, and 9,000 audiovisual items. Selection policy, catalog card entry format, author-title-subject index. (Supplemented like Wilson catalogs.)

Hodges, Elizabeth D. *Books for Elementary School Libraries: An Initial Collection.* American Library Association, 1969. Brief, descriptive annotations of over 3,000 books for initial library services, K-8.

Junior High School Library Catalog. 3rd ed. Wilson, 1975. Similar in format to *Children's Catalog;* includes books only. Useful for the junior high school grades. A new edition is published every 5 years with annual supplements.

McDaniel, Roderick. *Resources for Learning: A Core Media Collection for Elementary Schools*. Titles of media in all formats are listed by subject, with the fullest information given in title/author index. Annotations and a producer/distributor directory are given.

Media Review Digest. Pierian Press, 1974. Replaced *Multi-Media Reviews Index*. A comprehensive index to and digest of reviews, evaluations, and descriptions of all forms of nonbook media appearing in a great variety of periodicals and reviewing services. Two separate volumes: Part 1 contains films, videotapes, filmstrips, and miscellaneous media; Part 2 is concerned with musical and spoken-word records and tapes.

Senior High School Library Catalog. 10th ed. Wilson, 1972. Similar in format to *Children's Catalog*; includes books only. Useful for senior high school grades. A new edition is published every 5 years with annual supplements.

Wynar, Christine L. *Guide to Reference Books for School Media Centers*, and its *1974-75 Supplement*. Libraries Unlimited, 1973 and 1976. Contains 2,575 annotated entries of reference books and selection tools for use in elementary, junior, and senior high schools.

[Two useful charts which show recommended distribution of books are included at the conclusion of this policy.]

Periodicals

Audiovisual Instruction. Association for Educational Communications and Technology, Washington, DC. Monthly September through May with combined June/July issues.

The Booklist. American Library Association, Chicago, IL. Semimonthly, except August.

Bulletin of the Center for Children's Books. University of Chicago Press, Chicago. Monthly, except August.

The Horn Book Magazine. Horn Book, Inc., Boston, MA. Bimonthly.

Instructor. Instructor Publications, Inc., Dansville, NY. Nine times yearly, with May/June and August/September issues.

Learning. Education Today Co., Inc. Palo Alto, CA. Nine times a year during the school year.

Media and Methods. North American Publishing Co., Philadelphia, PA. Nine times per year, September through May/June.

Previews. R. R. Bowker Co., New York. Monthly, September through May.

School Library Journal. R. R. Bowker Co., New York, NY. Monthly, September through May.

Teacher. Macmillan Professional Magazines, Inc., Greenwich, CT. Nine times per year, September through May/June.

Top of the News. American Library Association, Chicago. Quarterly.
Wilson Library Bulletin. H. W. Wilson Co., New York. Monthly,
except July and August.

CONSIDERATION FILE

All through the year the learning resources director or aide should keep
an order file of the books most suitable for the needs of the Learning
Resources Center. This is a consideration file. It also contains replacement
copies and second copies needed. The cards in the consideration file are
filed by class number. This makes it easier to select materials in a particular
category in which the collection is weak. Thus, a balanced collection is
maintained.

Class No.		Author	
Title			
SBN			
Publisher and place	Year	List price	Cost
Edition or series	Vol.		No. of copies
Requested by		Dept. for which recommended	
Reviewed in			

PERIODICALS

Periodicals support the curriculum of the school and reflect the interest
of school-age groups. They are essential for many reasons. They give
current information and some information that never gets into hardback
form. They are used both for recreational reading and for reference
purposes.

The Texas Education Agency recommends periodicals that are curriculum-related, represent pupil interests, and have divergent editorial viewpoints and numbers of subscriptions as follows:

	LEVEL I	LEVEL II	LEVEL III	LEVEL IV
Elementary	10-15 titles	15-25 titles	25- 40 titles	40- 75 titles
Junior High	25-50 titles	50-60 titles	60- 75 titles	75-125 titles
Senior High	50-75 titles	75-90 titles	90-125 titles	125-175 titles

General criteria for selection are:

1. Buy those that will entice the reluctant reader.

2. Buy with as high standards as will be suitable for the Learning Resources Center.

3. Buy some, with permanent value, that are worth binding.

4. Selection may be influenced by *Readers' Guide to Periodical Literature*.

5. Include magazines with current information and current events in different areas such as science, sports, hobbies, and homemaking.

NEWSPAPERS

The Texas Education Agency recommends the following distribution:

	LEVEL I	LEVEL II	LEVEL III	LEVEL IV
Elementary	1 title	1 local & 1 state	3-6 titles	3-6 titles
Junior High	3 titles	4 titles	5 titles	6-10 titles
Senior High	3 titles	4 titles	5 titles	6-10 titles

When second and third newspaper subscriptions are added, local, state, and national publications are represented.

PAPERBACKS

The inclusion of paperback books in the School Learning Resources Center collection has added a new dimension to the program at all grade levels. Their format appeals to students, they are easy to carry, they are inexpensive, and there are many good titles available. The evaluation of those titles which are purchased as duplicate copies of hardback editions is no great problem because the latter have already been evaluated. Some publishers of children's books are now issuing paperback editions in the same size and with the same illustrations as the original hardcover publications.

School Learning Resources Centers directors should be alert for reliable paperback listings which are frequently cited in professional magazines. The following bibliographies also will be helpful:

Cohen, David. *Recommended Paperback Books for Elementary Schools.* Book Mail Service. Lists 1,000 books and includes a full alphabet index. The latest edition also identifies books about Afro-American and other multiethnic groups. Free, if request is on official school letterhead.

Fader, Daniel N. *Hooked on Books: Program and Proof.* Putnam, 1968. Describes the author's program for getting students to enjoy reading by using paperbacks, magazines, and newspapers instead of traditional textbooks. A list of 1,000 paperbacks which constitute the reading list is included.

Gillespie, John T. *Young Phenomenon: Paperbacks in Our Schools.* American Library Association, 1972. Classroom and school library media center use of paperback books, case studies, helps in selection, and suggestions for book fairs are among the subjects discussed.

The Paperback Goes to School. Bureau of Independent Publishers and Distributors. Lists books which have been screened by a committee of publishers and school librarians for their suitability for secondary schools. It is not comprehensive or selective but selected. Will be useful as a beginning.

Simmons, Beatrice. *Paperback Books for Children.* Citation, 1972. Compiled by a committee of the American Association of School Librarians. Annotates more than 700 recommended books for grades K-6. Arranged by subject areas. Includes author and title indexes and a directory of publishers.

VERTICAL FILE

A vertical file is made up of material which, because of its format, its size, or its value, is not suitable for treatment as a book. This file should always be legal-size since many materials do not fit into a letter-size file. The most common types of vertical file materials are pamphlets, bulletins, clippings, excerpts, pictures, and book jackets. To assure maximum use of these resources, a system of subject cataloging for vertical file subject folders may be represented in the card catalog along with books and other media. Each item added to the vertical file should be placed in a folder which is assigned a specific subject heading from the standard list used for all books and materials. The heading on each subject folder is then recorded at the head of a form catalog card, the body of which reads, "Additional material on this subject will be found in the vertical file under the above heading." These subject entry cards are treated in the catalog exactly as if they were subject entries for books with appropriate cross references made.

> VOLCANOES   Additional material on this subject
> will be found in the vertical file
> under the above heading.

If there is a date on the pamphlet or clipping, this should be circled with a red colored pencil to call attention to the date. Otherwise, the date on which the material is placed in the file should be stamped on the material. The date helps to determine the continuing value of each piece when the vertical file is weeded. Clippings should be mounted on either heavy paper or lightweight cardboard.

PROCEDURE FOR HANDLING OBJECTIONS

The suitability of particular books or other materials may be questioned. The complainant should be invited to file the form, *Request for Reconsideration of Library Materials*. [See Part III for a similar sample form.] This form shall be sent to the assistant superintendent for instruction, with duplicate copies to the principal and librarian of the school involved.

The material in question shall be reviewed by a committee of 5 composed of the assistant superintendent for instruction, building principal, coordinator of library services, teacher in the appropriate subject field, and Parent-Teacher Association representative or other interested lay person.

The Review Committee shall function at the call of the assistant superintendent upon receipt of a complaint. The material shall be considered with the specific objections in mind. The committee shall report back to the complainant. Appeal may be made to the Board of Education through proper channels.

The books or materials questioned shall be removed from the library during the period of examination. The review of questioned materials shall be treated objectively and as an important matter. Every opportunity shall be afforded those persons or groups questioning the school materials to meet with the committee and to present their opinions. The school librarian and other persons involved in the selection of the questioned material shall have the same opportunity. The best interests of the students, the curriculum, the school, and the community shall be of paramount consideration.

INSTRUCTIONS TO EVALUATING COMMITTEE

Bear in mind the principles of the freedom to learn and to read and base your decision on these broad principles rather than on defense of individual material. Freedom of inquiry is vital to education in a democracy.

Study thoroughly all materials referred to you and read available reviews. The general acceptance of the materials should be checked by consulting standard evaluation aids and local holdings in other schools.

Passages or parts should not be pulled out of context. The values and faults should be weighted against each other and the opinions based on the material as a whole.

WITHDRAWING

Books are withdrawn from the center if they are worn beyond repair and if they are not suitable for rebinding. The following procedure is used for withdrawing books:

1. Remove the borrower's card and arrange alphabetically by author.

2. Type a list by fund (regular or Title fund) of books being withdrawn in triplicate.

3. File one copy, giving the withdrawal date.

4. Send 2 copies of the list to the office of the coordinator of library services.

5. Note on the shelflist card (and at the elementary level on the union card) that the book has been withdrawn and give the date.

6. If the book is to be reordered, file the shelflist card in the consideration file.

7. If the book is not to be reordered and if this is the only copy, remove the cards from the card catalog and clip them to the shelflist card.

8. "WD" is the abbreviation used for a book which is withdrawn. Usually a book is not considered lost until after a period of 6 months or even an entire school year of 10 months. The date is added after the symbol.

INVENTORY

An inventory is an accounting of all cataloged books, bulletins, bound magazines, and audiovisual materials housed in the Learning Resources Centers. Before starting the inventory, the learning resources director may close circulation so that the collection will be as complete as possible. The time of year that inventory is taken is optional but, at the elementary level, the beginning of the school year is advocated. This procedure allows learning resources directors and aides to become acquainted with the collection and the Learning Resources Center will be closed at a time when the demands for service are at a minimum because of the time required to establish the administrative and instructional programs. The principal should assist the learning resources director or aide in the accomplishment of this inventory by providing student help and by informing the faculty of the necessity for such an inventory. Aides or personnel who are new to the inventory procedure may call on the coordinator for special instructions.

Audiovisual equipment is to be checked out from a designated area, as prescribed by the building principal, and inventory and summer storage should be completed with property cards so marked before school is closed for the summer. This will help you to become familiar again with what is available at your campus. Periodic spot check should be made in the middle of the year. Inventory information forms are usually distributed in early May.

WEEDING

Weeding is the process of clearing the collections in the Learning Resource Center of those materials which have outlived their usefulness. Withdrawing materials is a continuing process but weeding the collection is a carefully planned procedure almost as important as selecting new books of high quality. The American Library Association's Small Libraries Project (supported by the Texas Education Agency) offers the following reasons for weeding a collection:

1. To utilize in the best and most economical way the available space in your Learning Resource Center, relying on other sources such as your nearest city library or your county, regional, or state library for those little-used materials which would crowd your shelves or strain your budget.

2. To give your Learning Resource Center a reputation for reliability.

3. To remove an outward illusion of a well-stocked Learning Resource Center in the eyes of those who do not use it and may oppose your appeals for a better book budget.

4. To give your Learning Resource Center a fresh, inviting appearance.

5. To have a collection which is up-to-date.

6. To find books which need repair, rebinding, or replacing.

7. To be able to give the best possible service through a collection of materials of quality.

An annual weeding of the collection would not be out of order, but a complete weeding every 3 or 4 years is imperative. The persons who do the best job of weeding the collection are those who have a thorough understanding of the school's curriculum and of the existing collections. Other qualities needed are an adequate background in literature and knowledge about the characteristics of a good book, an understanding of the interests, needs, and abilities of the age group served, and a background of information about the community and other resources available.

In general, we will consider for discard, for any or all of the following reasons, books that are:

1. Unattractive in appearance because of yellowed paper, fine print, etc.

2. In poor physical condition as to ragged binding, a torn or dirty page, etc.

3. Seldom circulated.

4. With old copyright date that makes the books outmoded in content, use, or accuracy.

5. Mediocre or poor in quality. These may include:

   a. Poorly written books, with stereotyped characters and plots, popular when relatively few children's books were available.

   b. Series books of mediocre quality which were popular one or more generations ago.

   c. "Old fashioned" stories which are so written or illustrated that they are not appealing to children today. These may also include those with a dialect or moralizing tone, once thought to be exemplary reading for the young.

   d. Fictionalized representations of life in this country and other countries which have contributed to the development of false and stereotyped concepts of minority groups in our country and of people in other countries.

6. Duplications with several copies of titles no longer in heavy demand.

7. Of a subject matter or treatment not suitable for children served by the center.

8. Textbooks, except those single copies that have reference value. (Sets of textbooks or supplementary texts do not belong on shelves in the Learning Resource Center reading room.)

9. Sets of books (especially in the literature and history sections) which have gathered dust for years. Except for general or special encyclopedias, most sets of books "set." Titles in sets with the same binding, by standard authors, should be replaced by good reprint editions if needed and the others discarded.

10. Superseded by new or revised editions.

11. Of passing interest at the time of publication, such as travel and biographies of persons who were known in their generation but not likely to be of interest again.

Reference books should be checked against reviews in the *ALA Booklist*. Older sets of recommended encyclopedias are used in the classroom. Sets that are not recommended should be examined with a view of removing them from the collection.

When the collections are weeded, one classification should be handled at a time. As the books are taken from the shelves, they should be placed in three stacks: (1) those to be replaced, (2) those to be discarded, and (3) those to be rebound. The value of those in the "replacement" stack will be assessed carefully by checking with standard selection tools and by careful consideration of their place in the collection in relation to the needs of the pupils.

Materials no longer useful in the collection should be stamped "DISCARDED" over the ownership name inside of the covers of the books, on the title page, and on the identification page. Then the standard procedures for withdrawing should be followed.

Discarded books should usually not be given to teachers, to students, to paper drives, to most organizations, etc., as this may result in poor public relations. Since some citizens do not understand that destroying old, outdated books does not obviate the need for newer, more accurate and informative ones, it is best to dispose of discards with as little fanfare as possible.

THEFT OR VANDALISM

Any type of vandalism or theft of school equipment should be reported to the building principal. Reports need to be made with the proper authorities so replacement claims can be made.

CHART I   McAllen Independent School District
Basic Book Collection Titles—Elementary

SUBJECT	MINIMUM PERCENT	STANDARDS BOOKS	NUMBER ON HAND	PERCENT ON HAND	School BOOKS NEEDED	PERCENT NEEDED
Ready Reference	1.0	45				
Behavior, Manners, Understanding Self and Others	.5	30				
Religion	.3	7				
Holidays	.6	30				
Social Science	4.0	120				
Myths, Fairy Tales	7.0	203				
Language	1.6	15				
Natural Science	10.0	300				
Applied Science	7.0	210				
Sports, Hobbies, Games and Handicraft	3.0	90				
Fine Arts	2.0	60				
Literature	4.0	120				
History, Geography, Travel	12.0	360				
Biography	7.0	210				
Easy	15.0	450				
Fiction	25.0	750				
Total		3000				

CHART II   McAllen Independent School District
Basic Book Collecion Titles—Secondary

School _____

SUBJECT	MINIMUM PERCENT	STANDARDS BOOKS	NUMBER ON HAND	PERCENT ON HAND	BOOKS NEEDED	PERCENT NEEDED
Ready Reference	1.0	52				
Behavior, Manners, Understanding Self and Others	.5	45				
Religion	.3	15				
Holidays	.6	30				
Social Science	4.0	150				
Myths, Fairy Tales	7.0	30				
Language	1.6	30				
Natural Science	10.0	300				
Applied Science	7.0	203				
Sports, Hobbies, Games and Handicraft	3.0	150				
Fine Arts	2.0	150				
Literature	4.0	300				
History, Geography, Travel	12.0	450				
Biography	7.0	345				
Fiction	25.0	750				
Total		3000				

Fort Wayne Community Schools Media Centers

PHILOSOPHY

The media center is an integral, fundamental, and indispensable part of the instructional, guidance, and enrichment program of the school. The media center is a place to learn to investigate, to study, and to enjoy as it provides a boundless opportunity for education. Recognizing that both print and nonprint materials are relevant and valuable sources of information and stimuli, all types of materials and equipment are supplied by the media center.

The instructional and administrative staff, aided by media personnel, strive to become familiar with resource materials that are available in the media center and to make intelligent and efficient use of the center and those resources. The media personnel, aided by the entire staff, endeavor to teach students the skills of acquiring information through various channels and attempts to make them familiar with reference materials and media center resources. All members of the school population cooperate in developing and working within a media center program that provides for the informational and recreational needs of all.

SELECTION

The collection of materials in a school media center is provided to support and enhance the educational program of the school and to provide opportunities for users to develop personal interests. The school strives to be an effective agent in the development of the whole child—academic, social, physical, aesthetic. Therefore, the school must begin the educative process at the level of the individual child. It follows then that media center collections need to include instructional materials on various levels of

Fort Wayne Community Schools Media Centers, Fort Wayne, IN 46802

difficulty and maturity, related to all curricular areas and to a variety of individual interests.

In the Fort Wayne Community Schools, media personnel at the individual schools are responsible for planning and supervising orders for materials to be added to the school media center collection. The administrative and instructional staff depend upon them to exercise their best judgment in final evaluation of items considered for purchase and in selection of high quality materials which will support and enhance the curriculum and provide individual enrichment opportunities to the students and staffs. In the elementary schools where much of this important task is assigned to the media clerks, the supervisor of elementary instructional media has major responsibilities in providing inservice training, monthly selection lists, opportunity for preview, and other assistance in the selection process.

Since the instructional materials are intended to help provide for the interests and educational needs of the entire school community, administrative and teaching staff of the individual school, subject area consultants, and students share with media personnel the responsibility of this selection process. All should be familiar with the Fort Wayne Community Schools policies, procedures, and criteria for selecting media center materials and with professional selection aids. Even though competent individuals share this selection responsibility, media personnel need to be very familiar with the curriculum of the individual school, as well as the reading levels and interests of the students. Especially important is the need for media personnel to be familiar with all types of media on a wide variety of topics and interests and to keep up-to-date on current publications.

All materials—printed, visual, and recorded—should be selected for their contribution to the interests and enlightenment of the students and teachers who use them. Instructional and recreational materials are considered valuable when the subject matter, the style and/or viewpoint of the author, and the format of the media make a contribution to the users' interests and enlightenment. It is possible for the same information to be needed in a variety of forms and in varying degrees of difficulty for use with different individuals or groups. Such variation also provides opportunities for variety in presentation.

Both printed and audiovisual materials are effective in stimulating an individual's growth in factual knowledge, literary appreciation, aesthetic values, and ethical standards. At times, one instructional medium, used alone, can best present the concept being taught; at other times, a combination of printed materials and another medium can present the concept most effectively. Therefore, equal care should be taken in selecting the various types of media.

The type of material selected should be determined on the basis of which available medium most effectively conveys or interprets the desired concept; in many instances, materials of different format are most valuable when used to supplement one another.

Materials which deal with current topics should be up-to-date. Whenever practical, extensive provision should be made for presenting various points of view concerning the problems and issues of current times—international, national, state, and local. Those items which reflect a biased point of view should make the prejudice recognizable. Materials on subjects such as religion should be available; they should be factual, unbiased, and broadly representative. Factual material on an appropriate reading level should be available concerning those political ideologies which exert strong influence on government, education, or any other phase of our common life. Inclusion of profanity or frank treatment of sex should not automatically rule out books or other materials. It does, however, necessitate a searching evaluation of the merits—literary quality, truth of life, relevance to the curriculum—that the material in question may possess.

Gift items may be accepted by a school library media center if approved by the school personnel whose responsibility it is to select media center materials.

The media center collection in each school—books, pamphlets, monographs, documents, brochures, pictures, art prints, filmstrips, filmloops, tape recordings, phonograph recordings, transparencies, microforms, models, realia, and other educational materials—needs to meet a number of standards of excellence. To assure the desired excellence in quality, a number of policies and procedures such as those that follow need to be implemented.

CRITERIA FOR EVALUATION OF MULTIMEDIA

1. Materials may be selected that are recommended for school libraries in critical reviews published in educational, literary, and/or professional journals.

2. Materials may be selected from lists prepared by teachers, librarians, and other professional groups.

3. Items may be selected that have been personally examined by teachers, administrators, and/or media personnel.

SPECIFIC CRITERIA FOR EVALUATION OF MULTIMEDIA

1. Author, producer, director, or person of comparable responsibility may be considered responsible for the item under consideration.

   a. Academic preparation, specialization, and experience may be used in judging the competency of the person or persons responsible for the media.

2. Publisher, distributor, or producer share responsibility for quality.

   a. The reputation of a publisher, distributor, or producer in relation to desirable media for school media centers may be considered in selection.

3. Content is of major importance.

   a. The factual material should be authentic, up-to-date, accurate.

   b. The content should relate to the maturity level, experience, and understanding of the readers, viewers, or listeners for whom the material is recommended.

   c. The content should be free from materials such as:

- Propaganda discrediting American institutions and the ideals of democracy.
- Prejudice against class, race, creed, or nationality.

   d. The sentence structure, vocabulary, form, and style of expression should be suitable for the user for whom the material is intended.

   e. The content should stimulate thinking and inquiry rather than mere memorizing of fact.

   f. The content should suggest or lead to worthwhile learning or recreational activities.

   g. The content should deal with curricular concepts and with a variety of general topics.

4. Illustrations (including photographs, drawings, prints, maps, charts, diagrams, models, realia) should make a significant contribution to the item.

   a. Illustrations should be appropriately chosen for the concept being interpreted.

   b. Illustrations should have good art quality as measured by aesthetic principles and the standards of taste and skill.

- Illustrations depicting real people, places, or objects should be realistic and up-to-date.
- Illustrations depicting imaginary people, places, or objects should appeal to the reader and develop his/her imagination along desirable lines.

c. Illustrations should correlate with the written script or commentary; in printed materials the illustrations should be placed on the same page as the related text or on the page facing the text.

d. Illustrations should show recognition of the equal worth of people with respect to race, color, national origin, religion, and sex.

e. Illustrations should be related to the maturity level of the reader.

CRITERIA APPLICABLE TO BOOKS AND OTHER PRINTED MATERIALS

1. Format.

   a. Binding (books) and dust covers.

   - Binding should be made of durable fabric. Expendable materials may be in paperbacks, if so desired.

   - Color and design of binding should have artistic merit and should be appropriate to the age level.

   - The method of binding should permit the item to be held open with ease.

   - When feasible, dust covers should remain on the book and be protected by plastic book jackets.

   b. Size.

   - Printed materials should be of convenient size for handling by the age group for which they are intended.

2. Paper and ink.

   a. Paper should be of good quality.

   b. Black ink is preferable.

   c. There should be color contrast between page and print colors.

3. Printing and press work.

   a. Type should be clear and legible.

   b. Size of type should vary to suit maturity level of user.

4. Page makeup.

   a. Spaces between letters and words and lines, length of line, and number of lines on page should be conducive to legibility.

b. Margins should be wide enough to produce the appearance of an uncrowded page and to permit satisfactory rebinding.

c. Layout should be suitable to the maturity level of the reader.

5. Features.

   a. Where necessary, provision should be made for easy location of information contained in the material through such means as:

   - Footnotes.
   - Index(es).
   - Tabulations, charts, maps, scales.

   b. Provision should be made for defining and pronouncing unusual, difficult, and technical words through such means as:

   - Footnotes.
   - Glossary.
   - Explanation by study of context.

   c. Related study aids, suggested readings, word lists, and appendices have a high degree of usefulness.

CRITERIA APPLICABLE TO NONPRINT MEDIA

1. General considerations.

   a. The item should be of proper length for the intended user.

   b. The value of the item should be commensurate with cost, time, and effort required to use it.

2. Technical considerations.

   a. Illustrations should be clear and undistorted.

   b. Sound quality should be free from distortion and interference.

   c. Editing should have produced no break in continuity.

   d. The base material should be of high quality.

   e. Media which will be frequently handled should be of sturdy construction.

3. Aural content (sound media).

   a. The aural content should suit the concept being described or explained.

b. The aural content should supplement and interpret the illustrations with which it is used.

4. Features.

a. Provision should be made for easy location of information contained in the media.

- Labels.

- Tables of contents.

b. Aids such as study helps, suggested readings, word lists, and appendices are useful.

PROCEDURE FOR HANDLING RECONSIDERATION REQUESTS

The following procedure is recommended for handling problems which may arise when a particular media center acquisition is questioned.

1. Initiation of complaint.

a. Complainant should call in person at the office of the school principal. The complainant may obtain a copy of the questionnaire *Request for Reconsideration of a Media Center Acquisition* and a copy of the *Library Bill of Rights*. [See Part III for a sample form and Appendix I for current statement.]

b. The school principal or teacher may initiate a complaint by completing the *Request for Reconsideration of a Media Center Acquisition* form.

2. Consideration of complaint.

a. Composition of committee.

- Elementary—A committee will reevaluate the questioned media. The committee will be composed of the faculty advisory committee for media programs and the supervisor of elementary instructional media or 3 teachers selected by the school principal, the media clerk, and the supervisor of elementary instructional media. The school principal may elect to become a committee member if s/he so desires.

- Secondary—A committee composed of 3 teachers selected by the principal, the department head of the media center, and the subject area department head will reevaluate the questioned media. The school principal may elect to become a committee member if s/he so desires.

- A reading of the source material(s) cited when the item was originally selected should be considered by the committee, as well as the *Library Bill of Rights*.

b. The committee will jointly make a written response to school principal justifying its recommendation as to the reevaluation and the disposition of the item.

c. The school principal will make a decision concerning the request.

d. The school principal will arrange an interview with the complainant, inform the complainant of the decision, and support that decision in an appropriate manner.

e. The school principal will file copies of a report of the incident in his/her office, with the proper school media center person, with the proper elementary or secondary director, and with the director of instructional media. The report will consist of the following:

- The complainant's report.

- The committee's statement.

- A statement of action taken.

Newton Falls Exempted Village School District Libraries

PURPOSE

The purpose of the library is to participate in and support the educational program by providing and assisting in the use of an accessible collection of print and nonprint resources for the students, the faculty, and the administration.

OBJECTIVES

The school district strives to prepare the whole child for his/her role as a contributing member to our society. The freedoms to read and to develop an awareness of humanity's diverse heritage are essential rights in a democracy. It is the responsibility of the library to provide a collection of materials representative of all fields of interest and geared to the many needs of the students and faculty. The selection of media shall be in accordance with the following objectives: (1) to enrich the curriculum and (2) to further the development of youth intellectually, emotionally, spiritually, and culturally.

RESPONSIBILITY FOR SELECTION

The most important part of acquisitions work takes place before materials are actually ordered. It involves the planned selection of items best suited to strengthen the schools' resources for learning and instruction.

The Board of Education gives to qualified media personnel the responsibility of selecting resources for purchase. The scope of selection lies

Newton Falls Exempted Village School District Libraries. Newton Falls, OH 44444

within the entire school community and recommendations are provided by faculty and students. The final consideration rests with the media staff who attempt to choose materials from all forms of media which are carefully balanced for interest, vocabulary, and maturity and ability levels of all students within the schools served.

SELECTION PROCEDURE

All library materials and audiovisuals are selected and recommended for purchase by the librarian and the media specialist. In selecting materials for purchase, the existing collection is evaluated and decisions for acquisition are determined by consulting reputable, unbiased, professionally prepared selection aids and specialists from all departments and/or all grade levels. The book order is compiled, assigned a purchase order, and sent to the superintendent for approval.

SELECTION AIDS

The following bibliographies and reviewing publications shall be consulted in the choice of materials but selection is not limited exclusively to those cited:

AAA Science Booklist
Booklist
Books for You
Bulletin for the Center of Children's Books
Children's Catalog
Choice
Core Media Collection for Secondary Schools
Doors to More Mature Reading
Educational Media Catalog
Elementary School Library Collection
Gateways to Readable Books
High School Catalog
Magazines for School Libraries
Previews
Reference Books for School Libraries
School Library Journal
Vertical File Index
Wilson Library Bulletin

SELECTION CRITERIA BY SUBJECT AREA

Literature

1. Some indication of literary quality in regard to:

   a. Theme.

   b. Plot.

   c. Characterization.

   d. Use of language.

2. Special criteria for specific types of fiction:

   a. Historical fiction.

   - Accuracy of detail in regard to setting.

   - Accuracy of chronology.

   b. Science fiction.

   - Validity of alternative value and moral systems.

   - Maturity of students in understanding the possible satire and social criticism being expressed.

   c. "Best Sellers."

   - Conflict between what students want and quality and appropriateness.

   - Decide whether or not objectionable language, excessive violence, and/or explicit sexual scenes contribute to the overall effect of the material or are not really necessary.

   d. Realistic young adult fiction.

   - Avoidance of stereotyped characterization and "one-dimensional" characters.

   - Would the story be better understood if presented in nonfiction format rather than as a novel?

   - Will the topic be of interest for a period of time or will it be short-lived?

Social Studies

1. Select materials which emphasize the interdisciplinary approach.

2. Select materials which express a variety of viewpoints.

3. Maps, charts, and pictures should be easy to comprehend.

4. Materials should be up-to-date.

5. Resources should be written by a qualified author.

6. What is the scope of the media's coverage?

7. Avoid stereotypes of women and racial and ethnic groups.

8. Consider the use of primary source materials in comparison with secondary resources.

9. Determine the format which would provide the most recent data, e.g., periodicals, newspapers, government publications, and pamphlets.

10. Materials which present opinions and theories should be carefully evaluated for bias and accuracy.

Science and Mathematics

1. Reliability of author publisher and/or producer.

2. Choice of physical format best suited to convey the fact or concept.

3. Quality of technical production, e.g., photographs, audio, art work.

4. Currency and accuracy of information.

5. Vocabulary and illustrations suited to age and ability.

6. Interrelationships with other disciplines.

SELECTION CRITERIA BY MEDIUM

Print Resources

1. Fiction.

   a. Literary merit.
   b. Style.
   c. Popular appeal.
   d. True and constructive portrayal of life and character.
   e. Quality of physical format.
   f. Relationship to collection.
   g. Cost.

2. Nonfiction.

   a. Authority of author.
   b. Scope of subject matter.

    c. Accuracy.

    d. Acceptable format (binding, illustrations, print, etc.).

    e. Date of publication.

    f. Reputation of publisher.

    g. Relationship to collection.

    h. Arrangement of materials, e.g., indexes, bibliographies.

    i. Cost.

3. Special areas.

    a. Pamphlets.
   - Same criteria as for nonfiction.
   - Need.
   - Demand.

    b. Periodicals.
   - Demand.
   - Indexing in periodical indexes.
   - Authority and objectivity.
   - Local interest.
   - Format, e.g., bound volumes, microfilm.

    c. Newspapers.
   - Local interest.
   - Geographical representation.
   - Objectivity.
   - Demand.

    d. Paperbacks.
   - Out-of-print or not obtainable in other format.
   - Heavy demand for temporary current interest.
   - Multiple copies for class assignments.
   - Older and rarely used titles.
   - Same criteria as fiction and nonfiction.

    e. Documents.
   - Local interest.
   - Same critera is nonfiction.

Nonprint Resources

1. Interest and ability level of intended audience.

2. Relevancy to subject matter.

3. Technical quality, e.g., color, sound, art.

4. Authenticity of characterization.

5. Artistic and/or literary quality.

6. Up-to-dateness.

7. Appeal of format.

8. Organization of data.

9. Reputation of producer.

10. Storage and accessibility.

11. Availability of hardware for utilization.

12. Cost.

QUESTIONED MATERIALS

1. Procedure.

Objections may occasionally be made to selections although qualified persons attempt to select valuable materials for student and teacher use. A review of challenged materials should be treated objectively, unemotionally, and as an important routine matter. Criticisms must be submitted to the superintendent on a form which must be signed and must include specific information as to author, title, publisher, and definite citation of objection. [See Part III for a similar sample form.]

2. Review Committee.

The material in question shall be reviewed by a committee of 5:

a. Building principal.

b. Teacher from the building involved in the subject field of the questioned material.

c. Department head of the subject field in question.

d. Representative appointed by the Parents and Teachers Organization.

e. Representative from the Public Library Board of Trustees.

The Review Committee shall function when needed by the superintendent upon receipt of a complaint. The review process shall be considered with the specific objections in mind. The review process shall be limited to a maximum of 4 weeks. A decision by this committee shall be completed as soon as possible and given to the complainant. If the complainant is not satisfied with the decision, a complaint can be filed with the superintendent, who will take it to the Board of Education.

POLICY RELATING TO SPECIAL AREAS

1. *Duplication*. The duplication of titles depends upon the size of the book budget and the demand for a given title.

2. *Replacement*. The replacement of titles is contingent upon the titles' current value to the collection.

3. *Gifts*. Gift books are accepted in the library if they conform to the established criteria cited previously. Gift books are accepted with the understanding that those which are unsuitable for the collection may be disposed of at the discretion of media personnel.

4. *Weeding*. The discarding of library materials is selection in reverse. Resources are weeded for the following reasons: damage, obsolescence, insufficient use, and unserviceability.

5. *Binding*. Physical attractiveness is of special consideration in user appeal. Binding is preferable to mending if a title is expected to have long-term usefulness. Titles should be replaced when binding costs are comparable or greater than the purchase price. Paperbacks may require prebinding to withstand use and periodicals may need binding for preservation. An irreplaceable title of importance should be retained regardless of condition and a decision for care of its appearance should be determined by the effect upon its value.

POLICY REVISION

This policy shall be reviewed annually and revised as times and circumstances require.

Chambersburg Area School District Library Media Centers

OBJECTIVES

The Chambersburg Area School District Library Media Centers are learning centers that provide materials, services, and facilities for the instructional program needs of the District's students and teachers and endorse the responsibilities outlined in the *Library Bill of Rights* as approved by the American Association of School Librarians. [See Appendix I for current statement.]

RESPONSIBILITY FOR SELECTION OF MATERIALS

Books and other materials are selected by school librarians in consultation with faculty and administrators, and when deemed appropriate, students and parents. This is a cooperative, continuing process with major responsibility vested in the librarians.

CRITERIA FOR SELECTION

Books and materials selected for the school's library media center should meet high standards of quality involving the following criteria:

1. *Authority*—determined by the author's qualifications and sources of information used in preparation of the materials.

2. *Scope*—determined by adequacy of coverage in relation to the subject presented.

3. *Reliability*—determined by accuracy and recency.

Chambersburg Area School District Library Media Centers, Chambersburg, PA 17201

4. *Treatment*—determined by noting the author's purpose (reference, recreation, etc.).

5. *Readability*—determined by noting suitability for grade and interest levels, appropriate print and vocabulary, and illustrations.

6. *Subject interest*—determined by skill of presentation in relation to grade and interest level.

7. *Format*—determined by examination of cover, print, size, binding, illustrations, and other visual presentations.

8. *Special features*—determined by examination for appropriate indexes, bibliographies, outlines, etc.

9. *Potential uses*—consideration of the following:

   a. Meet curricular needs.
   b. Provide curriculum enrichment.
   c. Meet general reference needs.
   d. Provide additional factual information.
   e. Promote social and emotional development.
   f. Provide inspirational value.
   g. Serve reluctant readers.
   h. Furnish mature readers.
   i. Provide for recreational reading.
   j. Develop aesthetic taste.

BOOK AND MEDIA SELECTION AIDS

1. Books:

   AAAS Science Booklist
   American Historical Fiction, Dickenson
   Basic Book Collection for High Schools, ALA
   Basic Book Collection for Junior High Schools, ALA
   Children's Catalog (and Supplements)
   Elementary School Library Collection, Brodart
   Gateways to Readable Books, Strang
   Guide to Reference Books (and Supplements), Winchell
   Junior High School Library Catalog (and Supplements), H. W. Wilson
   Notable Children's Books, ALA
   Senior High School Library Catalog

2. Periodicals:

   Booklist and Subscription Books Bulletin
   Bulletin of the Center for Children's Books

Horn Book Magazine
Instructor
Media Index
Previews
School Library Journal
Teacher
Wilson Library Bulletin

3. Other Sources:

South Central Regional Library Media Examination Center
Conference Exhibits

DUPLICATION

Need is the criterion for duplication of books and materials. A variety of different titles is usually preferred to duplicate copies of a single copy. When the need for duplication arises, additional copies are usually purchased in controlled numbers and in paperback when available and suitable.

GIFTS

Gifts to the library media collections must be evaluated and satisfy the same criteria as purchases for the collection. It is left to the discretion of the school librarians whether gift materials are acceptable.

MAINTENANCE OF THE COLLECTION

1. *Inventory.* The collections shall be inventoried regularly, at least once every year.

2. *Weeding.* In order to develop and maintain quality collections of books and materials, librarians employ a periodic evaluation of these collections. This weeding process enables them to rid the collections of out-of-date, inappropriate, useless, worn-out books and materials.

PROCEDURE FOR HANDLING CHALLENGED OR QUESTIONED BOOKS AND MATERIALS

1. It is recommended that, upon receiving a complaint, the librarian hold a conference with the citizen making the complaint. The principal of the building will be notified and may be present at the conference.

2. If the problem cannot be resolved in the conference, the citizen will be given a complaint form. [See Part III for a similar sample form.]

3. The citizen will return the completed form to the building librarian who will give a copy to the building principal and the library coordinator. (The form must be completed in its entirety to be acceptable for a review of the book).

4. The building principal will appoint a committee to review the complaint. This committee should be composed of the school librarian, the building principal, the library coordinator, two teachers (one from the discipline or grade representing the subject matter of the book and one from a different discipline or grade), and another member of the school community. (This person could be from the PTA or other parent interest group).

5. The committee will review the complaint and make a written report and recommendation to the superintendent.

6. Final disposition authority to keep or remove a book or other material rests with the Board of School Directors of the Chambersburg Area School District.

7. A letter stating the decision will be sent to the complainant.

Sonoma Valley Unified School District Library Media Centers

OBJECTIVES

The primary objective of the Sonoma Valley Unified School District's educational media centers is to implement, enrich, and support the educational programs of the schools. It is the duty of each center to provide a wide range of materials on all levels of difficulty, with diversity of appeal, and the presentation of different points of view.

To this end, the Board of Education of the Sonoma Valley Unified School District reaffirms the objectives of the *Standards for School Media Programs* of the American Association of School Librarians and the *Library Bill of Rights*. [See Appendix I for current statement.]

PHILOSOPHY

Today, in America, the home and family are in transition. How change will permanently affect the present young people is questionable. They are as perturbed as adults with the conflict in ideologies among world powers; they share the anxiety of the future. As adolescents, they are unsure and insecure. Four major adjustments face them: (1) becoming acquainted with their bodies and their changes, (2) forming mature sexual relationships, (3) freeing themselves from control of parents and becoming responsible agents, and (4) forming values and decisions on professions and goals. Young people need the opportunity to recognize and practice individual enterprise and competition. They need encouragement to excel, but excellence cannot be achieved unless they have the ability to understand their places in historical reference and to practice critical thinking, too often alien practices, in view of the brain-pounding of modern advertising and publicity. Providing the right instructional media assists these unfolding abilities.

Sonoma Valley Unified School District Media Centers, Sonoma, CA 95476

RESPONSIBILITY

The Sonoma Valley Unified School District Board of Education is legally responsible for all matters relating to the operation of Sonoma Valley Unified School District schools. The responsibility for the selection of instructional materials is delegated to the professionally trained personnel employed by the school system. Selection of materials involves many people: principals, teachers, supervisors, and media specialists. The responsibility for coordinating the selection of instructional materials and making the recommendation for purchase rests with the professionally trained media personnel.

GUIDELINES

The expansion of school library programs to include a diversity of materials is a natural outgrowth of the acceptance of the concept of the library as an integral aspect of the instructional program of the school. It is the function of the library to provide materials which undergird the school curriculum, and it is no longer realistic to think of teaching and learning materials only in terms of the printed word. To support an educational program, a school needs material in many forms related to all curriculum areas.

Intelligent selection of these materials is a time-consuming task which requires professional competence, as well as the ability to profit by the professional competence of others. The first requisite is depth of knowledge of the curriculum and the second is knowledge of the needs, interests, and abilities of the school clientele. Related factors are the amount of money available, the materials already available in the school library, and materials available from other sources.

Selection of the type of material, printed, pictured, or recorded, should be made on the basis of the medium available that most effectively conveys or interprets the content or the concept; in many instances, material in one format is useful in supplementing that in another. The same material may be needed in various media for use with individuals and groups with varying abilities and interests as well as to provide opportunities for variety in presentation. All materials selected for the school library, in whatever format, should meet high standards of excellence. Materials which deal with current topics should be up-to-date; those which reflect a biased point of view should make the prejudice recognizable.

CRITERIA

Needs of the individual school based on knowledge of the curriculum and of the existing collection are given first consideration. Requests from faculty, library volunteers, and students are given consideration. Materials for purchase are considered on the basis of:

1. Overall purpose.

2. Timeliness or permanence.

3. Importance of the subject matter.

4. Quality of the writing/production.

5. Readability and popular appeal.

6. Authoritativeness.

7. Reputation of the publisher/producer.

8. Reputation and significance of the author/artist/composer/producer, etc.

9. Format and price.

PROCEDURES

In selecting materials for purchase, the media specialist evaluates the existing collection and consults:

1. Reputable, unbiased, professionally prepared selection aids.

2. Specialists from all departments and/or all grade levels.

3. The media selection committee appointed by the media specialists to serve in an advisory capacity in the selection of materials.

Reviews are the most familiar form of critical expression concerning new publications. These reviews may be in the form of essays or short notices. Although much variation of opinion is expressed by different reviewers, it is generally possible to obtain a consensus of judgment. Some instructional materials selection tools, apart from the general literary periodicals and contemporary works of literary criticism, are specifically for library use, including: *Previews, Book Review Digest, School Library Journal, Horn Book, Media and Methods,* etc.

In specific areas the media specialist follows these procedures:

1. Gift materials are judged by basic selection standards and are accepted or rejected by these standards.

2. Multiple items of outstanding and much-in-demand media are purchased as needed.

3. Worn or missing standard items are replaced periodically.

4. Out-of-date or no longer useful materials are withdrawn from the collection. Sets of materials and materials acquired by subscription are examined carefully and are purchased only to fill a definite need.

Salesmen must have permission from each school office before going into the school.

TYPES OF MATERIALS

Instructional materials include textbooks, trade (or library) books, newspapers, pamphlets, magazines, charts, globes, maps, recordings, films, filmstrips, pictures, collections or specimens of real objects, models, exhibits, and any other media of communication which may contribute to teaching and to learning.

In choosing instructional materials, the following needs must be considered: (1) the purchase in teaching, (2) the characteristics of the children to be taught, (3) the situation, to decide what types of materials would be most stimulating and would motivate the best learning, (4) the materials that are available that might be considered and their potential, (5) the ultimate decision as to ''the best thing to use with this group or this child to teach those things at this time.''

The process of selection includes the following areas of consideration:

1. The potential value of the various types of materials.

2. The materials available from which to choose.

3. The materials themselves (specific books, recordings, films, etc., that are outstanding).

4. The standard lists that recommend materials.

5. The criteria to apply in evaluating various types of materials.

6. The current periodicals that review materials.

7. How to motivate children and young people to use materials intelligently and with satisfaction.

8. How to use these materials in teaching.

For specific media, considerations are as follows:

Books

1. Is the subject matter or story appropriate for the group or individual who will use it?

2. Will it interest them?

3. For factual material, is it dependable, accurate, and up-to-date?

4. For imaginative material, does it encourage appreciations, attitudes, understandings, or insights that are worthwhile?

5. Is the style appropriate for the type of book? Does it encourage appreciation for good literature, skillfully told with beauty and feeling? Or does it encourage appreciation for clarity of explanation, logic, respect for facts and their objective presentation?

6. Does it have a valuable purpose for young readers? Examples: (1) understanding of our country and its development; (2) understanding of people in other countries and their problems; (3) understanding the facts and methods of science; (4) appreciation of art, music or literature; (5) recognition of one's personal abilities, interests, problems; (6) insight into the feelings and problems of others; and (7) encouraging creative or other worthwhile activities on the part of the reader?

7. What values might there be for children or young people in using this book?

8. Is the format satisfactory:

    a. Is the appearance interesting and appropriate for the type of book and reader?

    b. Is the binding durable, attractive?

    c. Is the book well designed?

    d. Are the illustrations appropriate, useful assets to the book?

9. If choosing for purchase, is this the best possible value for the cost, considering the type of material, the content, and format?

Films, Filmstrips

1. Is the film/filmstrip designed to teach effectively the information, attitudes, skills, or understandings pertinent at this point in the teaching-learning situation?

2. Can it be easily understood by the group to be taught?

3. Is it of suitable length for use with this age group or for this purpose in teaching?

4. Are the photographic and sound qualities good?

5. Is the film/filmstrip convincing, clear, interesting, and stimulating in its presentation?

6. What will this group of children and young people learn from this film/filmstrip? What might some individuals in this group learn?

7. Is the film/filmstrip based on dependable information? Is it a true representation of experience? Is it up-to-date, or, if dated, still useful?

8. Is this the best film/filmstrip available for this purpose and this group of learners?

Tape and Disc Recordings

1. Is this recording designed to reach or encourage the desired attitudes, understandings, skills, or appreciations?

2. Is it appropriate for this group of learners in style, content, length?

3. Is the tone quality clear?

4. If a dramatic presentation combining background music or other sound, narration, dramatization, is there unity of effect, skillfully developed?

5. Is this the best recording available for this purpose?

6. Will it encourage intelligent listening?

7. If choosing for purchase, is it nonbreakable, and is it worth the cost?

Globes

1. Is it durable? Sturdy, for easy handling? Large enough (at least 16 inches) for adequate representation and for ease in visual use?

2. Are the symbols easy to distinguish, used consistently all over the globe?

3. Are the colors pleasing, and when used as symbols, used consistently?

4. Is the type good, the legend complete, and clearly printed?

5. Is the mounting flexible? (A cradle mounting is most flexible.)

6. Is the information dependable, up-to-date, presented clearly and fairly?

7. Is this the type of globe suitable for this teaching situation?

Maps

1. Is the format good, with adequate, clearly printed, and consistently used symbol language, pleasing colors, and flexible mounting? (Single copies of maps are most desirable since they are most useful school-wide. Folded maps may be handled and stored easily.)

2. Is the information (physical areas, size of cities or areas, historical data, facts of production or natural resources, geographical items) dependable and up-to-date?

3. For world maps, is the mapping done on an equal area projection? (See title for this information.) Are sufficient parallels (10° to 15° intervals) shown? Are they straight lines spaced equal distance apart? Do the 60th parallels measure approximately one-half the length of the equator? Do the meridians converge at the poles? Are there at least 2 or more standard meridians?

4. Is this the best value for the money?

Slides

1. Are they dependable as to information, clear as to purpose?

2. Are they appropriate for this teaching-learning situation?

3. Are they technically good, with good photography or other graphic presentation, with no scratches or blemishes?

4. Are they well designed for general effectiveness?

5. Are they worth the cost?

CHALLENGED MATERIALS

Occasional objections to a selection will be made by the public, despite the care taken to select valuable materials for student and teacher use and the qualifications of persons who select the material. The board must uphold and defend all media selections made by the media specialist who acts as its agent. Without this support, no librarian will attempt any but the most timid efforts to stock the shelves, and library service in its fullest sense will not exist.

A file is to be kept on materials likely to be questioned or considered controversial. If a complaint is made, the procedures are as follows:

1. Be courteous but make no commitments.

2. Inform the complainant that s/he must submit to the media committee a written objection, in triplicate, on a form which is provided. [See Part III for a similar sample form.]

3. Temporarily withdraw the material, pending a decision of the committee.

4. Inform the superintendent and the media supervisor.

5. The Board of Education will appoint a committee to reevaluate the media materials and make recommendations. This review is to take no longer than 2 weeks to complete. The Review Committee should be composed of the school principal, one other administrator, the librarian, and 2 teachers chosen by the principal to make a committee of 5. Every effort is to be made to meet with the person questioning materials to consider his/her objection, keeping in mind the best interests of the students, the community, and the curriculum.

6. The media committee will:

   a. Read and examine the material in the light of the objection made.

   b. Check general acceptance of the material by reading reviews.

   c. Weigh values and faults of the material as a whole and form opinions based on full examination.

   d. Meet to discuss the material and prepare a report on it. This report is to be filed and a copy sent to the complainant.

   e. The ruling of the committee may be appealed to the board. The decision of the board shall be final.

Fairfield Public School Library Resource Centers

PHILOSOPHY

The library exists primarily for educational purposes. The purpose of a school library resource center should be to implement classroom activity and serve as an integral part of the curriculum, paralleling it at all points. It offers enrichment and provides materials selected from all forms of media to serve as a basis for independent study and individualized instruction for interest, for vocabulary maturity, and at the ability levels of all students within the school.

OBJECTIVES

Fairfield's Public School Library Resource Centers are an essential part of learning. They are centers where books, pamphlets, periodicals, and other nonbook materials are organized for use by the teachers and pupils. Their objectives are to:

1. Enrich and supplement the basic texts in the classroom.

2. Serve as a basis for a working laboratory for the investigation of classroom problems and the satisfaction of intellectual curiosity.

3. Satisfy, through the development of library skills, the needs of study and research.

4. Provide an opportunity to learn about the use of books and other nonbook materials.

5. Stimulate an enjoyment and appreciation of materials to attract students to reading, viewing, and listening as sources of pleasure and recreation over and above needed subject content.

Fairfield Public School Library Resource Centers, Fairfield, CT 06430

6. Develop the competencies in students to use and produce media for communication.

7. Contribute to development of the social, intellectual, and spiritual values of the students.

No statement of school library objectives is complete without inclusion of the *Library Bill of Rights,* the *Freedom to Read,* and *Intellectual Freedom* statements, which are included in this policy. [See Appendix I for current statements.]

SELECTION

The basic policy is to choose the best new materials and replace and duplicate the older titles which have proven their worth.

Materials should be judged on their own merits and considered also in relation to the budget, the need, the collection as a whole and in relation to the intellectual, emotional, and physical maturity of the pupils for whom they are intended.

RESPONSIBILITY

Selection of materials for the library is the responsibility of the library teacher and the coordinator of learning resources.

CRITERIA FOR SELECTION

The selection of materials is a continuous process because of the changing curriculum content and the publishing of new materials. Materials include books, charts, pictures, posters, 8mm and 16mm films, filmstrips, games, globes, maps, kits, models, microforms, disc and tape recordings, slides, transparencies, and video tapes. The selection process is as follows:

1. Materials may be recommended for selection by teachers, administrators, citizens, and students.

2. The library teachers and the coordinator of learning resources may be aided in their final selection by consulting authoritative reviews, recommended lists, and standard bibliographic tools. It is recommended that materials should be previewed or examined if evaluative, reliable reviews are not available. It is further recommended that nonprint materials be previewed prior to purchase.

3. The following evaluative criteria are used as they apply:

   a. The materials meet high standards of quality in factual content and are appropriate to the ability and needs of the pupils.

   b. Most materials are selected, based upon the curricular needs of the students.

   c. The materials contribute to literary appreciation or have aesthetic value.

   d. The materials are objectively and impartially selected to provide a balanced collection for the library.

   e. The materials are selected for their clarity of sound, effective use of sound track, narration, dialogue and/or captions, photographic quality, use of color where needed, and suitability for curriculum use.

CRITERIA FOR SELECTION OF CONTROVERSIAL MATERIALS

Materials should be selected for their strengths rather than rejected for their weaknesses.

In selecting materials in controversial areas, the following criteria are given consideration:

1. Materials on controversial issues represent a particular point of view, and a sincere effort is made to select equally representative materials covering contrasting points of view.

2. The material does not unfairly, inaccurately, or viciously disparage a particular race or religion. A writer's expression of a certain viewpoint is not to be considered a disparagement when it represents the historical or contemporary views held by some persons or groups.

3. The materials on religion are chosen to explain rather than convince and are selected to represent the field as widely as necessary for the school purposes.

4. The selection of materials on political theories and ideologies or on public issues is directed towards maintaining a balanced collection, representing various views.

5. The use of profanity or the treatment of sex in a literary work of established quality is not an adequate reason for eliminating the material from the school library.

6. Materials on physiology, physical maturation, or personal hygiene should be accurate and in good taste.

INQUIRY PROCEDURES

Occasional objections to a selection will be made by individuals, despite the care taken to select valuable materials for student and teacher use and the qualifications of persons who select the materials.

If any complaint is made, the procedures are as follows:

1. Be courteous, but make no commitments.

2. Invite the complainant to discuss his/her objection or objections with the building administrator and the library teacher for the purpose of resolving the objection or objections.

3. Inform complainant of the option to file his/her objections in writing and offer to have him/her complete the proper questionnaire, so that s/he may submit a formal complaint to the building principal. [See Part III for a similar sample form.]

4. The principal of the building, upon receiving the complainant's request, will then inform the superintendent of schools, the assistant superintendent of instruction, the director of elementary education, and the coordinator of learning resources.

5. The building administrator will:

   a. Read and examine materials referred to him/her.

   b. Review with the library teacher the selection criteria and objectives used and prepare a report.

   c. File copies of the report with the superintendent of schools and the coordinator of learning resources.

6. The library teacher will prepare a report and file copies with the superintendent of schools and the coordinator of learning resources.

7. The superintendent of schools should submit to the complainant his/her recommendations in 2 weeks with a copy to the building administrator, library teacher, and coordinator of learning resources.

GIFTS

The library welcomes books and other resources from individuals and organizations but reserves the right to refuse unsuitable materials. The materials, to be acceptable, must meet the same high standards and criteria established for the selection of all library materials. A special book plate will be placed in the front of the material to recognize the giver.

MEMORIALS AND BEQUESTS

Citizens and organizations often consider memorials or bequests to libraries, in the form of funds, for the enrichment of the lives of the youth in general or in specified areas of knowledge. The coordinator of learning resources and school officials will gladly work with any individuals or organizations in the formation of policies regarding such memorials or bequests.

SELECTION AIDS

Ideally, all materials added to the library should be read or previewed before purchase. Where circumstances make such reviewing impossible, skilled use should be made of selection aids, such as: basic general lists, current general lists, special bibliographies for reference books and particular subject materials, and book reviewing journals. No one publication should be relied on exclusively.

Council Bluffs Public Schools Media Centers

REASONS FOR POLICY

The Board of Education of the Council Bluffs Public Schools has directed the administration to develop a policy for the selection of instructional materials.

The advantages of a written policy for the selection of materials are numerous: (1) It encourages thinking on the part of librarians, teachers, administrators and parents about the needs of that particular school library; (2) it promotes cooperation among many groups; (3) it stimulates critical evaluation of materials and improved selection; (4) it brings understanding to the practices and problems facing those selecting materials and helps with the interpretation of those problems; (5) it provides a positive approach to controversial or challenged materials; (6) it insures wise use of funds; and (7) it is an answer to the gift book problem.

Of major importance is the fact that the United States Constitution guarantees the right to read in the First Amendment. Additionally, the board recognizes the principles of the *Students' Right to Read*, as approved by the National Council of Teachers of English, and the *Library Bill of Rights*. [See Appendix I for current statement.]

OBJECTIVES

The primary objectives of the schools' educational media centers are to implement, enrich, and support the educational programs of the schools and to aid the individual student in the pursuit of continuing education and the creative use of leisure time. It is the duty of the centers to provide a wide range of materials on all levels of difficulty, with diversity of appeal and the presentation of different points of view.

Council Bluffs Public Schools Media Centers, Council Bluffs, IA 51501

RESPONSIBILITY FOR SELECTION

The Council Bluffs Board of Education is legally responsible for all matters relating to the operation of the Council Bluffs Community Schools.

The authority for the selection of instructional materials is delegated to the professionally trained personnel employed by the school system.

Selection of materials involves principals, teachers, coordinators, and media specialists. The responsibility for coordinating the selection of instructional materials rests with the professionally trained media personnel.

CRITERIA FOR SELECTION

Needs of the individual school based on knowledge of the curriculum and of the existing collection are given first consideration.

Consideration of the criteria below, when relevant, shall provide the basis for selection of materials.

1. Authority—Reputation and significance of author/artist/composer/ producer.

2. Reputation of publisher/producer.

3. Scope—Overall purpose.

4. Reliability—Accuracy, recency, timeliness or permanence.

5. Subject matter importance or interest.

6. Treatment of material—Purpose, bias, level (technical or general).

7. Readability and popular appeal.

8. Quality of writing/production.

9. Format:

Print

Paper of good quality.
Print adequate and well-spaced.
Adequate margins.
Effective illustrations (pertinent).
Firmly bound.
Adequate and accurate index.
Bibliographies, projects, charts, maps, glossary.

Nonprint

High artistic quality.
Technical quality—satisfactory visual image, clear and intelligible sound reproduction, effective use of color, synchronization of sound and visual.
Medium appropriate for message.

10. Potential use for reference, dealing with personal problems and cultural understanding, understanding current events, developing special interests, aesthetic tastes, and inspirational values.

11. Standard selection tools—Reliable professional selection tools should be used as guides. Lists issued by the American Library Association, the Association for Educational Communications and Technology, the Iowa Department of Public Instruction, the National Education Association, the National Council of Teachers of English, the American Association for the Advancement of Science, and other comparable professional publications may be used as selection guides. An examination of the materials themselves is the best guide for purchase.

PROCEDURES

In selecting materials for purchase, the media specialist evaluates the existing collection and consults reputable, unbiased, professionally prepared selection aids. Teachers, principals, and other staff members from all departments and/or grade levels are consulted. Suggestions from parents and students are always considered. The principal has the ultimate responsibility for those materials to be used in his/her building.

GIFTS

Gift materials are judged by the basic selection standards in this policy and are accepted or rejected by those standards. All gifts may be accepted with the stipulation that the principal or his/her designee reserves the right to dispose of unneeded materials.

MULTIPLE COPIES

Multiple copies of outstanding worth may be purchased where warranted by use or need. Worn or missing standard items are replaced periodically.

WITHDRAWALS

Materials to be withdrawn are judged by the same basic standards as those for purchase. Those found unsuitable because of content, age, or condition are no longer useful and are withdrawn.

FREE AND INEXPENSIVE MATERIALS

Free and inexpensive materials may be acquired and used, provided they are unbiased quality materials without reference to a specific make of product and deal with a general field of accepted educational value.

CONTROVERSIAL AREAS

Since the following subjects are sometimes controversial, these shall be our policies concerning them:

1. *Religion.* Factual, unbiased material which represents major religions of the world shall be included in the library collections.

2. *Ideologies.* The libraries shall, without making any effort to sway reader judgment, make available basic factual information on the level of their reading public any ideology or philosophy which exerts a strong force, either favorable or unfavorable, in government, current events, politics, or other phase of life.

3. *Sex and profanity.* Materials with accents on sex shall be subjected to a stern test of literary merit and reality by the media specialist who shall take into consideration the community, the laws, and the accepted public moral standards. While we would not in any case include the sensational, overdramatic, or pornographic, the appearance of sexual incidents or profanity shall not automatically disqualify a book. Rather the decision shall be made on the basis of whether the book presents life in its true proportions, whether circumstances are realistically dealt with, and whether the book is of literary value. Factual material of an educational nature on the level of the reader shall be included in the literary collections.

4. *Race.* Materials representative of the many ethnic and cultural groups and their contributions to our American heritage shall be provided. Materials should be well written, objective, and when taken as a whole should not attempt to sway the emotions of the student toward or against any one group.

5. *Narcotics, alcohol, and tobacco.* State law requires that we teach about the harmful effects of their use. To be avoided are presentations on the methods of taking or administering these substances and pleasurable effects of their use.

CHALLENGED MATERIALS

Occasional objections to a selection will be made despite the care taken to select valuable materials for student and teacher use and the qualifications of persons who select the materials.

The principles of the freedom to read and of the professional responsibility of the staff rather than the materials must be defended.

Steps to be followed are:

1. Invite the complainant to file objections in writing on a questionnaire. [See Part III for a similar sample form.]

2. Determine whether materials may be sufficiently in question to warrant immediate withdrawal pending a decision of a Reconsideration Committee.

3. The complainant should be asked to return his/her formal written objection to the principal of the building involved. When this is done, the complainant may request a hearing before the Reconsideration Committee. Such complaints should be handled at the building level where possible.

4. A reasonable amount of time will be given for all members of the Reconsideration Committee to read and evaluate the material in question.

5. The Reconsideration Committee will meet with the complainant and carefully consider all facets involved.

6. The Reconsideration Committee will hold a session for discussion and evaluation. A recommendation with an explanation will be made to the superintendent.

7. The superintendent will notify the complainant of the decision.

8. The complainant, if not satisfied, may ask for a hearing before the Board of Education.

9. The decision of the Board of Education is final.

10. This process should be brought to its conclusion within a period of 3 months.

RECONSIDERATION COMMITTEE

The Reconsideration Committee shall be made up of 11 members:

1. One principal designated annually by the superintendent.

2. One teacher designated annually by the superintendent.

3. One school media specialist designated annually by the superintendent.

4. One member of the central administrative staff designated annually by the superintendent who will serve as chairman of the committee. (This position will normally be filled by the supervisor or person responsible for the district's media services.)

5. Five members from the community appointed annually by the Executive Committee of the Parent-Teacher-Student Association.

6. Two high school students selected annually from and by the Student Advisory Committee.

Oak Lawn Community High School Media Center

LEGAL RESPONSIBILITY

The Board of Education of Oak Lawn Community High School is legally responsible for all matters relating to the operation of the school. This includes the operation and contents of the school library-media center.

SELECTION PERSONNEL

The Board of Education, operating through the administrative staff of the school, provides qualified professional personnel to select the materials for the library-media center and to direct its operation.

OBJECTIVES

The library-media department should be the main resource center for learning activities of the school. Its primary objective is to implement, enrich, and support the educational program of the school by:

1. Acquiring, organizing, and making available a variety of relevant materials and equipment for their use.

2. Furnishing students and teachers with guidance and instruction in the location, use, and evaluation of these materials and equipment.

RESPONSIBILITIES

As professional educators, the staff of the school library-media department is concerned with the development of informed and responsible citizens. To this end, it is the responsibility of this department to provide:

Oak Lawn Community High School Media Center, Oak Lawn, IL 60453

1. A comprehensive collection of instructional materials, plus equipment for their use, selected in compliance with basic written selection principles, and to give maximum accessibility to these materials and equipment, by providing:

   a. Materials that will support the curriculum, taking into consideration individual needs, varied interests, abilities, socioeconomic backgrounds, and maturity levels of the students served.

   b. Materials for teachers and students that will stimulate growth in knowledge and develop literary, cultural, and aesthetic appreciations and ethical standards.

   c. Materials which accurately reflect all religious, social, political, and ethnic groups, and their contributions to our American heritage as well as a knowledge and appreciation of world history and culture.

   d. Materials on all sides of controversial issues, beliefs, and ideas so that young citizens may develop, under guidance, the practice of critical analysis of all media.

   e. A comprehensive collection of instructional materials which, when selected in compliance with basic selection principles, can be defended on the basis of their appropriateness for the users of the center.

2. The necessary qualified personnel for the organization, maintenance, and operation of the department to fulfill its stated objectives.

SELECTION PROCEDURES

In order to fulfill the stated objectives of the library-media department, the professional selection personnel will consult with the school administration, faculty, students, and parents as needed in making selections.

Selection of materials will be assisted by reading, examination, and checking of standard evaluation aids, standard catalogs, and reviews which are reputable, unbiased, and professionally prepared.

CRITERIA FOR SELECTION

1. Needs of the individual school program:

   a. Based on knowledge of the curriculum and of the existing collection.

   b. Based on knowledge of youth and of the local school community.

    c. Based on requests from administrators, teachers, students, and parents.

2. Merit of material to be purchased, judged on the basis of:

    a. Overall purpose.

    b. Timeliness or permanence.

    c. Importance of the subject matter.

    d. Quality of the writing or production.

    e. Readability and popular appeal.

    f. Authoritativeness.

    g. Reputation of the publisher or producer.

    h. Reputation and significance of the author, artist, composer, and producer.

    i. Format and price.

PROCEDURES FOR HANDLING COMPLAINTS CONCERNING MATERIALS

We believe that parents have the right to choose the reading of their own children. We do not believe they have the right to control that of other children.

Many well-meaning persons wish to restrict school materials to those that do not mention unsavory aspects of our society. They do not want children exposed to materials in which people drink or swear or do many of the things commonly featured in daily newspapers, on television, or in motion pictures. Schools have a responsibility to lead their students to understand all aspects of their culture and society—the good and the bad. An unwise course of action into which the school can be stampeded may lead to undermining the morale of teachers and the unnecessary disappearance from the curriculum of materials useful in helping the student understand his/her world.

1. Criticisms of materials should be submitted in writing to the superintendent, who will inform the Board of Education.

    a. If the complainant telephones, listen courteously, and invite him/her to file his/her complaint in writing. Make no commitments, admissions of guilt, or threats.

    b. If s/he writes, acknowledge the letter promptly and politely.

c. In either case, offer to send the complainant a questionnaire so that s/he can make a formal statement. [See Part III for a similar sample form.]

d. Do nothing else until a formal, written complaint has been received. Idle troublemakers may well be discouraged from taking action. The responsible objector has learned the channels and procedures for his/her complaint and should be satisfied that s/he will be properly heard.

2. The written form will:

a. Formalize and make official the complaint.

b. Indicate specifically the material in question.

c. Reveal the size of the complainant's backing.

d. Require the complainant to clarify his/her thinking on the material in order to make an intelligent statement on the specific objection.

e. Cause him/her to evaluate the material.

f. Establish to what extent s/he is familiar with the material.

g. Give him/her an opportunity to recognize the criticism and intent of the material or to realize his/her failure to understand it.

h. Give, finally, alternative actions which s/he may take on the material.

3. Allegations thus submitted will be considered by a committee selected by the superintendent. This committee will include a member of the library-media department, one or more faculty members qualified in the subject field of the questioned material, a member of the administration, and any other qualified and concerned persons the superintendent may choose.

4. The materials involved will be withdrawn pending a decision in writing by the above committee.

5. Appeals from the decision may be made through the superintendent to the Board of Education for final decision.

Cashton Public Schools Instructional Materials Center

OBJECTIVES

The function of the Cashton Public School Instructional Materials Center is to select books and media for its clientele that will contribute to a well-balanced collection that will enhance educational and recreational growth. It is the duty of the center to provide a wide range of materials on all levels of difficulty, with diversity of appeal and presentation of different points of view.

It is important that we support the book selection principles contained in the American Library Association's *Library Bill of Rights,* approved by the American Association of School Librarians. [See Appendix I for current statement.]

RESPONSIBILITY FOR SELECTION OF MATERIALS

The Instructional Materials Center (IMC) director, charged with book selection, is appointed by the Board of Education. This policy statement, when filed with the Board of Education, enables the board to back the stand of the Instructional Materials Center director or to notify the director if they feel the policies are not being carried out as originally intended.

The IMC director has the ultimate decision as to whether or not material for the library shall be purchased or accepted as a gift, although any and all members of the staff, parents, and students will be encouraged to give suggestions.

CRITERIA USED IN MEDIA SELECTION

General Criteria

The primary objective of a school library is to implement, enrich, and support the educational program of a school. Criteria for instructional materials selection should implement this basic objective. Criteria for the selection of all instructional materials are both general, as found in the professional literature, and specific in terms of the needs of the community. General criteria are stated in terms of significant descriptors of the subject, integrity of treatment, and quality of the medium (style, clarity, originality). Specific criteria are determined by a study of the characteristics of the schools' instructional program and the needs of students as affected by the community, as follows:

1. Needs of the individual school program.
   a. Based on knowledge of the curriculum.
   b. Based on requests from administrators and teachers.

2. Needs of the individual student.
   a. Based on knowledge of children and youth.
   b. Based on requests by parents and students.

Needs from these several sources will require a wide range of instructional materials, for an acceptance level of quality on all levels of difficulty, with a diversity of appeal, and presentation of different points of view (ethnic, religious, political, and cultural).

Specific Criteria

1. *General book selection.* The following will be evaluated in the selection of print

   a. Bibliographical data.
   b. Subject matter.
   c. Treatment.
   d. Authority.
   e. Literacy qualities.
   f. Bibliographical characteristics.
   g. Format.
   h. Possible uses.
   i. Available aids in evaluation.

2. *Nonbook material.* The following criteria will be evaluated in the selection of

   a. Authenticity.
   b. Appropriateness.

    c. Scope.
    d. Interest.
    e. Organization.
    f. Technical aspects.
    g. Special features.
    h. Physical characteristics.
    i. Library potential.
    j. Selection aids.
    k. Cost.

SELECTION AIDS

The best selection of media is done by personal examination and evaluation of materials. However, this is not always possible and, consequently, reliable selection lists are employed. Authoritative, unbiased, professionally prepared selection aids will be used. This IMC will use many of the lists recommended by the American Association of School Librarians.

POLICY RELATED TO SPECIAL MATERIALS

Periodicals, Pamphlets, Newspapers

Periodicals will be selected to supplement the curriculum and IMC collection of materials. A factor in selection will be the indexing of the periodicals in standard indexes used in the IMC. When selecting periodicals, the director will use the same criteria as for selecting books. The same criteria will be used for selecting pamphlets for the vertical file. The newspapers will include local, statewide, and nationally circulated papers.

Series Books or Materials

Media presented as a series will be evaluated as individual titles, both with and without regard to the series as a whole, and will be included when they meet previously stated criteria. Series by authors in which familiar characters are carried through many different experiences and which serve a real purpose in maintaining children's interest may be selected.

Local History

Material on state and local history is essential in the school media center. Material should meet previously established criteria for evaluation.

Professional Collection

The school IMC must provide materials for teachers and administrators. This collection should represent all areas of instruction and be both practical and innovative.

POLICY RELATED TO SPECIAL AREAS

Gifts

Gifts of books and other material will be welcomed provided they meet the same standards of book selection as those applied to original purchases, and provided they can be integrated into the general library collection and do not need special housing. Inside the book on a special card or plate will be the donor's name. The library staff reserves the right to dispose of the gift at its discretion if it is in bad physical condition, not warranting the cost of repair, or if it is out-of-date.

Duplicates

There will be duplicate copies of material if there is definite need for them. It is usually more important to provide a variety of materials rather than several copies of a single item.

Replacement

If materials have proven their worth they will be replaced if lost, damaged or worn. The replacement of material will depend on the number of media on the same subject in the IMC, the number of duplicates, and the possibility of newer material on the same subject of better quality.

CONTROVERSIAL MATERIALS

Religion

Specific religious teaching has been excluded as inappropriate but versions of the Bible have been provided. Materials on religious subjects will be factual, unbiased, and broadly represented.

Sex Education, Drugs, Immoral or Indecent Books and Materials

The IMC director will refrain from selecting materials that are sensational, overdramatic, and that glorify profanity, sex, or drugs.

Human Relations and Ethnic Groups

Books or media will not be disqualified on the basis of race. Materials should be selected to represent many different national, religious, and ethnic backgrounds. Media should demonstrate wholesome attitudes of mutual respect and understanding among all people. Books or material will also be included if they demonstrate truth about an ethnic group's experience at a particular time.

Political Ideologies

Media dealing with politics will be selected if not overly biased. Different opinions and views of many political ideologies will be provided.

PROCEDURE FOR HANDLING CRITICISM OF MEDIA

The following procedure is to be followed in case a book or other media in the school IMC are questioned. A copy of the National Council of Teachers of English complaint form will be forwarded to the complainant, with the request that he fill it out and return it to the librarian or principal. [See Part III for a similar sample form.]

1. The material in question will be removed from circulation after a signed complaint has been turned into the superintendent, principal, or librarian. The material will be reviewed by a committee.

2. The committee will consist of one faculty member in the area in which a complaint is made, the principal, 4 adults from the school district, and the librarian.

3. The lay members of the committee shall be appointed by the principal.

4. The committee will make the final decision on materials which are challenged.

5. The committee's decision may be appealed to the Board of Education.

Mountain Heritage High School Media Center

CRITERIA AND PROCEDURES FOR SELECTION

The media center collections of Yancey County, in addition to conforming with the American Library Association's *Library Bill of Rights,* approved by the American Association of School Librarians [see Appendix I for current statement], need to reflect the basic philosophies and objectives of each individual school. The criteria for the selection of all materials should be based on the needs of each school, teacher, and student.

Media center materials should be chosen through use of the following guidelines:

1. Materials meet the curriculum needs in the individual school.
2. Materials meet the need of each student and teacher.
3. Materials are authoritative, appealing, and up-to-date.
4. Materials feature good format.
5. Materials provide a wide scope of levels of difficulty and different points of view.

In the process of selecting media, all available resources should be utilized and should include bibliographies and reviews prepared by qualified professional educators, examination collections and exhibits, preview copies from publishers and producers, and specialists in different fields of study.

Each type of media has some unique features and therefore can provide a unique contribution. Each item of media should be selected for the contributions that it can make, and, in the case of materials, should be selected for the contribution that its content and method of delivery together can provide. It is important that all materials and equipment be acquired in relation to well-defined purposes for the improvement of instruction.

Mountain Heritage High School Media Center, Yancey County Schools, Burnsville, NC 28714

In evaluating the existing media collection as a basis for selection, the media specialist should count only one copy of a title, for a true picture of subject distribution.

RESPONSIBILITY FOR SELECTION

The Yancey County Board of Education is legally responsible for all matters relating to the operation of Yancey County Schools.

The coordination of the selection and acquisition of materials and equipment related to media should be the delegated responsibility of the media coordinator and media specialists.

In order to assist the media coordinator and media specialists in each school to determine selections on the basis of school objectives and priority of needs, consideration should be given to forming a committee consisting of the media specialist and teachers representing all subject or grade areas in the school. The total selection process should involve many people: media coordinator, media specialists, supervisors, principals, teachers, and students.

POLICY RELATING TO SPECIAL AREAS

1. *Gifts* should be judged by the same standards as other materials in the collection.

2. *Duplicates* should be added as use indicates need.

3. *Reference materials* should be kept up-to-date, with encyclopedias being replaced at regular intervals. Authoritative selection aids should be referred to before purchasing any sets of expensive reference books.

4. *Nonbook materials* should include filmstrips, recordings, realia, pictures, maps, globes, microfilm, slides, and tapes and should be selected by the same criteria as printed materials.

5. *Weeding and discarding* should be on a consistent and systematic basis in order that all materials will meet standards as set in the selection policies of the Yancey County School Media Centers.

6. *Rebinding* should be done on a consistent and systematic basis in order that all materials to be rebound will meet the same standards as set in the selection policies of the Yancey County School Media Centers.

7. *Challenged materials* should be reconsidered. The complaint's concerns should be submitted in writing on a form adapted from *The*

Students' Right to Read and forwarded to the media coordinator, who will notify the principal concerned and the superintendent, for action by a committee composed of administrators, media personnel, and teachers. In studying the questioned materials, the committee should use specialists in the subject matter field and approved selection aids. A written report of the committee's decision on the challenged materials should be filed in the school where the materials are located and in the central office. A copy should also be mailed to the complainant. If the matter is not resolved at this point, the complainant and the members of the committee who handled the complaint will meet with the members of the Board of Education in an effort to decide further action to be taken. It is important to note that a decision to remove materials from a media center is to be followed through only under legal guidelines as adopted by the American Library Association Council.

WEEDING MATERIALS

Systematic weeding of materials is necessary in media operation. Additionally, preventive maintenance and repair to ensure that the media remain useful at all times is a must in an effective media program. Media collections should contain only quality media with recency and should exclude obsolete, badly worn, and inappropriate items.

Materials which have become obsolete or worn out are to be discarded by the media specialist, who should consider the following areas:

1. Materials too worn to be mended or rebound.

2. Materials with worn or missing pages or parts.

3. Materials with fine print which causes difficult reading.

4. Materials beyond comprehension of the readers.

5. Materials with content out-of-date.

6. Textbooks not useful for reference.

7. Mediocre materials, including some series.

8. Sets of materials out-of-date or beyond comprehension.

9. Government documents not valuable.

10. Out-of-date vertical file materials.

The procedure for discarding is simple:

1. Discard the item by writing DISCARD on it.

2. Pull all cards for the item from the shelflist and card catalog. If item is to be replaced, file catalog cards in withdrawal file.

3. Write DISCARD on the shelflist card or in the appropriate column in the accession book. If shelflist method of accessioning is used, hold shelflist card in file marked DISCARDS until after inventory for current school year.

New York City Public Schools Library Media Centers

INTRODUCTION

1. The Board of Education and the chancellor, as the governing body of all New York City public schools, are legally responsible for the final selection of instructional materials. However, their function is policy-making and, in practice, they have delegated to the professional staff the actual task of selecting these materials.

2. The Board of Education, through the Center for Library Media, establishes policy for the selection of library materials with a clearly defined method for handling contested materials.

OBJECTIVES GOVERNING THE SELECTION OF MATERIALS

1. The primary objectives of a good school library media center are to:

   a. Implement, enrich, and support the educational program of the school and reflect the varied interests, abilities, and maturity levels of the students.

   b. Enable and encourage pupils to further develop their full potential as creative and responsible individuals.

2. To achieve these two basic objectives, it is important to provide easy access to a centrally cataloged and comprehensive collection of materials at appropriate levels of difficulty in order to:

   a. Generate an understanding of American freedoms and a desire to preserve those freedoms through the development of informed and responsible citizenship.

New York City Public Schools Center for Library Media and Telecommunications, Brooklyn, NY 11201

b. Foster a breadth and depth of insight which will stimulate growth of ethical standards and a sensitivity to social, intellectual, aesthetic, and spiritual values.

c. Represent fairly the many religious, ethnic, and cultural groups and their contribution to our American heritage.

d. Evoke a love of reading and learning which will assure continuing self-education and a fruitful source of personal enjoyment.

e. Develop reading skills, literary and aesthetic taste and discrimination in choice of materials.

f. Encourage pupils to locate, use, and evaluate material on opposing sides of controversial issues so that they may develop, under guidance, the practice of critical examination and thinking.

g. Provide practical instruction in the use of library media centers and their resources.

h. Encourage the professional growth of the faculty.

CRITERIA FOR SELECTION

1. Selection of books, periodicals, and other printed materials should be based on the following criteria:

a. Satisfaction of needs of students and faculty:

- Curriculum needs.
- Recreational reading.
- Developmental needs.

b. Quality of content:

- Accuracy and recency of factual information.
- Qualification of author.
- Unstereotyped presentation of religious, ethnic, or cultural groups and free of sexist bias.
- Readability.
- Interest level.
- Appropriateness to levels of instruction and maturity of students.
- Organization of materials.
- Treatment of controversial subjects:

  Political philosophy. Is the material factually accurate and objective in presentation or is it an authentic presentation of a particular point of view? Is there excessive emotionalism or sensationalism?

Sex and family living. Is it appropriate to the instructional and maturity level intended?

Sex and violence. The incidence of sexual episodes, profanity, or violence shall not automatically disqualify library material. Does the material present life in its true proportion? Is it appropriate to the maturity level of the students? Is it sensational or extraneous to the development of character and plot?

   c. Quality of format:

- Typography.
- Illustrations.
- Binding.

2. Nonprint materials:

   a. Same criteria as listed for printed material.

   b. Technical quality:

- Satisfactory visual image including effective use of color.
- Clear sound reproduction.
- Synchronization of sound and image.

3. Gifts of library materials will be accepted only if they meet the stated selection criteria.

PROCEDURES FOR SELECTION

1. The responsibility for the selection of library media center materials is that of professionally qualified library media specialists.

2. Provision should be made for input and communication by administrators, curriculum specialists, teachers, parents, and students.

3. Final decision on purchases should rest with the professional personnel in accordance with the formally adopted policy.

4. The process of selection of materials should be assisted by examination, reading, and checking of bibliographies, book and audiovisual review media such as:

AAS Science Book List
AAS Science Book List for Children
American Association of School Librarians Book Lists
Appraisal
AV Guide

Audiovisual Instruction
Best Books for Children
Black Experience in Children's Books (N.Y.P.L.)
Booklist
Bulletin for the Center for Children's Books
Children's Catalog and Supplements
Choice
Horn
Junior High School Catalog and Supplements
Library Journal
Media and Methods
National Council for the Social Studies Book Lists
National Council of Teachers of English Book Lists
National Science Teacher's Association Book List
New York Times Book Reviews
Science Book: A Quarterly Review
Senior H.S. Catalog and Supplements
Subscription Books Bulletin Reviews
Wilson Library Bulletin

5. Selection should be a continuing process throughout the school year.

PROCEDURE FOR HANDLING COMPLAINTS ABOUT LIBRARY MATERIALS

The following review process shall be set up to handle complaints about instructional material. It is noted here that no books or material shall be removed from the school during the review process.

1. Complaints about any instructional material within a school must be submitted in writing to the principal on a form. [See Part III for a similar sample form.]

2. If a book which is on the Board of Education Approved Library Book Lists is involved, the form may be referred to the Center for Library Media where appropriate action will be taken through reevaluation of the materials by the appropriate Standing Committee. Its recommendation will then go to the executive director of the Division of the Educational Planning and Support for final decision.

3. For nonlisted materials selected by the individual school, it is recommended that the principal set up a Review Committee who will evaluate the complaint in line with the selection criteria and any other criteria set up by the community school district. Consultation with the Center for Library Media may be requested.

4. In all cases a Review Committee will:

   a. Read and examine materials referred to it.

   b. Check general acceptance of the materials by reading reviews.

   c. Weigh values and faults against each other and form opinion based on the material as a whole and not on passages pulled out of context.

5. The Review Commitee in each affected school may be made up of the following:

   a. Principal of the school.

   b. Librarian of the school.

   c. A teacher representative chosen by the faculty from the area or grade involved.

   d. District librarian (if applicable).

   e. Two parent members in good standing of the Executive Committee of the Parents' Association certified by the president as the representatives.

6. After consideration of the recommendation, final decision should be made by the appropriate administrator designated by the district, for example, the principal or community superintendent.

Anchorage School District Library Media Centers

OBJECTIVES

The school district library/media centers will strive to:

1. Provide materials that will enrich and support the curriculum, taking into consideration the varied interests, abilities, and maturity levels of the pupils served.

2. Provide materials that will stimulate growth in factual knowledge, literary appreciation, aesthetic values, and ethical standards.

3. Provide information which will encourage and enable students to think independently and make intelligent judgments in their daily lives.

4. Provide materials representative of many religious, ethnic, and cultural groups and their contributions to our American heritage.

5. Place principle above personal opinion and reason above prejudice in the selection of quality materials in order to assure a collection appropriate for users of the materials.

RESPONSIBILITY

Selection shall be governed by:

1. Curriculum.

2. Maturity, abilities, and backgrounds of students.

3. Interests of students.

4. Quality and accuracy of available materials.

Anchorage School District Media Services, Anchorage, AK 99502

Instructional materials selection shall be a cooperative, continuing process in which administrators, teachers, lay persons, and students shall participate, coordinated by the professional staffs of media centers, district and school.

The director of the Audiovisual Services and Library Resources Departments will be responsible for the following selection-related activities at the district level:

1. Organize and administer a districtwide reviewing network for materials.

   a. Maintain liaison with all curriculum committees to ensure coordinated preview and evaluation.

   b. Arrange for preview privileges for material when examination copies are unavailable.

   c. Provide facilities for and encourage visits to the materials examination center by individuals and/or groups.·

   d. Provide an exhibit collection of current books and other print and nonprint media representing at least the current and immediate past publishing and producing seasons.

   e. Maintain a file of current commercial catalogs of materials and equipment.

   f. Act as a clearinghouse for new bibliographies and selection aids that should be brought to the attention of media personnel and as a dissemination point for the lists produced in individual schools.

   g. Purchase and make available expensive or specialized reviewing sources that normally would not be purchased or made available by individual schools.

   h. Coordinate preview of films and other audiovisual materials by curriculum committees and/or other appropriate persons or groups of persons.

   i. Maintain a permanent file of reviews of locally reviewed items and disseminate this information.

2. Supervise selection of films and unit material to be purchased for circulation from the district wide audiovisual center, verifying that all such materials have been appropriately previewed and recommended for purchase.

3. Provide for re-review of building-level materials as follows:

   a. Print and nonprint materials purchased for unit (individual school) media centers are selected from a variety of sources as indicated below. Although many of these items have been reviewed prior to selection by the librarian or other unit staff members, this is not always possible.

b. All new-to-the-district materials for unit media centers must, however, pass through the Library Resources Department for technical processing before they are delivered to the individual building media centers. At this point, these new materials are surveyed by the cataloger, who handles each new-to-the-district title, both print and nonprint. The cataloger, a professional staff member, retains any materials for which suitability might be questioned. Items so identified are then reviewed by Media Services staff members, school librarians, and, in some cases, principals, teachers, nurses, parents at the grade levels for which the materials were ordered.

c. If the item is determined to be inappropriate for the grade levels of the ordering school, it is made available to other levels and transferred to a school of appropriate level. If the item is determined to be inappropriate for any level, it is discarded.

4. Maintain a union file of materials holdings within the district.

The school media center professional staff, under the direction of the unit principal, will be responsible for the following selection-related activities at the individual school level:

1. Involve as many persons as possible from the school and the community in the selection process.

2. Route bibliographies and other selection aids to appropriate persons, requesting purchase suggestions.

3. Give high priority in the selection process to materials listed in the bibliographies included in adopted texts.

4. Be aware of curriculum changes; attend and participate in department or grade-level faculty meetings, discussing future acquisition plans.

5. Maintain liaison with the district Media Services Department and jointly coordinate activities.

6. Preview materials made available by district Media Services.

7. Conduct interest inventories with students to determine what topics interest them most and least.

8. Consult basic commercially produced selection aids:

   a. *Children's Catalog*
   b. *Elementary School Library Collection*

   c. *Junior High School Catalog*
   d. *High School Catalog*
   e. *Vertical File Index*
   f. *Booklist* and *Subscription Books Bulletin*
   g. *Wilson Library Bulletin*
   h. *School Library Journal*
   i. *Horn Book*
   j. *Previews*
   k. Professional magazines from subject departments
   l. Other current periodicals

9. Incorporate, where appropriate, suggestions from exchange of materials with neighboring-district schools, visits to exhibits and displays, examination of vendors' stocks and publishers' samples, reading lists from other school systems, etc., with emphasis on suggestions from teachers, students, Parent-Teacher Associations, and individuals of the community.

10. Coordinate requests for materials and present recommendations for purchase to the unit principal.

CRITERIA

Factors applicable to all materials:

1. Where appropriate to the subject, is the material current and up-to-date?

2. Is the item suitable for the grade level for which it is selected?

3. Does the item meet curriculum needs at that level?

4. Is any aspect of the material likely to be viewed as objectionable by any segment of the community? If so, do specific values outweigh possible objections?

5. Have materials been carefully reviewed to eliminate items reflecting biased attitudes toward race, religion, and/or sex?

6. Does each collection contain materials in significant quantity which present the roles of minority groups and of women in society in an honest and straightforward manner?

7. If material on a controversial issue is included, are all points of view regarding the topic represented in the collection?

Factors applicable to specific media:

1. Books:

   a. Fiction:

   - If a work of realistic fiction, is it relevant to the lives of the students? Does it reflect a complex reality? Does it reflect the human condition honestly?

   - Are the characters worthy of the reader's enthusiasm?

   - Do the incidents seem forced or are they plausible, considering the characters and situations depicted?

   - Will the book contribute to the academic and/or personal growth of the reader?

   b. Nonfiction:

   - Are the concepts and ideas presented within the understanding of students for whom the material is designed?

   - Are the content and subject significant? Is the material a real contribution to the subject? Is the information accurate?

   - Is the treatment of the subject balanced and original?

   - Is the author an authority in the field or, if not, has his/her research been objective and comprehensive?

   - Is the presentation of material interesting and appealing?

   - Is the writing smooth, clear, and dynamic?

   - Is the book properly indexed?

   - Are bibliographies selective and up-to-date?

   c. Other criteria applicable to both fiction and nonfiction:

   - Are the size of the book, its shape, and the illustrations and the size of the type appropriate to the contents and for the readers for whom the book is intended?

   - Is the binding durable and attractive? Is the design and makeup attractive and appropriate to the contents?

2. Audiovisual materials:

   a. Films:

   - Is the film pertinent to the educational needs of the students?

- Is the educational intent of the film best accomplished with motion pictures? How effectively are the purposes of the film accomplished?

- Is the film sufficiently limited in scope to permit adequate treatment of specific concepts contained in it?

- Is the continuity logical and satisfactory?

- Are interest and vocabulary level appropriate to the intended grade level(s)?

- Is the treatment appropriate to the main theme?

- Are color, sound effects, narration, and photography satisfactory?

- What is the effect of the film on attitudes?

b. Filmstrips (including sound filmstrips), slides, transparencies, study prints, and other still picture presentations:

- Does the subject lend itself to this format?

- Does the material relate to and does it contribute meaningful content to the topic under discussion or study?

- If so, are the visuals in sufficient quantity and quality to convey the messages adequately?

- Is the photography of good quality? Are the pictures clear, sharp and interesting?

- Is there a manual or other notes included? Does the material suggest follow-up activities?

- Is there a clearly defined sequence in the materials?

- Are captions and subtitles (if present) large enough to be read with reasonable ease?

- If there is accompanying sound, are the sound and the visual images well synchronized?

c. Audio recordings:

- Is the voice of the narrator pleasant, the diction good, and the enunciation clear and understandable?

- Is sufficient variation provided in the production so that the listening span of the student will not be taxed?

- Is the story told or dramatized at a pace that will permit the student to comprehend as he listens?

- Will the interpretation give pleasure to the student?
- Are performance and production of music recordings of good quality technically?

d. Kits, models, realia, etc.:

- Are all parts of an item related to the subject and of equal quality?
- Where appropriate, are size relationships made clear?
- Are parts suitably and permanently labeled?
- Do the colors and composition of materials help stress important features?
- Is the item durable and easy to reassemble?
- Is there an accompanying manual with follow-up activities?

CONTROVERSIAL MATERIALS

When the suitability of instructional material is questioned, the principal of the school where the question is raised will attempt to solve the problem by discussing the matter with the person(s) presenting the complaint. If the matter remains unresolved, the following procedure will be pursued:

1. Rational discussion of controversial issues is an important part of the school program. Teachers should assist students in identifying relevant information, learning techniques of critical analysis, and making independent judgments. Teachers should help students become sensitive to the continuing need for objective reexamination of issues in light of new information and changing conditions and attitudes in society.

2. It is recognized that, from time to time, various portions or elements of educational programs may be viewed as controversial by one or more segments of the community. When written objections are raised to the use of controversial matter in one or more of the schools, such objection should initially be directed to the assistant superintendent for instructional services who will in turn direct the objection to the appropriate teacher(s) or administrator(s) for responses.

3. If this procedure does not resolve the objection within 15 school days of the filing of the original written objection, the objecting party shall so notify the superintendent of schools who shall have the matter submitted to the District Controversial Materials Review Committee. This committee shall consist of 9 members, selected as follows:

a. Three employees of the school district designated by the superintendent, one of whom shall be designated as the voting chairperson of the committee.

b. Six persons who are not employed by the district, selected from each of the district's 6 regional Advisory Educational Concerns Committees by the membership of each such committee.

4. Members of the committee shall be designated at the beginning of the school year and shall serve for the remainder of that school year. The 6 persons not employed by the district may not serve consecutive terms.

5. The committee shall take appropriate steps to conduct an objective review of the material in question. These steps shall include, among other things, an opportunity for those persons or groups questioning the material and for staff members to present their concerns regarding the material.

6. Upon completion of the review, the committee shall submit its report (including any minority reports) to the School Board for consideration. The committee must submit its report to the School Board within 20 school days of the date on which a matter is submitted to it for review. The decision of the board shall be final.

Laredo Independent School District Learning Resources Centers

PHILOSOPHY

The Laredo Independent School District holds the belief that every citizen of our country is entitled to receive the highest quality of education. In view of this, it has designed an educational program which will encourage and enable each student to become intellectually and socially competent, to value moral integrity and personal decency and to achieve self-understanding and self-realization. The goals of our Learning Resources Center program are to instill in all students the lifelong love of books, to enable them to utilize all types of media for information, enlightenment, and enjoyment, and to introduce them to their rich cultural heritage and to encourage citizenship.

The Laredo Independent School District Learning Resources Centers function as an integral part of the total educational program.

OBJECTIVES

The following objectives will help in achieving the goals of the Learning Resources Centers Program:

1. To provide a planned program which will arouse in students an interest in books and other types of media and to broaden this interest through service and guidance in a pleasant atmosphere.

2. To provide materials that enrich and support the curriculum, taking into consideration the varied interests, abilities, and maturity levels of the students served.

Laredo Independent School District Media Services, Laredo, TX 78040

3. To provide materials representative of the many religious, ethnic, and cultural groups and their contributions to our American heritage.

4. To provide materials on opposing sides of controversial issues so that young citizens may develop under guidance the practice of critical reading and thinking.

RESPONSIBILITY FOR SELECTION

While the legal responsibility for the purchase of all instructional materials is vested in the school board, the board in turn delegates authority for final selection and purchase of Learning Resource Center materials to the Learning Resource Center director, with recommendations from the faculty and students and the approval of the principal.

CONSIDERATIONS

1. Paperbacks may be purchased as the need arises only with regular funds.

2. Duplication will be made if deemed necessary by the Learning Resource Center director or upon teachers' requests.

3. Replacement of lost, missing, or damaged materials will be made if material is still relevant to the existing collection.

4. Periodicals and microfiche may be purchased to supplement the curriculum and for pleasure reading.

5. A vertical file will be maintained for students and teachers.

6. Fines for overdue materials will be charged, and lost or damaged materials will be paid for.

SELECTION TOOLS

1. Sources for selection of print materials:

   A Basic Book Collection for Elementary Grades, ALA
   A Basic Book Collection for Junior High Schools, ALA
   A Basic Book Collection for High Schools, ALA
   Children's Catalog, Wilson
   Junior High School Library Catalog, Wilson
   Senior High School Library Catalog, Wilson
   Elementary School Library Collection, Brodart Foundation

Gateway to Readable Books, Wilson
Good Reading for Poor Readers, Garrard
Your Reading—A Book List for Junior High, NCTE
The Teachers' Library: How to Organize It, NEA
Booklist, ALA
Horn Book Magazine
Library Journal, Bowker
School Library Journal, Bowker
Science Books; A Quarterly Review, AAAS
Wilson Library Bulletin, Wilson
School Selection Guide, Baker & Taylor

2. Sources for selection of nonprint materials:

Educational Technology Magazine
Guides to Newer Educational Media (films, filmstrips, phono records, radio, slides and television), ALA
Film Review Digest, Film Library Association
Index to 16mm Educational Films, NICEM
Index to 35 mm Educational Films, NICEM

3. Sources for Selection of Equipment:

Audio Visual Equipment Directory, National Audiovisual Association
Audiovisual Market Place, A Multimedia Guide, Bowker

FREE AND INEXPENSIVE MATERIALS

Free and inexpensive instructional materials are produced in many forms and comprise an important segment of the area of instructional materials. They should be accepted and used only when they contributed to the educational goals of the Laredo Independent School District. These materials should be of the same high quality and purpose as are all other types of instructional materials. When suggestions are made for obtaining free and inexpensive instructional materials from commercial firms or government bureaus, it should be made clear that no more than one pupil per class or grade should write to the same source.

SPONSORED MATERIALS

In evaluating sponsored materials, evaluation and selection committees may use the same criteria which have been set up for evaluating all other types of instructional materials. Sponsored materials should not attempt to establish the exclusiveness of a particular product or service. The sources of funds and sponsoring organizations of the materials should be known so that the point of view and propaganda content presented may be identified and evaluated. If the material meets these criteria and the product is in good taste, the appearance of the name of this sponsor on the material is acceptable.

GIFTS

District Learning Resource Centers and Campus Learning Resource Centers are frequently offered gifts of books which do not meet the standards set up in the book selection policies for the Laredo Independent School District. In such cases, it is difficult to refuse the gift without offending the would-be donor and discouraging interest in the media services. The procedures to be followed include:

1. Gift books are to be judged by the same standards as books which are purchased. Items that do not meet the blanket approval criteria must be reviewed by the Adoption Committee.

2. If books are accepted, it should be understood that they will be treated as other books in the Learning Resource Center. A recommended way of giving recognition to friends who present books to the Learning Resource Center is to use bookplates bearing the names of the donors in all gift books.

3. Friends of the Learning Resource Center should be encouraged to give books from a list prepared by the media specialist or librarian, instead of giving at random. In this way they can contribute to the building of a balanced, well-chosen collection to meet the needs of the particular school.

TYPES OF MATERIALS

Instructional materials, other than textbooks, are those items designed to assist the learner in the teaching-learning process. They take many forms and may be consumable or expendable and vary greatly in their anticipated useful life. Instructional materials include such items as:

Library books	Films	Charts	Tape	Program
Magazines	Filmstrips	Maps	recordings	materials
Newspapers	Transparencies	Globes	Phonograph	Workbooks
Curriculum	Video tapes	Models	records	Kits
guides	Microfilms	Pictures	Specimens	Games
Manuals			Slides	

PROCESS

The diagrams show the components in the process of identifying, evaluating, selecting, and reevaluating instructional materials and indicate who is involved at each juncture.

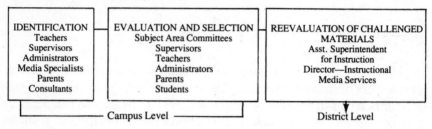

IDENTIFICATION Teachers Supervisors Administrators Media Specialists Parents Consultants	EVALUATION AND SELECTION Subject Area Committees Supervisors Teachers Administrators Parents Students	REEVALUATION OF CHALLENGED MATERIALS Asst. Superintendent for Instruction Director—Instructional Media Services

——————————— Campus Level ———————————　　　　　　District Level

IDENTIFICATION

There are many sources for identifying instructional materials for evaluation: vendors, publishers, catalogs, professional journals, periodicals, advertisements, workshops, inservice activity (book fair), parents, consultants, teachers, and student requests are some of the sources for identification.

Media specialists, librarians, and subject-area supervisors take the initiative in identification of materials and equipment for evaluation. However, teachers, administrators, and students are consistently called upon for recommendations. Two basic approaches are in operation:

1. *Informal method (ongoing).*

   a. Scan advertisements.
   b. Review catalogs of major publishers.
   c. Meet with sales representatives.
   d. Send for sample copies.
   e. Arrange for previews.
   f. Gather lists and samples at conferences.
   g. Consult with colleagues.

2. *Organized approach.*

   a. Determine needs for particular item(s) and search for appropriate materials.

   b. Designate particular staff members to focus on the identification of particular media, topics, or objectives.

   c. Send questionnaires to teachers and administrators for specific suggestions.

d. Send questionnaires to staff on a regular basis for general input.

e. Maintain a card file or list on a continuing basis.

f. Arrange for regular appointments with sales representatives.

g. Send a form letter to publishing houses and sales representatives requesting complimentary copies of instructional materials for specific courses.

EVALUATION AND SELECTION

The learning resources specialists or librarians assigned to each Campus Learning Resource Center (K-12) are responsible for organizing and scheduling evaluation committees on that campus. The size and composition of the group may be influenced by:

1. Nature of the tasks.

2. Expertise required.

3. Type(s) of materials.

4. Amount of material to be evaluated.

5. Diversification of viewpoint of committee members.

It is axiomatic that a representative group of those who will use the materials to be evaluated be involved. Teachers should make up the bulk of the evaluators. It is recommended that parents or other citizens also be invited to participate. Student involvement at the high school level is encouraged.

In some disciplines, it may be necessary to organize a committee which meets several times a year. Other subject areas may find it more workable to form committees as the need arises. In some cases, evaluation of materials may accompany a curriculum-writing workshop. Federal programs will form evaluation committees to respond to materials selection (other than textbook) from their advisory committees chosen from the community.

The District Learning Resource Center will be responsible for procuring and returning preview films. The District Learning Resource Center film librarian will be calling on Laredo Independent School District staff to evaluate films and filmstrips on a continuing basis. Subject area supervisors, teachers, and department heads may also initiate the request for particular titles. Most major film companies send new releases automatically, especially in the areas of major concern.

BLANKET AND AUTOMATIC APPROVAL

There are sources of instructional materials whose publications or offerings are of such consistently high quality that individual evaluation is not necessary. Individual item evaluation of these sources would be a total waste of time. For the most part, these sources are public institutions, foundations, magazine publishers, and government publications.

Following are the types of materials which have blanket approval:

1. All media, both print and nonprint, except 16mm films, which are favorably reviewed in professional journals or are listed in standard bibliographies, are automatically approved for use in the Laredo Independent School District. Acceptable standard bibliographies may be obtained from the District Learning Resource Center.

2. Reprints from any periodical reproduced by Webb County political entities (i.e., Webb County Historical Commission or Laredo Public Library).

3. Any item listed in a course of study published by Laredo Independent School District.

4. Curriculum-related pamphlets.

5. Materials that support a pilot program which has had prior approval.

6. Materials supporting Laredo Independent School District/Channel 8 school television.

7. Materials issued by agencies of the state of Texas.

8. Materials pertaining to an approved textbook, which are an integral part of the text and published by the same publisher, are automatically approved for purchase.

9. Instrument and choral sheet music.

There may be occasions when materials are technically covered by blanket approval but may still be of a sensitive nature for a particular school. In this event, the evaluator is to refer the material to the director of instructional media services. Materials may be routed to the assistant superintendent for instruction if the director of instructional media judges the nature of the content to warrant formal review.

Instructional materials for the Campus Learning Resource Centers not covered by blanket approval may be purchased by the following procedure:

1. Submit a completed *Evaluation of Instructional Materials* form to the director of instructional media within 30 days of the arrival of the items accompanied by a completed shelflist card for each item. [See Part III for form.]

2. If the items do not receive approval, they will be retired from the collection. If they are approved, the shelflist card will be stamped by the authorizing source (i.e., media director or assistant superintendent for instruction).

EVALUATION AND SELECTION OF INSTRUCTIONAL MATERIALS

General Criteria

	Yes	No	NA
1. Authenticity and scholarship.			
a. Is the material authentic?	☐	☐	☐
b. Is the material up-to-date?	☐	☐	☐
c. Are the authors and/or producers well-qualified?	☐	☐	☐
d. Does the material have high scholarship?	☐	☐	☐
e. Are the illustrations of good quality?	☐	☐	☐
f. Is the format well-organized?	☐	☐	☐
g. Are the indices and appendices sufficient and conveniently organized?	☐	☐	☐
2. Appropriateness.			
a. Does the material focus upon the goals and objectives of the Laredo Independent School District curriculum?	☐	☐	☐
b. Are any parts of the material objectionable?	☐	☐	☐
c. Is the material appropriate in vocabulary?	☐	☐	☐
d. Are the concepts presented appropriately?	☐	☐	☐
e. Are the methods of presentation based upon good learning theory?	☐	☐	☐
3. Content.			
a. Is controversial material presented impartially?	☐	☐	☐
b. Does this material present information that currently approved sources do not?	☐	☐	☐
c. Does this material present a new dimension or direction the currently approved materials do not?	☐	☐	☐

Yes No NA

d. Does the material evidence on the part of the writer, author, and editors fair treatment of minority groups? □ □ □

e. Is the material free of racial, religious, ethnic, and sexual bias and stereotyping? □ □ □

4. Motivational qualities.

a. Will the materials gain and hold the interest of the users? □ □ □

b. Will the materials stimulate curiosity of the users? □ □ □

c. Are the motivational techniques such that the content is not compromised? □ □ □

d. Are the illustrations, cover, and general format attractive? □ □ □

5. Technical quality.

a. Is the quality of the paper sufficient? □ □ □

b. Is the binding strong enough for intended use? □ □ □

c. Is the cover attractive and of sufficient durability? □ □ □

Library Books

Fiction

1. Purpose.

a. What is the purpose, theme, or message of the book? Does the author accomplish this purpose? □ □ □

b. If the story is humorous, is the humor the type that will appeal to children? □ □ □

c. If the story is fantasy, is it the type that has imaginative appeal and is suitable for children? □ □ □

For young adults? □ □ □

d. Will the reading of the book result in more compassionate understanding of human beings? □ □ □

e. Does it offer an opportunity to better understand and appreciate the aspirations, achievements, and problems of various minority groups and women? □ □ □

f. Does it present a positive picture of the role of women and avoid stereotyping? □ □ □

Yes No NA

g. Are any questionable elements of the story an integral part of a worthwhile theme or message?   ☐ ☐ ☐

2. Content.

   a. If the story is set in modern times, does it give a realistic picture of life as it is now?   ☐ ☐ ☐

   b. Does the story avoid an oversimplified view of life, one which leaves the reader with the general feeling that life is sweet and rosy or ugly and meaningless, or the like?   ☐ ☐ ☐

   c. When factual information is given, is it presented accurately?   ☐ ☐ ☐

   d. Is prejudicial appeal readily identifiable by the potential reader?   ☐ ☐ ☐

   e. Are concepts presented appropriate to the ability and maturity of the potential reader?   ☐ ☐ ☐

   f. Is there good plot construction with logical development and a minimum of coincidence?   ☐ ☐ ☐

   g. Do characters speak in a language true to the period and section of the country in which they live?   ☐ ☐ ☐

   h. Are characters created with individual human qualities?   ☐ ☐ ☐

   i. Is the book written so as not to offend the sensibilities of women or a minority group by the way it presents either the chief character or any of the minor characters?   ☐ ☐ ☐

   j. Does it include contributions of women to society when appropriate?   ☐ ☐ ☐

   k. Is the book written so as not to be preoccupied with sex, violence, cruelty, brutality, and aberrant behavior that would make this book inappropriate for children or young adults?   ☐ ☐ ☐

   l. Is the language in good taste?   ☐ ☐ ☐

   • If there is use of offensive language, is it appropriate to the purpose of the text? For children?   ☐ ☐ ☐

   • For young adults?   ☐ ☐ ☐

	Yes	No	NA
• Is dialect authentic?	☐	☐	☐
• Is the book free from derisive names and epithets that would offend minority groups?	☐	☐	☐
• Children?	☐	☐	☐
• Young adults?	☐	☐	☐
• Women?	☐	☐	☐
m. Does the book have literary and human values?	☐	☐	☐
• Is the book well-written?	☐	☐	☐
• Does the story have appeal?	☐	☐	☐
• Does the story give a broader understanding of human behavior without stressing differences of class, race, color, sex, education, religion, or philosophy in any inimical way?	☐	☐	☐
• Does the book make a significant contribution to the history of literature or ideas?	☐	☐	☐

3. Technical quality.

	Yes	No	NA
a. Is the size of the book appropriate for use at the intended level?	☐	☐	☐
b. Is the binding durable and strong?	☐	☐	☐
c. Is the cover attractive?	☐	☐	☐
d. Is the paper durable and opaque?	☐	☐	☐
e. Is the typography clear and easy to read?	☐	☐	☐
f. Is the type size appropriate for the level intended?	☐	☐	☐
g. Are the page layouts well designed?	☐	☐	☐
h. Is the space between the lines appropriate and in for the level intended?	☐	☐	☐
i. Illustrations.			
• Are the illustrations appropriate and in good taste?	☐	☐	☐
• Are the illustrations realistic in relation to the story?	☐	☐	☐
• Do the illustrations avoid stereotypes and/or ethno-centrism?	☐	☐	☐

Yes No NA

- Is the art or photographic quality acceptable (sharpness, composition, distortion, color)? ☐ ☐ ☐

- Are the captions readable? ☐ ☐ ☐

- Are illustrations located properly for greatest usefulness? ☐ ☐ ☐

4. Supporting opinion.

   a. Does it appear on one or more reputable book lists or selection aids? ☐ ☐ ☐

   b. Has it been favorably reviewed by experts in the field? ☐ ☐ ☐

Nonfiction

1. Purpose.

   a. Does the author accomplish the overall purpose of the book? ☐ ☐ ☐

   b. Is the purpose accomplished in good literary style? ☐ ☐ ☐

2. Author and publisher.

   a. Is the author competent and qualified in the field? ☐ ☐ ☐

   b. Is the author of significant reputation in his field? ☐ ☐ ☐

   c. Is the material published by a reputable publisher? ☐ ☐ ☐

3. Authenticity.

   a. Is the material factually accurate and objective in presentation? ☐ ☐ ☐

   b. Is the material up-to-date? ☐ ☐ ☐

   c. Are information sources well-documented? ☐ ☐ ☐

   d. Are translations and retellings faithful to the original? ☐ ☐ ☐

4. Appropriateness.

   a. Does the material promote the educational goals and objectives of the curriculum? ☐ ☐ ☐

   b. Is it appropriate to the level of instruction intended? ☐ ☐ ☐

      - Is the vocabulary appropriate? ☐ ☐ ☐

      - Is the presentation of concepts appropriate to the ability and maturity of the student? ☐ ☐ ☐

Yes No NA

- Illustrations:

  - Are they appropriate to the subject and age level? ☐ ☐ ☐

  - Do they portray realistic human qualities? ☐ ☐ ☐

  - Do they avoid stereotype? ☐ ☐ ☐

- Are the methods of development appropriate? ☐ ☐ ☐

  - Is a logical scope and sequence developed? ☐ ☐ ☐

  - Is it readable, clear, and appropriate for the level and subject? ☐ ☐ ☐

  - Does it have literary merit? ☐ ☐ ☐

c. With respect to controversial material:

- Are the sources, purposes, and points of view readily identifiable? ☐ ☐ ☐

- Is prejudicial appeal readily identifiable? ☐ ☐ ☐

- Are other materials available that present different and representative points of view concerning the problems and issues? ☐ ☐ ☐

d. Is the interest level appropriate to the user? ☐ ☐ ☐

- Will the material stimulate the curiosity of the user? ☐ ☐ ☐

- Will the material appeal to many students? ☐ ☐ ☐

5. Content.

a. Is the content of this material well-presented by providing adequate scope, range, depth, and continuity? ☐ ☐ ☐

b. Have the principles of learning (e.g., reinforcement, transfer) been followed in developing the material? ☐ ☐ ☐

c. Is the material in each chapter presented logically and clearly? ☐ ☐ ☐

d. Does the material achieve its stated purpose? ☐ ☐ ☐

e. Does this material present information not otherwise available? ☐ ☐ ☐

f. Does this material give a new dimension or direction to its subject? ☐ ☐ ☐

Yes No NA

g. Where appropriate, does it treat women and minority groups in a way that highlights their problems and their contributions? ☐ ☐ ☐

h. Is the content clearly outlined in the table of contents? ☐ ☐ ☐

- Is the pagination definite and clear? ☐ ☐ ☐

- Are chapter titles and subtitles clearly outlined? ☐ ☐ ☐

i. Is appended material useful? ☐ ☐ ☐

j. Are pupil aids to learning provided? ☐ ☐ ☐

- Is there a glossary? ☐ ☐ ☐

- Are aids to pronunciation and meaning provided? ☐ ☐ ☐

- Are summaries and reviews provided where appropriate? ☐ ☐ ☐

- Are exercises and activities appropriate and provocative? ☐ ☐ ☐

- Are various related materials listed? ☐ ☐ ☐

k. Is the index adequate for pupils at the level for which the book is intended? ☐ ☐ ☐

l. Do the visual aids (e.g., pictures, maps, graphs, charts) contribute to the development of the text? ☐ ☐ ☐

- Are they attractive? ☐ ☐ ☐

- Are they placed for greatest usefulness? ☐ ☐ ☐

- Are they adequate in number? ☐ ☐ ☐

- Where appropriate, are the illustrations multiethnic and free from stereotype? ☐ ☐ ☐

m. Is the copyright date a significant factor in evaluating usefulness of content? ☐ ☐ ☐

6. Technical quality.

a. Is the size of the book appropriate for use at the interest level? ☐ ☐ ☐

b. Is the binding durable and strong? ☐ ☐ ☐

c. Is the binding sewn? ☐ ☐ ☐

d. Is the cover attractive? ☐ ☐ ☐

	Yes	No	NA

e. Is the paper durable and opaque? ☐ ☐ ☐

f. Is the typography clear and easy to read? ☐ ☐ ☐

g. Is the type size appropriate for the level intended? ☐ ☐ ☐

h. Are the page layouts well designed? ☐ ☐ ☐

i. Is the space between the lines appropriate for the level intended? ☐ ☐ ☐

j. Illustrations.

  • Is the art or photographic quality acceptable (sharpness, composition, distortion, color)? ☐ ☐ ☐

  • Is there a good balance between artistic technique and educational need? ☐ ☐ ☐

  • Are the captions readable? ☐ ☐ ☐

  • Are the illustrations and captions suitable for teaching and learning purposes? ☐ ☐ ☐

  • Are illustrations located properly for greatest usefulness? ☐ ☐ ☐

  • Are the illustrations adequate in number? ☐ ☐ ☐

7. Supporting opinion

  a. Does it appear on one or more reputable book lists or selection aids? ☐ ☐ ☐

  b. Has it been favorably reviewed by experts in the field? ☐ ☐ ☐

Charts

1. Is the content of this material well-organized and well-balanced? ☐ ☐ ☐

  a. Is the material presented logically and clearly? ☐ ☐ ☐

  b. Does the material achieve its stated purpose? ☐ ☐ ☐

  c. Does the chart aid conceptualization of subject matter? ☐ ☐ ☐

  d. Is the content presented as clearly and simply as possible for the level intended? ☐ ☐ ☐

  e. Is material arranged in logical sequence? ☐ ☐ ☐

  f. Are charts presented in a series? ☐ ☐ ☐

Yes No NA

g. Is the scale or size such that comparisons can be made between or among charts? ☐ ☐ ☐

h. Are symbolizations adequately explained? ☐ ☐ ☐

2. Is the technical quality of this material acceptable? ☐ ☐ ☐

   a. Is printed material sharply and clearly defined? ☐ ☐ ☐

   b. Is the media used durable and opaque? ☐ ☐ ☐

   c. Is some provision made for display? ☐ ☐ ☐

     • Are the charts provided with wall attachments? ☐ ☐ ☐

     • Are the charts mounted on a tripod or other floor display holder? ☐ ☐ ☐

     • Is the holder easy to manipulate? ☐ ☐ ☐

     • Does the holder take only a reasonable amount of space? ☐ ☐ ☐

Films, Filmstrips, Cartridge, Films, Slides, and Transparencies

1. Is the content of this material well-organized and well-balanced? ☐ ☐ ☐

   a. Have the principles of learning (e.g., reinforcement, transfer) been followed in developing the material? ☐ ☐ ☐

   b. Is the material presented logically and clearly? ☐ ☐ ☐

   c. Is the sequence developed adequately? ☐ ☐ ☐

   d. Is data sufficiently comprehensive to be useful? ☐ ☐ ☐

   e. Is the content appropriate for this type of presentation? ☐ ☐ ☐

   f. Is the material imaginative when imagination is really needed? ☐ ☐ ☐

   g. Is the quality of the script or commentary satisfactory? ☐ ☐ ☐

   h. Is the music or background satisfactory? ☐ ☐ ☐

   i. Are the titles, labels, or captions appropriate? ☐ ☐ ☐

   j. Is all material essential? ☐ ☐ ☐

2. Is the technical quality of this material acceptable? ☐ ☐ ☐

   a. Is the visual image satisfactory? ☐ ☐ ☐

Yes No NA

- Is the photography clear and artistic? ☐ ☐ ☐
- Does it have enough close-ups? ☐ ☐ ☐
- Are printed items adequate in size? ☐ ☐ ☐

b. Is the quality of sound clear and intelligible? ☐ ☐ ☐

c. Is color used effectively? ☐ ☐ ☐

d. Are sound and visual image synchronized? ☐ ☐ ☐

Globes

1. Is the content of this material well-organized and well-balanced? ☐ ☐ ☐

a. Is the material presented logically and clearly? ☐ ☐ ☐

b. Does the material achieve its stated purpose? ☐ ☐ ☐

c. Are latitude and longitude lines or indicators provided? ☐ ☐ ☐

d. Are color symbolizations pleasing but distinctive in quality? ☐ ☐ ☐

e. If raised-relief techniques are used, is vertical exaggeration excessive? ☐ ☐ ☐

2. Is the technical quality of this material acceptable? ☐ ☐ ☐

a. Will materials used in the construction of the globe resist denting and breakage? ☐ ☐ ☐

b. Are jointures on globes smooth and relatively unnoticable? ☐ ☐ ☐

- Are map segments well registered? ☐ ☐ ☐
- Are places where parts of a globe are joined in construction prominent? ☐ ☐ ☐

c. Is the base firm and heavy enough to resist tipping in use? ☐ ☐ ☐

d. Will connections of movable parts wear well? ☐ ☐ ☐

e. Is there an axis provided for the globe? ☐ ☐ ☐

f. Is a place provided for the storage of an axis pin if it is removable? ☐ ☐ ☐

g. Is the surface soil-resistant and cleanable? ☐ ☐ ☐

h. Is the surface made to be marked upon? ☐ ☐ ☐

Maps   Yes No NA

1. Is the content of this material well-organized and well-
   balanced?   ☐ ☐ ☐

   a. Is the material presented logically and clearly?   ☐ ☐ ☐

   b. Does the material achieve its stated purpose?   ☐ ☐ ☐

   c. Is the projection suitable for use at the level intended?   ☐ ☐ ☐

   d. Is the projection suitable for the content to be shown?   ☐ ☐ ☐

   e. Is the map scale suitable for the purpose intended?   ☐ ☐ ☐

   f. Is the legend adequately and clearly presented?   ☐ ☐ ☐

   g. Are color symbolizations pleasing but distinctive in
      quality?   ☐ ☐ ☐

   h. If raised-relief technique is used, is vertical exaggera-
      tion in good proportion?   ☐ ☐ ☐

   i. Are latitude and longitude clearly delineated?   ☐ ☐ ☐

   j. Are contents dated when this is a significant factor in
      their utilization?   ☐ ☐ ☐

   k. Are the contents developed on a comparable basis if
      the map is part of a series?   ☐ ☐ ☐

   l. Is the detail appropriate to the intended use?   ☐ ☐ ☐

2. Is the technical quality of this material acceptable?   ☐ ☐ ☐

   a. Is the durability of the material upon which the map is
      reproduced adequate for the purposes intended?   ☐ ☐ ☐

      • Is the map constructed so it will not curl along the
        edges?   ☐ ☐ ☐

      • Is the map constructed of a material that will not
        crack, split, or tear easily?   ☐ ☐ ☐

   b. Are printed materials acceptable in terms of legibility
      and placement?   ☐ ☐ ☐

   c. Is the mounting device durable?   ☐ ☐ ☐

   d. Is the mounting device appropriate for the intended
      use?   ☐ ☐ ☐

   e. Is the surface washable?   ☐ ☐ ☐

Yes No NA

  f. Is the surface as nonreflecting as possible? ☐ ☐ ☐

  g. Can marking devices be used on the surface? ☐ ☐ ☐

Programed Materials

1. Is the content of this material well-organized and well-balanced? ☐ ☐ ☐

  a. Have the principles of learning (e.g., reinforcement, transfer) been followed in developing the material? ☐ ☐ ☐

  b. Is the material presented logically and clearly? ☐ ☐ ☐

  c. Does the material achieve its stated purpose? ☐ ☐ ☐

  d. Is the program consistent with the behavioral objectives which are desired? ☐ ☐ ☐

  e. Does the program emphasize the major objectives which are desired? ☐ ☐ ☐

  f. Does the program offer the type of response (e.g., multiple choice, constructed response) that is desired? ☐ ☐ ☐

  g. Does the program orient the student to a problem and prepare him for new information? ☐ ☐ ☐

  h. Does the program use interesting and novel cues? ☐ ☐ ☐

  i. Are those cueing techniques being used most appropriate for the kind of behavioral outcomes desired? ☐ ☐ ☐

  j. Is the program cued adequately? ☐ ☐ ☐

  k. Does the program raise questions for discussion at different intervals in order to further learning? ☐ ☐ ☐

  l. Can the teacher develop problems from the programed activities to be performed as follow-up activities in the program? ☐ ☐ ☐

  m. Is there an efficient way to refer to specific content? ☐ ☐ ☐

2. Is the technical quality of this material acceptable? ☐ ☐ ☐

  a. Does the program provide a record of the performance of the participant which can aid in diagnosis of individual learning problems? ☐ ☐ ☐

  b. Does the program require a separate answer sheet? ☐ ☐ ☐

Yes No NA

c. Does the learner participate actively at each step of the program? ☐ ☐ ☐

d. Does the program reinforce, after each student's answer, by telling him immediately whether he has responded correctly or not? ☐ ☐ ☐

e. Does the program provide an adequate number of responses within a frame before correction or reinforcement? ☐ ☐ ☐

f. Does each frame provide too much reading? ☐ ☐ ☐

g. Is the program easy to handle physically? ☐ ☐ ☐

h. Is the size of type appropriate for the grade level? ☐ ☐ ☐

Tape and Phonograph Records

1. Is the content of this material well-organized and well-balanced? ☐ ☐ ☐

   a. Have the principles of learning (e.g., reinforcement, transfer) been followed in developing the material? ☐ ☐ ☐

   b. Is the material presented logically and clearly? ☐ ☐ ☐

   c. Does the material achieve its stated purpose? ☐ ☐ ☐

   d. Is the content appropriate for presentation in recorded form? ☐ ☐ ☐

   e. Does the material complement printed and visual teaching resources in the same subject area? ☐ ☐ ☐

   f. Is the quality of the script or commentary satisfactory? ☐ ☐ ☐

2. Is the technical quality of this material acceptable? ☐ ☐ ☐

   a. Is the recording clearly labeled? (Title, number indicating playing sequence, and speed.) ☐ ☐ ☐

   b. Is the type of material used for the record or tape durable? ☐ ☐ ☐

   c. Is the quality of sound satisfactory? ☐ ☐ ☐

   • Are the speakers' or actors' voices clear and understandable? ☐ ☐ ☐

   • Is the music free from distortion? ☐ ☐ ☐

Flat Pictures and Study Prints

Yes No NA

1. Is the content of this material well-organized and well-balanced? ☐ ☐ ☐

   a. Is the material presented logically and clearly? ☐ ☐ ☐

   b. Does the material achieve its stated purpose? ☐ ☐ ☐

   c. Do the colors used (including black and white) contribute to learning? ☐ ☐ ☐

   d. Is the size commensurate with the purpose for which it is intended? ☐ ☐ ☐

   e. Has the composition been planned to illustrate or emphasize the intended purpose? ☐ ☐ ☐

   f. Is explanatory material provided? ☐ ☐ ☐

   g. Are the captions a good interpretation of the material yet not distracting? ☐ ☐ ☐

   h. Is there a recognizable sequence if the picture is part of a series? ☐ ☐ ☐

   i. Is the material such that it will not be out of style too quickly? ☐ ☐ ☐

2. Is the technical quality of this material acceptable? ☐ ☐ ☐

   a. Is the definition sharp and clear? ☐ ☐ ☐

   b. Are the color reproductions accurately registered? ☐ ☐ ☐

   c. Is the base material durable and opaque? ☐ ☐ ☐

   d. Is the surface as nonreflecting as possible? ☐ ☐ ☐

   e. Is the material constructed so as not to curl, split, or tear easily? ☐ ☐ ☐

Other Types: Workbooks, Answer Sheets, Ditto Masters, Puzzles, Games

1. Is the content of this material well-organized and well-balanced? ☐ ☐ ☐

   a. Have the principles of learning (e.g., reinforcement, transfer) been followed in developing the material? ☐ ☐ ☐

   b. Is the material presented logically and clearly? ☐ ☐ ☐

   c. Does the material achieve its stated purpose? ☐ ☐ ☐

	Yes	No	NA
d. Is the content developed for use with a specific text?	☐	☐	☐
e. Is the content adaptable to basic courses of study in the designated field?	☐	☐	☐
f. Does the content provide drill in basic skills?	☐	☐	☐
g. Can the teacher develop problems from the programed activities to be performed as follow-up activities?	☐	☐	☐
h. If examples or directions are needed, are they stated clearly?	☐	☐	☐
i. Are visual aids to learning provided when appropriate?	☐	☐	☐
j. Is there an efficient way to refer to specific content?	☐	☐	☐
2. Is the technical quality of this material acceptable?	☐	☐	☐
a. Is the size of the material appropriate for use at the intended level?	☐	☐	☐
b. Is the material attractive?	☐	☐	☐
c. Is the material durable?	☐	☐	☐
d. Is the typography clear and easy to read?	☐	☐	☐
e. Is the type size appropriate for the level intended?	☐	☐	☐
f. Are the layouts well-designed?	☐	☐	☐

SEX ROLE STEREOTYPE CHECK LIST

The prevention of sex role stereotyping in instructional materials is a major concern of parents and educators. In the evaluation and selection process, in addition to other criteria, apply the following check list when appropriate.

	Male	Female
1. Number of stories where main character is	_____	_____
Number of illustrations of	_____	_____
Number of times children are shown		
in active play	_____	_____
using initiative in solving problems	_____	_____
earning money	_____	_____
receiving money	_____	_____
receiving recognition	_____	_____

	Male	Female
involved in sports	_____	_____
tearful, helpless, or receiving help	_____	_____
Number of times adults are shown		
in different occupations	_____	_____
playing with children or taking children on outings	_____	_____
teaching skills	_____	_____
giving tenderness	_____	_____
scolding children	_____	_____
biographically	_____	_____

2. Are boys allowed to show emotions as well as girls? Does the book avoid portraying females as emotionally uncontrolled?

3. Are girls rewarded for intelligence rather than for beauty? Are girls portrayed as intelligent?

4. Does the book avoid derogatory comments directed at girls in general?

5. Are girls shown as competent?

6. Are mothers shown working outside the home? Are there stories about one-parent families? Families without children? Are baby-sitters shown?

7. Are minority and ethnic groups treated naturally?

8. Are terms and titles which use the generic term ''man'' to represent humanity avoided? Are occupational terms which ignore the existence of women workers avoided?

REEVALUATION OF CHALLENGED MATERIALS

When a concern that cannot be handled on a local school level is expressed by a citizen or group, the school administrator or supervisor is requested to consult with the assistant superintendent for instruction. If the concern warrants follow-up, the assistant superintendent will forward a *Request for Reconsideration of Instructional Materials* form to the citizen. [See Part III for a similar sample form.] The Instructional Material Review Committee will follow through by reviewing the data and submitting a recommendation to the assistant superintendent for instruction.

The assistant superintendent for instruction will recommend materials for consideration to the District Materials Review Committee. The standing Review Committee will be composed of the following: director of instructional media services, 3 school administrators (elementary, junior high, high school), 3 teachers (appropriate to subject matter under consideration), 2 supervisors (library supervisor, subject area supervisor, and librarians from campuses involved), 2 parents (from Parents-Teachers Association or a federal program), 2 students, director of secondary curriculum (ex officio), and assistant superintendent for instruction (ex officio).

In the event language, ideas, or illustrations in any of the materials have been identified as controversial or offensive to the community or to particular groups in the community, it is the responsibility of the program supervisor or principal to take the following steps:

1. Submit the materials with the evaluation form.

2. Identify the specific items or sections which are questionable.

3. Arrange for a conference with the assistant superintendent for instruction.

The assistant superintendent for instruction will review the materials and organize them for presentation to the Instructional Materials Review Committee. In the event that materials are, in the judgment of the assistant superintendent for instruction, obviously of a noncontroversial nature or represent a pilot or experimental program, s/he may authorize the materials for use until official review is accomplished.

No parent or group of parents has the right to determine the reading matter for students other than their own children.

The Board of Education does, however, recognize the right of an individual parent to request that his/her child not have to read a given book, provided a written request is made to the appropriate building principal.

If a specific problem or concern can not be satisfactorily resolved at the assistant superintendent's level, the problem or concern is to be directed to the superintendent and, should s/he deem advisable, to the Board of Education.

PART II
PARTIAL POLICIES

List of Schools and Districts— Library Media Centers—Partial Policies

Introductions
Hunterdon Central High School, Flemington, NJ 08822

Philosophy
Shaler Area School District, Glenshaw, PA 15116
Salem Public Schools, Salem, OR 97302
Amherst Central High School, Amherst, NY 14226
Bad Axe High School, Bad Axe, MI 48413
Anderson Union High School, Anderson, CA 96007

Objectives
Jenison Public Schools, Jenison, MI 49428
Natchez-Adams County Public Schools, Natchez, MS 39120
Spearman Public Schools, Spearman, TX 79081
Emerson-Hubbard Community Schools, Emerson, NE 68733
Heuvelton Central School District, Heuvelton, NY 13654
Tracy Public Schools, Tracy, MN 56175

Responsibility
Jenison Public Schools
Arlington County Public Schools, Arlington, VA 22207
Sachem Central School District, Holbrook, NY 11741

Recommendations
Sachem Central School District

Criteria—General

Austin Independent School District, Austin, TX 78752
Cocalico School District, Denver, PA 17517
Novato Unified School District, Novato, CA 94947
Norman Public Schools, Norman, OK 73069
Kalamazoo Public Schools, Kalamazoo, MI 49008
Montgomery County Public Schools, Rockville, MD 20850

Criteria—Special

Greenwich Public Schools, Greenwich, CT 06830
Azusa Unified School District, Azusa, CA 91702
Boulder Valley Schools, Boulder, CO 80301
Columbia County Schools, Appling, GA 30802
Jefferson County School District 509-J, Madras, OR 97741
Southwest School Corporation of Sullivan County, Sullivan, IN 47882
Montgomery County Public Schools

Interlibrary Loan

Coffeyville Unified School District 445, Coffeyville, KS 67337

Weeding

Greenwich Public Schools
Jackson Local School District, Massilon, OH 44646

Challenged Materials

Boulder Valley Schools
Coleman High School, Coleman, MI 48616
Hood River County School District 1, Hood River, OR 97031
Mount Pleasant Community Schools, Mount Pleasant, IA 52641
New Prague Public Schools, New Prague, MN 56071

Introductions

Hunterdon Central High School

To select materials in print and nonprint form which will meet the needs of students, teachers, and the school community, every district needs a carefully developed materials selection policy.

Such a policy will:

1. Guide in the building of quality collections which will support and enrich the curriculum.

2. Focus the attention of school library media specialists on their responsibilities and opportunities in the selection process.

3. Aid in interpreting the selection process in the school and community.

4. Provide a means of meeting the challenges of censorship and pressure groups.

DEVELOPMENT

The library media specialist will:

1. Explore with administrators the need for a policy and the means by which this may be accomplished.

2. Stimulate the interest of the faculty.

3. Serve on a committee appointed by the administrator to draft the policy. This districtwide committee should have representation from the Board of Education, administration, library media specialists, faculty, students, and the community.

4. Acquire and distribute to the committee members appropriate materials.

5. Participate in drafting and revision of the policy statement.

ADOPTION

The committee will:

1. Present the final draft to the faculty and administration for recommendations.

2. Submit the final selection policy to the superintendent for presentation to the Board of Education for adoption. In order to become an accepted school policy, the document must be read into the official minutes of the Board of Education.

CONTENTS

Although each school system will develop a policy to fit its own needs, each policy should include all of the following:

1. A philosophy of selection, such as the American Library Association's *Library Bill of Rights*, as supported by the American Association of School Librarians. [See Appendix I for current statement.]

2. A statement of the legal responsibility for the selection of books and materials, both purchased and donated. This statement should make clear that the local Board of Education determines the criteria, methodology, and procedures but delegates the responsibility for selection of individual items to qualified professionals.

3. Selection criteria and principles for developing multimedia collections.

4. Procedures for responding to criticisms of materials.

REVIEW AND REVISION

Any policy, however excellent, should be periodically reviewed to reflect changing needs and current educational trends.

Philosophy

Shaler Area School District

The Board of Education of the Shaler Area School District, believing that each American citizen is entitled to a quality, optimum education, has designed an educational program which will encourage and enable each student to become intellectually and socially competent, to value moral integrity and personal decency, and to achieve self-understanding and self-realization.

The following objectives provide unity, direction, and guidance in both the design and implementation of the educational program:

1. To provide ample opportunity for each student to build his "house of intellect" commensurate with his mental potential.

2. To provide learning experience which will meet uniquely and adequately individual student needs, interests, goals, abilities, and creative potential.

3. To provide learning experiences and teaching guidance which will enable and encourage each student to build a positive set of values.

4. To provide teaching and learning experiences which will enable and encourage each student to understand, to appreciate, and to value his cultural, social, political, and economic heritage as an American, as a world citizen, and as a human being.

5. To provide teaching and learning experiences which have been structured as a progressive continuum of related fundamentals from kindergarten through grade 12.

6. To provide ample opportunity for each student to become conversant with the techniques of critical, analytical, reflective, logical, and creative thinking.

The school libraries function as an integral part of the total educational program. The goal of the school library program is to facilitate and expedite realization of the attainment of a quality, optimum education for each student. To reach this goal, the following objectives give purpose and direction to the library program:

1. To provide an educationally functional and effective library program which will meet adequately the developmental needs of the curriculum and the personal needs, interests, goals, abilities, and creative potential of the students.

2. To provide informed and concerned guidance in the use of library service and resources which will personalize teaching and individualize learning.

3. To provide a planned, purposeful, and educationally significant program which will be appropriately integrated with the classroom teaching and learning program.

4. To provide library resources which will stimulate and promote interest in self-directed knowledge building.

If the librarian is to have a significant part in instruction, s/he must involve him/herself in the whole curriculum. S/he must participate in developing curriculum, in planning instruction, in carrying out the teaching and learning activities involved in implementing curriculum, and in evaluating the success of the instructional program. The librarian is a teacher who works with the whole curriculum.

The principal and the librarian establish the overall policies governing school library service with the assistance of a faculty library committee. As the instructional leader of the school, the principal is in the best position to make important decisions to relate library services to the rest of the instructional program.

The librarian will work with the classroom teachers, textbook selection committees, and subject area supervisors in the selection of materials. By participating in planning, librarians can bring their knowledge of materials to the design of curriculum while accomplishing their goal of teacher participation in selection. This will avoid collections being chosen in isolation.

Using the recommendations of the total staff, the librarian will compile the total order for the school library within their school budget figure and submit it to the building principal for his/her approval.

Salem Public Schools

The educational philosophy of the Salem public schools opens with this statement: "We believe that to develop and preserve our democratic society, with its individual rights and responsibilities, our schools must constantly strive to promote the growth of each individual physically, emotionally, socially, spiritually, and intellectually."

To educate each student to the fullest, a wide variety of instructional materials to fill curriculum and personal needs should be supplied. These instructional materials are both printed materials (library books, textbooks, periodicals, pamphlets, and newspapers) and audiovisual materials (films, film-strips, slides, recordings, transcriptions, tapes, and other educational media).

As criteria guiding the selection of instructional materials within the district, the School Board readopts the statement of *Our Educational Philosophy*, as adopted by the board in 1960, and accepts the principles of the American Library Association's *Library Bill of Rights*, as endorsed by the American Association of School Librarians. [See Appendix I for current statement.]

Amherst Central High School

An adequate school library is an essential resource for learning. "Use" is the keystone of our philosophy. We believe that:

1. The library program should help the student use the library effectively and efficiently for a variety of purposes, personal or academic.

2. Only well-informed, participating citizens can produce effective representative government. Thus, the library should have and offer materials relevant to general student concerns as well as to specific content area studies.

3. Man is a social being and the analysis of his social problems is an integral part of the school experience. The school is more than a mirror image of the community; it is a force for social change. The school library should supply resources that will facilitate such experience.

4. Man is an aesthetic being. The school fosters a continuing response to aesthetic experiences.

5. Each can become all s/he is capable of being. The library should provide materials for optimum individual growth.

The Amherst Central Senior High School faculty and administration endorse and reaffirm the philosophy expressed by the American Library Association's *Library Bill of Rights*, as endorsed by the American Association of School Librarians. [See Appendix I for current statement.]

We strive to assist each student in becoming a thinking, contributing, and constructive citizen of our democratic society. We emphasize and encourage the development of these aspects in each child's character:

1. *Adaptability*—to accept the inevitable, yet ever working for a better life.

2. *Appreciation*—to acquire an admiration for that which is genuine and beautiful.

3. *Responsibility*—to assume obligation and carry through in the personal, vocational, and civic tasks of life.

4. *Understanding*—to be aware and well-informed of diverse opinions, attitudes, and beliefs and to keep an open mind so that personal differences may be resolved through fraternal communication.

The fundamental functions of selecting instructional materials for the library media center should be:

1. To implement, enrich, and support the curriculum of the school, taking into consideration the varied interests, abilities, and degrees of sophistication of the users served.

2. To stimulate growth in factual knowledge, reading skills, literary appreciation, aesthetic values, ethical standards, and discrimination in choice of materials.

3. To alert users to new developments in academic, religious, ethnic, and cultural subjects.

4. To provide information on opposing sides of controversial issues and background knowledge to enable users to make intelligent judgments and practice critical thinking.

5. To evoke a love of reading and learning which will assure a continuing self-education and establish desirable intellectual habits that last for life.

6. To encourage professional growth of the faculty.

Bad Axe High School

1. A written statement will be available in the principal's office to all interested parties of the specific book selection practices of the school.

2. The responsibilities of the participating individuals and the limits of their responsibilities will be clarified.

3. Written criteria will serve as a basis for common agreement for those responsible for materials selection.

4. Both the North Central Association of Colleges and Secondary Schools and the University of Michigan require such a policy for member high schools.

5. A written policy will expedite the handling of complaints.

Anderson Union High School

The administrative staff of the Anderson Union High School District endorses the tenets set forth in the following:

1. *Library Bill of Rights* (American Library Association, endorsed by the American Association of School Librarians).

2. *The Freedom to Read* (American Library Association).

3. *Policies on Intellectual Freedom in Libraries* (California Association of School Librarians).

4. *The Students' Right to Read* (National Council of Teachers of English).

Objectives

Jenison Public Schools

1. Accreditation requirements:
   a. University of Michigan accreditation standards mandate that there will be a written book selection policy supported by the Board of Education (Standard VIII, Library).
   b. The North Central Association of Colleges and Secondary Schools requires that the professional staff will develop a statement of policy, with board approval, for the selection of reference materials, instructional materials for the library, and textbooks (Standard VIII, Instructional Media Program).
2. To insure uniformity of policy in program development.
3. To guarantee continuity of program in spite of instructional, media, and administrative staff changes.
4. To protect against unwise expenditures.
5. To eliminate or control personal interest pressures.

Natchez-Adams County Public Schools

The purpose of the media program is to be a partner in knowledge management, with its function to support, to implement, to enrich, to vitalize, and to humanize the educational program as it strives to attain excellence in content, process, and product. It will share with all other instructional agents their responsibility for systematically designing, carrying out, and evaluating the total process of learning and teaching.

The media program offers laboratories for learning. Each media center will function as a learning laboratory where the students/teachers come to work intensively and productively with ideas. The central media center will be a supportive endeavor.

The media program offers depth, breadth, and relevance to learning. This objective involves content and process, which demands that learning be individualized, purposeful, unrestricted, open-ended, expanded, and enriched; it also demands that learning embrace the total cognitive and affective domains.

The media program offers scientific design or a master plan for the development and management of the total program so that it is integrated with the day-to-day, ongoing instructional program.

Since the media program is well-established and all schools meet the AA state requirements, and the Southern Association requirements, the district supervisor must look at the total program for strengths and weaknesses and guide progress toward excellence.

1. The philosophy and goals of the media program will reflect the philosophy of the total educational program.

2. The school board shall provide adequate budget, staff, and facilities for the media program to meet state and regional standards.

3. The school board will continue supporting a districtwide coordinator/ director to plan, develop, maintain, lead/guide the operation of the master plan for the total media program, plus provide staff and budget to meet the needs of educational excellence in the Natchez-Adams County School District.

4. The school board will continue to support the central center with short- and long-range plans to add printing services, graphics, production, and photography within the next few years as budget allows.

5. The central media center will continue being a service-oriented facility which supports each individual media program through centralized ordering, processing, inventorying, maintenance, and production.

6. The central center is a resource center housing the professional library, 16mm collection, videotape collection, exhibit and selection materials, expensive kits and collections, supplemental texts, minicourse materials, and infrequently used materials, and is organized for easy accessibility and use.

7. The central center is a coordinating agency, which will cooperate with all other schools, libraries, colleges, industries, businesses, etc., and the state department to make accessible all available resources for enriching and supplementing the educational program.

8. The media director will provide leadership in promoting media inservice teacher education in accordance with the needs.

9. The media director will be responsible for formulating and recommending policies concerning the media program and its budget, personnel, facilities, collection, and services so that continuous development, progress, maintenance, evaluation, and educational excellence will be realities.

10. The media director will carry on a continuous public relations program internally within the individual school programs via our students, faculty, and administration, and externally through the news media, face-to-face contacts, civic club meetings, and affiliation with other clubs and agencies.

11. The media director and the other media personnel will provide a cooperative venture of sharing materials between schools using interlibrary loan procedures.

12. The media director is knowledgeable of present facilities and inventories, shall prepare long-term financial support programs, shall prepare long-term plans for reaching the ALA-AECT standards, and shall formulate plans for continuous evaluation and make plans for needed changes.

13. The media director is a consultant/specialist in his/her field and a co-worker with other specialists working cooperatively to provide leadership for educational innovation.

14. Emphasis will be placed on personnel management for the purpose of increasing the individual employee's effectiveness. Through the use of good leadership conferences, surveys, good communications, good public relations, and evaluation, this objective will be fulfilled.

15. Annual interim evaluations will be improved, so that strengths and weaknesses of the media program can be identified. The district evaluation form will be used for this purpose.

16. The staff of each school media center will select and order, with the aid of standard and recognized tools, materials/equipment that will meet quantitative and qualitative standards set forth by the district policies and the state and Southern Association accrediting agencies to maintain the highest degree of accreditation.

Spearman Public Schools

In order to determine the objectives of the library program in the schools, we must first determine what a library is and what its concerns are.

A library is first of all a service agency. It is also a teaching agency, a materials center, and a reading center.

Its concerns are with:

1. The enrichment of the curriculum.

2. The encouragement of the reading program.

3. The provision for a program of guidance.

4. The provision of professional and cultural growth of the staff.

As a teaching center, the library must provide the service of teaching the effective use of library tools so that the materials can be most effectively used.

As a materials center, the library must provide those nonprint materials necessary to augment the printed materials.

As a reading center, the library must be a place for enjoying books, studying, and investigating problems. This means a librarian must be alert to people and books, understand needs, utilize the testing programs, be alert to reading problems and assist in dealing with these problems, be effective in relating the library to the world around us, and must do these things in such a way that others are not aware of these services.

In the concern of enrichment of the curriculum, the library should:

1. Strive to meet the needs of the pupils, teachers, parents, and other community members.

2. Help students to become skillful and discriminating users of libraries and of printed and nonprinted materials.

3. Work with teachers in selection and use of all types of materials which contribute to the teaching program.

In the encouragement of the reading program, the librarian should:

1. Cooperate with other librarians and community leaders in planning and developing an overall library program for the community.

2. Introduce pupils to community libraries as early as possible and co-operate with those libraries in their efforts to encourage continued education and cultural growth.

3. Provide up-to-date materials.

In guidance, the library should:

1. Provide experiences to develop helpful interests, to make satisfactory personal adjustments, and to acquire desirable social attitudes.

2. Provide materials and services appropriate and meaningful for growth and development as individuals.

3. Stimulate and guide pupils in their reading that they may find interesting enjoyment and satisfaction and that they may grow in critical judgment and appreciation.

Lastly, the adult users of the school library should be provided with professional and adult materials to assure a continuing growth, professionally and culturally. In summary, the library should be a service agency which seeks to supply, encourage, enrich, instruct, and enlarge the educational philosophy of the school.

Emerson-Hubbard Community Schools

1. To select materials with the dual purpose of supporting and enriching the curriculum of the school and at the same time serving the individual's reading needs, interests, abilities, knowledge, and enlightenment beyond the school program for the pupils.

2. To provide materials which will stimulate growth in factual knowledge, appreciation of literature, aesthetic values, and ethical standards.

3. To provide materials presenting all points of view concerning the problems and issues of our times in order to develop, under guidance, critical examination, thinking, and judgment.

4. To provide materials appropriate and meaningful to the growth and development of pupils as individuals capable of making intelligent judgments.

5. To generate an understanding of American freedoms and a desire to preserve those freedoms through the development of informed and responsible citizenship.

6. To provide materials which represent many religious, ethnic, and cultural groups and their contributions to our American heritage.

7. To promote a love for, as well as skills in, reading, viewing, listening, and learning which will continue as a source of education and enjoyment.

8. To place principle above personal opinion and reason above prejudice in the selection of materials of the highest quality in order to assure a comprehensive collection appropriate for the users of the media center.

Heuvelton Central School District

The selection should reflect and help implement the basic functions of a good school program. The materials chosen should:

1. Provide teachers and pupils with reference and supplementary materials which support and enrich the curriculum.

2. Enable and encourage pupils to further develop their full potential as creative and responsible individuals by meeting and stimulating the greatest possible diversity of interests and abilities, whether or not these materials are directly related to the curriculum.

To fulfill these two basic functions, there should be easy access to a centrally cataloged and comprehensive selection of a variety of materials at appropriate levels of difficulty to:

1. Evoke a love of reading and learning which will assure a continuing self-education and a fruitful source of recreation and personal enjoyment.

2. Generate an understanding of American freedoms and a desire to preserve those freedoms through the development of informed and responsible citizenship.

3. Develop reading skills, literary and aesthetic taste, and discrimination in choice of materials.

4. Foster a breadth and depth of insight which will stimulate growth of ethical standards and a sensitivity to social, intellectual, aesthetic, and spiritual values.

5. Encourage pupils to locate, use, and evaluate as much material as possible on opposing sides of controversial issues so that they may develop, under guidance, the practice of critical examination and thinking.

6. Fairly represent the many religious, ethnic, and cultural groups and their contribution to our American heritage.

7. Provide practical instruction in the use of libraries and their resources.

8. Encourage the professional growth of the faculty.

Tracy Public Schools

Selection is designed so that students can:

1. Derive the fullest benefit from their classroom instruction.

2. Extend the boundaries of their knowledge and experiences.

3. Pursue self-directed learning of all kinds.

4. Explore and satisfy their many curiosities and interests.

5. Find enjoyment in the rich stores of the imaginative expressions of creative artists.

6. Learn how to use libraries and to evaluate the materials of communication.

7. Obtain materials that meet their individual needs and abilities.

8. Establish desirable intellectual habits that last for life.

Selection is designed so that teachers and counselors can:

1. Achieve their instructional objectives to the fullest degree.

2. Enrich course content.

3. Prepare assignments that provide for the needs and abilities of individual students.

4. Motivate students to use materials for curricular and noncurricular purposes.

5. Have the materials needed in counseling students in many aspects of guidance work.

6. Use materials directly with students in the classroom.

7. Teach students how to use materials and libraries.

8. Have materials easily accessible and efficiently organized so that time is not wasted in locating materials for examination and use.

9. Keep abreast with the best ideas and practices in education.

10. Use materials to broaden their own knowledge and to derive personal enrichment.

Responsibility

Jenison Public Schools

1. *Legal.* The Board of Education of the Jenison Public Schools is legally responsible for the selection of school media materials.

2. *Supervision.* The Board of Education delegates the power of selection to the administrative staff and requires supervision.

3. *Implementation.* The administrative staff delegates the final selection to the media staff under the supervision of the district media coordinator. The selection policy and process is carried out in accordance with the board and administrative policies.

Arlington County Public Schools

The Arlington County School Board is legally responsible for the purchase of all instructional materials. In each school, the librarian has the delegated responsibility for the selection of print and nonprint materials to be used by students and teachers.

The supervisor of library services may make recommendations and/or suggestions, but the final decision to purchase materials for a given collection rests with the librarian, who exercises the best professional judgment as to the needs of the individual school.

Sachem Central School District

1. The Board of Education, as the governing body of the Sachem School District at Holbrook, is legally responsible for the selection of library materials.

2. The board, as a policymaking body, delegates the authority for the selection of materials to professional personnel of the district in accordance with the policy that materials for the school libraries should be selected by the professional personnel of the libraries in consultation with administration, faculty, and students. Final decision on purchase shall rest with the superintendent or his designees.

Recommendations

Sachem Central School District

1. A teacher's recommendation for purchase of materials is given immediate consideration. The library media specialist reserves the right to question the purchase of particular materials, but if they fulfill the criteria for selection, they should be ordered. The library media specialist should periodically solicit teacher recommendations, either through conversation or by providing each teacher with order cards on which s/he may indicate possible purchase.

2. An administrator's recommendation for purchase is given immediate consideration and ordered as soon as possible.

3. A student's recommendations shall also be considered. Materials may be ordered if:

    a. They have been recommended in one of the standard selection aids.

    b. They have not been recommended but otherwise meet the established selection criteria and will appeal to more than just the student making the request.

    c. Money is available.

Criteria—General

Austin Independent School District

1. Librarians should be guided in the selection of materials by examination at supply stores, exhibits, and other libraries; by review at area meetings; and by the judicious use of standard reviewing tools and authoritative lists.

2. Materials selected should support all phases of the curriculum, and librarians should base decisions on a knowledge of the curriculum and of the existing collection.

3. Selection should be guided by a knowledge of the abilities, needs, interests, problems, motivations, cultural patterns, and maturity levels of the students, who should be involved directly in the selection process. Materials should represent all levels of understanding and experience. A formal procedure for ensuring that the desires of students are processed to the librarians will be developed and communicated to students.

4. Materials should be provided which interpret the contemporary world and present varying opinions on controversial issues and social problems.

5. Two basic factors, truth and art, are to be considered in selection of media.

   a. Truth includes accuracy, timeliness, authoritativeness, and freedom from bias.

   b. Art includes aesthetic values, imagination, creativity, and style appropriate to the material and to the maturity of the student.

6. In selecting controversial materials, the following criteria should be given consideration:

   a. Materials on controversial issues should represent contrasting views.

b. The race, nationality, or political views of a writer should not prohibit inclusion of his work.

c. In a literary work of established quality, the use of profanity or the treatment of sex is not an adequate reason for eliminating the material.

d. Materials should be evaluated as a whole; the purpose, style, and theme should overshadow any isolated offensive section. The masking, clipping, or other alteration of an individual work should be avoided.

e. A writer's expression of a certain viewpoint is not to be considered a disparagement when it represents the historical or contemporary views held by some persons or groups.

f. Materials on physiology, physical maturation, or personal hygiene should be accurate and in good taste.

g. Materials should be selected for their strengths rather than rejected for their weaknesses.

7. The library media centers welcome books and other resource material from individuals and organizations but reserve the right of placement. The materials, to be acceptable, must meet the standards and criteria established within this selection policy.

Cocalico School District

1. Needs of the individual school based on knowledge of the curriculum and of the existing collection are given first consideration.

2. Materials for purchase are considered on the basis of overall purpose, timeliness or permanence, importance of the subject matter, quality of the writing/production, readability and popular appeal, authoritativeness, reputation of the publisher/producer, reputation and significance of the author/artist/composer/producer, and format and price.

3. General criteria to be applied to:

a. Content.

- Is the subject matter accurate?

- Is the subject matter up-to-date in its information?

- Is it suitable for the age and maturity level of the reader for whom it is intended?

- Is the material as high in quality or better than other books already in the collection and not a duplication of existing material?

- Is the reading interest level suitable for the age level of the group for which the materials are intended?

- Will the subject matter tend to develop aesthetic, ethical, and moral values?

- Is the author qualified to write in this particular field?

- Do the publisher's reputation and standards prove desirable for school library materials?

- Is the material of lasting value?

- What is the importance of the subject matter to the curriculum?

- Has the material been recommended by any of the selection aids or standard book lists for school libraries?

- Has the material been recommended or approved by faculty and/or students?

b. Physical features.

- Is the format of the material satisfactory in size, appearance, and quality?

- Is the print readable, legible, and clear?

- Is the material durable?

- Is the price of the material commensurate with other current needs?

- Is the material indexed adequately?

- Is the technical quality of nonprint items the best available?

4. Specific criteria to be applied to:

a. Duplication.

- Materials are duplicated on the basis of need. Most often different titles are purchased within a subject area rather than large numbers of just one title.

b. Gifts.

- Gifts are examined and evaluated by the same standards as purchased materials. If the gift material does not meet the preceding standards, it will not be added to the collection.

c. Replacements.

- Lost, damaged, or worn materials are not automatically replaced. The decision to replace materials is based on the availability of duplicated material, the number of other materials on the same subject, the availability of more recent or better material, and the continued demand for the material in question.

Novato Unified School District

Each item will be evaluated individually in terms of its own qualities, in terms of whether or not it will be a useful addition to the collections, and in relation to the goals of the school. The varying range of abilities and interests among students will be taken into consideration. The collection will be oriented towards meeting educational needs in the broadest sense.

Evaluation of individual materials will be in terms of the purpose of the author and how well it has been achieved, style, accuracy, authority, effective presentation, organization, format, design, binding, paper, and other pertinent factors.

1. *Reference collection.* The purpose of this collection will be to provide basic tools such as dictionaries, encyclopedias, atlases, yearbooks, and other source materials in major fields and subjects so that students can become familiar with the kinds of information to be found in such books and can learn to use them systematically. The reference collection will be expanded in the areas where information is most needed by students or faculty.

2. *Nonfiction.* Standard books of information in every general area will form the basis of the nonfiction collection. Books on special subjects may be added as demand indicates. Where use is heavy, circulating copies of reference books will also be made available. In a subject area which is changing rapidly and where recency is important, new books will be added as frequently as necessary.

3. *Fiction collection.* The importance of recreational reading as an educational tool cannot be underestimated. Fiction can be a means of acquiring insight into and understanding of all kinds of individuals and situations far beyond the boundaries of a student's ordinary personal experience and can offer an enrichment of life that is not possible through the use of strictly factual books. It can lead to the development of imagination and an appreciation of the beauty of language, enlarging the thinking of each reader in important ways. The collection for recreational reading achieves this purpose by including the best works of authors of both juvenile and adult books. Books will be considered for the following qualities:

a. Plot well-organized and believable within its own framework.

b. Characterization convincing.

c. Skilled use of language.

d. Originality.

e. Honest presentation of human emotions, values, and ideas.

f. Illustrations.

The collection will offer a diversity of appeal and wide range of subject coverage and reading levels. It will include the best editions of classics, as well as books which may not be of permanent literary value but which can serve as a bridge for those students who cannot handle a more demanding treatment. All books must meet the standards.

4. *Periodicals.* Periodicals will be chosen to present various points of view on current issues and ideas, particularly in areas of political, social, and scientific thought and in subjects of particular interest to students. They will supplement the book collection. Periodicals known to be biased in one direction may be made available for study purposes but must be balanced by other periodicals that cover the same material from another point of view.

5. *Newspapers.* Newspapers of general circulation, dealing with matters of local, national, and international importance, shall be available in the library for student use.

6. *Pamphlets.* Pamphlets will be acquired as needed to provide supplementary information on any topic. They must meet the same standards of timeliness and accuracy applied to all nonfiction material. The pamphlet collection is intended to emphasize current thinking as much as possible and will be kept up-to-date by periodic revision. Pamphlets whose source cannot be traced will be excluded or else treated as examples of propaganda.

7. *Free and inexpensive materials.* Free and inexpensive materials will be subject to the same standards of evaluation stated above. Materials whose main purpose is advertising or which is largely commercial in nature will be excluded.

Norman Public Schools

1. It is the policy of the Norman Public Schools to select materials for library resource centers in accordance with the following principles:

a. Instructional materials are chosen because they are of interest and have learning value for the students in the community. Materials are not excluded because of race, nationality, religion, or political views of the writer.

b. Insofar as it is practical, materials are provided which present all points of view concerning the international, national and local problems and issues of our times. Books and materials of sound, factual authority are not removed or banned from library resource center shelves because of partisan or doctrinal disapproval.

2. Certain factors are considered in the selection of library resource center materials:

   a. Selections are made for and in accordance with the different maturity levels of the students.

   b. Materials are selected which fill a need related to the curriculum and/or contribute to the development and enrichment of the student.

   c. In the selection of materials, reviewing tools such as standard catalogs are used. When possible, audiovisual materials are previewed before purchase or ordered with return privilege guaranteed.

   d. The following specific criteria are considered:

      • The overall purpose of the material and how well it is accomplished.

      • Reputation and significance of the author.

      • Timeliness or permanence of the material.

      • Importance of subject matter to the collection.

      • Accuracy of material.

      • Reputation and standards of the publisher or producer.

      • Readability and reader appeal.

      • Quality of writing and illustrations.

      • Appearance of the title in material selection aids.

      • Price.

   e. Nonfiction subjects which are topics of criticism are carefully considered before selection. Among these are:

      • *Religion.* Factual, unbiased materials which represent all major religions may be included in the library resource center collection.

Bibles and other sacred writings are acceptable. Publications from religious bodies may be selected if they have general value or appear in magazine indexes.

- *Ideologies*. The library resource center should, without making any effort to sway the reader's judgment, make available basic, factual information, on the maturity level of its reading public, on ideologies or philosophies that are of current or continuing interest.

- *Science*. Medical and scientific knowledge suitable to the developmental stage of the students should be made available without any biased selection of facts.

f. Fiction has assumed an important role as an educational medium. The sound treatment of significant historical, social and personal problems in books of fiction can contribute to the understanding of human problems and human relations. Fiction is acquired to supplement areas of the curriculum and to encourage and develop the reading interests of students.

Kalamazoo Public Schools

GUIDELINES

Print and Nonprint Material

1. What is the subject matter and scope? Does it have significant curricular content to justify its cost?

2. If print, does it have literary quality? If nonprint, is the item attractive and interesting with some aesthetic value of vitality, style, and imagination?

3. Is it well-researched, accurate, and authoritative?

4. Who is the publisher or producer and what is his reputation?

5. Is it readable or suitable for students of the age or grade levels at which it will be studied?

6. Is it up-to-date?

7. Does it duplicate or add to other material in the media center?

8. What features are included that will increase its usefulness: table of contents, index, bibliographies, maps, charts, thought-provoking captions, clear labeling, summaries, outlines, questions?

9. What is the need for it in the school? Is it worth the money it costs and the time and effort to use it?

10. How much does it cost? Is it expensive or inexpensive in relation to the total materials fund available? Would some less expensive item produce similar or better results?

11. If print, is it well made with good paper and print, large enough margins for easy opening, good illustrations? If nonprint, is it technically satisfactory in respect to photography, sound, color, type size, illustrations? Is it physically satisfactory in respect to intended use?

12. Is it educationally sound for the age group for which it is intended? Does it stimulate thinking and inquiry? Does it suggest or lead to worthwhile learning activities?

Nonstereotyped Roles in Material

1. Are both parents and children of each sex involved in household tasks?

2. Are fathers shown in roles other than going to work or doing male-type chores? Are there family concerns, community concerns, personal growth concerns?

3. Are mothers shown in roles other than housework or child rearing? Are there family concerns, community concerns, personal growth concerns?

4. Does the home look "lived in" by real, human people or is it a "ready-for-company," sterile home?

5. Are there accurate portrayals of one-parent families?

6. Are there accurate portrayals of multiple-parent (divorce-remarriage) families?

7. Do the male characters respect the female characters and respond to them as equals?

8. Are mothers employed outside the home? In a stereotyping or a creative job?

9. Are boys and girls portrayed with a range of human responses, with girls adventurous and aggressive as well as sensitive and boys gentle as well as strong?

10. Are boys and girls participating equally in physical and intellectual activities?

11. Are girls developing independent lives, independently meeting challenges and finding their own solutions?

12. Do girls have a variety of choices and aspire to a variety of goals?

This section is adapted from *Little Miss Muffett Fights Back*, a publication of Feminists on Children's Media, New York, 1971 and *Citizens' Study—Sex Discrimination in the Kalamazoo Public Schools*, 1972.

Minority Group Material

1. *Appropriate language*. If dialect must be used, it should be faithful to the region of the story. A heavy use of words or expressions fraught with connotations of disrespect and contempt is unsuitable.

2. *Illustrations* must be true to the people depicted, not caricatures or stereotypes.

3. *Theme*. Minority peoples should be portrayed in all aspects of life, in different living situations, jobs, and professions.

4. *Treatment of characters*. There should be emphases in characters to show that they are people faced with the universal problems of all mankind: earning a living, hating and loving, rejoicing and grieving, experiencing successes and failures, learning to find their way through a complex world of ideas, and living with other people.

Montgomery County Public Schools

GENERAL STANDARDS

1. Is the material authentic?

   a. Is the material factually accurate?

   b. Is the material up-to-date?

   c. Are the author and/or producer well-qualified?

2. Is the material appropriate?

   a. Does it promote the educational goals and objectives of the curriculum of Montgomery County?

   b. Might the material be considered objectionable?

   c. Is it appropriate to the level of instruction intended?

   - Is the vocabulary appropriate?
   - Are the concepts appropriate?
   - Are the methods of development appropriate?

   d. Is controversial material presented impartially?

   e. Is this material suitable to the curriculum?

   f. Does this material present information that currently approved sources do not?

   g. Does this material give a new dimension or direction to currently approved sources?

3. Will the material catch and hold the interest of the users?

   a. Will the material stimulate the curiosity of the user?

   b. Can the material be used to satisfy curiosity?

4. Is the cost of the material justified?

Criteria—Special

Greenwich Public Schools

VERTICAL FILE

A vertical file can be, to a school media center, a quick reference source for useful, ephemeral literature. It is also likely to become a time-consuming catchall for inconsequential miscellanies and wasteful of staff time and floor space. It is recommended that media personnel think twice before assigning material to the vertical file. It is easier to keep out marginally useful material than to weed it out. Some materials that should not be assigned to the vertical file are the following:

1. Reprints from encyclopedias already in the media center.

2. Articles from magazines that are accessible through the *Readers' Guide to Periodical Literature* and backfiled in the media center.

3. Trivia on subjects adequately covered in the book collection, including encyclopedias.

4. Outdated material ''still good for something'' but discarded from the collection for good reasons.

5. ''Free'' materials not worth bothering about if they weren't free, no matter how attractive.

6. Materials irrelevant to the curriculum or unsuitable to reading levels and interests of students.

There is a legitimate place in a vertical file for the following:

1. Pamphlets, summaries, and reports not available elsewhere in the media center on topics of current interest or of relevance to the curriculum.

2. Significant materials which fill gaps in the book collection. Make up the deficiency in books as soon as possible, but use the vertical file materials in the meantime.

3. Current information on subjects in constant need of updating: geographical units, Nobel prizes, book awards, etc. Current editions of the *World Almanac, Statesmen's Yearbook,* and encyclopedia yearbooks make this information obsolete in a short time but, in the meantime, it's worth keeping where it can be located quickly.

4. Difficult-to-find, esoteric materials needed for specific teachers' assignments. These materials become obsolete when teachers retire, leave the school, or change their course content and should be discarded when no longer needed.

Some suggested procedures for maintaining the vertical file are as follows:

1. Evaluate materials in accordance with principles outlined above. Discard unwanted material promptly or forward it to teachers directly concerned.

2. For items to be kept, assign subject headings, using standard list of subject headings already in use. Establish a current subject heading authority file. When entering an item, print the subject heading on it, stamp, and date it.

3. Weed relentlessly.

Azusa Unified School District

FREE MATERIALS

Free material should:

1. Conform to the California Education Code.

2. Supply information not readily available in regular instructional materials.

3. Meet the same standards that purchased materials do.

4. State the sponsorship clearly.

Free material should be rejected if it:

1. Distorts or omits pertinent facts.

2. Makes sensational appeals to the emotions.

3. Fosters passive acceptance or uncritical thinking with respect to economic, social, political, or religious problems.

4. Uses deceptive propaganda devices.

5. Is obsolete or unauthoritative.

6. Overadvertises.

However, some material can be used effectively for propaganda analysis or for showing a minority point of view if the teacher is careful to identify prejudice and to use the material with students who can evaluate it accurately.

Boulder Valley Schools

SPONSORED MATERIALS

Organizations, institutions, and individuals at times develop materials which are offered to schools free or inexpensively. As a general rule, sponsored materials present a particular point of view, and extreme care must be exercised in evaluating and using them. The responsibility for using sponsored materials rests with the certificated staff member who recommends their use. In any questionable instance, the principal should be informed and will decide whether their use is in the best interest of the students.

Sponsored material must meet the same basic selection criteria as any other learning material, as well as the following special criteria:

1. Any expression of a point of view should be clearly identified.

2. Any advertising that appears on or with any material should be in good taste and unobtrusive.

3. The source of all material should be clearly identifiable.

Columbia County Schools

EQUIPMENT

1. *Portability.* Is the equipment easy to handle and move about? Is it reasonably light in weight? Is it compact? Is it easy to lift and carry? Some equipment should be classroom- or auditorium-stationed or highly specialized, and portability may not be an important factor.

2. *Ruggedness.* Does previous performance show this piece of equipment to give good service with minimum trouble? Is it sturdy, with little vibration during operation? Are all joints, braces, etc., tight and strong? Are handles secure? Are control mechanisms strong?

3. *Cost.* Does the item compare favorably with similar brand items? Is the price reasonable?

4. *Operation.* Can the machine be operated easily by teacher and student? Is the operation easy to teach? Are the controls few in number and easy to understand and use? Is it free of operative peculiarities?

5. *Performance quality.* Will the machine do what it is expected to do? Does it fulfill objectives previously established?

6. *Design.* Is it attractive? Are all external parts free of unfinished or rough parts? Will the finish mar easily? Was it designed for rugged school use? Are desirable safety features included? Is it properly balanced?

7. *Maintenance and repair.* Is it easy to clean? Can minor adjustments be easily made? Are replacement parts readily available at reasonable cost?

8. *Manufacturer/distributor.* Does the manufacturer make the item primarily for school use? Is the company apt to stay in the school business?

9. *Local status.* Does the school actually need the item being evaluated? Is it practical to trade equipment that is still useful? Rather than trading equipment, is it more worthwhile to make an outright purchase at lower cost?

10. *Service.* Are repair and emergency service readily available? Are adequate stocks of replacement parts available? Who will pick up equipment for repair? Are transportation charges to be paid by the school or by the dealer?

Jefferson County School District 509-J

EQUIPMENT

The following are minimum considerations to be used in evaluating equipment prior to selection and purchase:

1. Each equipment item will be designed and manufactured in a manner that allows for convenient use by teachers and students (usability), that

a. An objective and systematic process will be used for establishing usability, functionality, and safety. The *User's Evaluation Form* developed by the Oregon Media Equipment Evaluation Network will form the basis for establishing usability and functionality. [This form is in Part III.]

b. Usability, functionality, and safety are best determined when each item of equipment is tested under field conditions. Whenever possible, equipment will be field-tested for a suitable length of time in a situation similar to where it will ultimately be used.

2. All electronic and mechanical equipment will be favorably evaluated by competent technical personnel prior to purchase.

a. Evidence acceptable for favorable technical evaluation includes:

- A positive review from Educational Products Information Exchange Institute (EPIE), *Library Technology Reports*, or other professional library media publication that review equipment.

- A positive equipment evaluation report from state or school district technical staff reports.

- A favorable evaluation by local technicians who have experience and training in servicing the type of equipment being evaluated.

b. Standard forms from the Oregon Media Equipment Evaluation Network will be used for gathering and reporting evaluation information.

3. Certain factors unique to the district should be considered when choosing between two competing models of equipment.

a. Standardization within the district.

- When two pieces of equipment are being evaluated as being relatively equal by the above criteria, special consideration will be given to models which the district has previously purchased in significant numbers.

- Care will be taken to assure the compatibility of an equipment item with components, accessories, and the collection of materials intended to be used with it.

b. Reputation, proximity, and stability of vendors will be considered in selecting between two relatively equal items.

c. The availability of maintenance and repair services will be considered prior to the purchase of an item of equipment.

4. The Board of Directors delegates authority for the evaluation and selection of media equipment to the professional personnel as outlined

above. Purchasing procedures will follow district purchasing guidelines. Requests for bids on equipment will specify the qualifications as determined by the preview/evaluation procedure.

5. Continuing evaluation of equipment should be maintained through the use of *User's Evaluation Form*. The Board of Directors delegates to the professional staff the ongoing evaluation necessary in maintaining a building and district equipment collection that is current with the media needs of teachers and students.

Southwest School Corporation of Sullivan County

EQUIPMENT

1. *Portability*.

   a. Equipment is easy to handle.

   b. Convenient sturdy handles.

   c. Compact and reasonably light in weight.

2. *Ruggedness*.

   a. Equipment gives good service with minimum of trouble.

   b. Sturdy in appearance and construction.

   c. Design attractive and functional.

   d. Surface does not mar easily.

   e. Control mechanisms are strong.

3. *Cost*.

   a. Reasonable and competitive in price.

   b. Maintenance and repair are not excessive.

4. *Ease of operation*.

   a. Teachers and students can learn operation easily.

   b. There are few controls.

   c. Controls are easy to work.

5. *Performance*.

   a. Equipment performs well.

   b. Equipment is dependable.

6. *Reputation of manufacturer.*

   a. The company honors all warranties.

   b. Production of school equipment is a major concern.

   c. The company has been in business at least 5 years.

   d. The company is likely to continue in business.

   e. The equipment will continue to be manufactured.

7. *Service of dealer.*

   a. Service and adequate parts are available.

   b. Emergencies can easily be cared for.

   c. Repairs are made quickly and efficiently.

   d. There is a pickup and delivery plan.

8. *Replacement.*

   a. Equipment will be replaced on a rotation plan.

   b. Maximum number years of service for equipment will vary.

   c. All projectors will be replaced in 8-10 years.

Montgomery County Public Schools

SPECIFIC STANDARDS

Free and Inexpensive Materials

Free and inexpensive instructional materials are produced in many forms and comprise an important segment of the area of instructional materials. They should be accepted and used only when they contribute to the educational goals of the Montgomery County Public Schools. These materials should be of the same high quality and purpose as are all other types of instructional materials.

Sponsored Materials

In evaluating sponsored materials, evaluation and selection committees may use the same criteria which have been set up for evaluating all other types of instructional materials. Sponsored materials should not attempt to establish the exclusiveness of a particular product or service. The source of funds and sponsoring organizations of the materials should be known so that the point of view and propaganda content presented may be identified and evaluated. If the materials meet these criteria and the products are in good taste, the appearance of the name of the sponsor on the materials is acceptable.

LIBRARY BOOKS AND TEXTBOOKS

Fiction and Other Literary Forms

The criteria established for the selection of fiction have much in common with the criteria established for the selection of nonfiction books. However, there are differences related to the author's purpose, development of the theme and story, and the level of the audience for whom s/he is writing. Suggestions for criteria for fiction are as follows:

1. Purpose.

   a. What is the purpose, theme, or message of the book? How well does the author accomplish this purpose?

   b. If the story is humorous, is the humor the type that will appeal to children? To young adults?

   c. If the story is fantasy, is it the type that has imaginative appeal and is suitable for children? For young adults?

   d. Will the reading of the book result in more compassionate understanding of human beings?

   e. Does it offer an opportunity to better understand and appreciate the aspirations, achievements, and problems of various minority groups and women?

   f. Does it present a positive picture of the role of women and avoid stereotyping?

   g. Are any questionable elements of the story an integral part of a worthwhile theme or message?

2. Content.

   a. Does a story about modern times give a realistic picture of life as it is now?

   b. Does the story avoid an oversimplified view of life, one which leaves the reader with the general feeling that life is sweet and rosy or ugly and meaningless, or the like?

c. When factual information is a part of the story, is it presented accurately?

d. Is prejudicial appeal readily identifiable by the potential reader?

e. Are concepts presented appropriate to the ability and maturity of the potential reader?

f. Is there good plot construction with logical development and minimum of coincidence?

g. Do characters speak in a language true to the period and section of the country in which they live?

h. Are characters created with individual human qualities or are they stereotypes of any cultural group?

i. Does the book offend in some special way the sensibilities of women or a minority group by the way it presents either the chief character or any of the minor characters?

j. Does it include contributions of women to society?

k. Is there preoccupation with sex, violence, cruelty, brutality, and aberrant behavior that would make this book inappropriate for children? For young adults?

l. Is the language in good taste?

   • If there is use of offensive language, is it appropriate to the purpose of the text? For children? For young adults?

   • Is dialect authentic or is it overdrawn and inconsistent, giving a false, author-created dialect or false idiom?

   • Is the book free from derisive names and epithets that would offend minority groups? Children? Young adults? Women?

m. Does the book have literary and human values?

   • Is the book well-written?

   • Does the story have appeal?

   • Does the story give a broader understanding of human behavior without stressing differences of class, race, color, sex, education, religion, or philosophy in any inimical way?

   • Does the book make a significant contribution to the history of literature or ideas?

3. Technical quality.

   a. Is the size of the book appropriate for use at the intended level?

   b. Is the binding durable and strong?

   c. Is the cover attractive?

   d. Is the paper durable and opaque?

   e. Is the typography clear and easy to read?

   f. Is the type size appropriate for the level intended?

   g. Are the page layouts well-designed? Ample margins?

   h. Is the space between the lines appropriate for the level intended?

   i. Illustrations:

   - Are the illustrations appropriate and in good taste?

   - Are the illustrations realistic in relation to the story?

   - Do the illustrations avoid stereotypes? Ethnocentrism?

   - Is the art or photographic quality acceptable (sharpness, composition, distortion, color)?

   - Are the captions readable?

   - Are the illustrations located properly for greatest usefulness?

4. Supporting opinion.

   a. Does it appear on one or more reputable book lists or selection aids?

   b. Has it been favorably reviewed by experts in the field?

Nonfiction

1. Purpose.

   a. What is the overall purpose of the book?

   b. How well is the purpose accomplished?

   c. For whom is it intended?

2. Author and publisher.

   a. Is the author competent and qualified in the field?

   b. What is the reputation and significance of the author and publisher in the field?

3. Authenticity.

   a. Is the material factually accurate and objective in presentation or is it an authentic presentation of a particular point of view?

   b. Is the material up-to-date?

   c. Are information sources well-documented?

   d. Are translations and retellings faithful to the original?

4. Appropriateness.

   a. Does the material promote the educational goals and objectives of the curriculum of Montgomery County?

   b. Is it appropriate to the level of instruction intended?

      • Is the vocabulary appropriate?

      • Is the presentation of concepts appropriate to the ability and maturity of the student?

      • Illustrations: Are they appropriate to the subject and age level? Do they portray realistic human qualities? Do they avoid stereotype?

      • Are the methods of development appropriate? Is a logical scope and sequence developed? Is it readable, clear, and appropriate for the level and subject? Does it have literary merit?

   c. With respect to controversial material:

      • Are the sources, purposes, and points of view readily identifiable?

      • Is prejudicial appeal readily identifiable? Excessive emotionalism?

      • Are other materials available that present different and representative points of view concerning the problems and issues?

   d. Is the interest level appropriate to the user?

      • Will the material stimulate the curiosity of the user?

      • Will the material appeal to many students?

5. Content.

   a. Is the content of this material well-presented by providing adequate scope, range, depth, and continuity?

   b. Have the principles of learning (e.g., reinforcement, transfer) been followed in developing the material?

   c. Is the material in each chapter presented logically and clearly?

d. Does the material achieve its stated purpose?

e. Does this material present information not otherwise available?

f. Does this material give a new dimension or direction to its subject?

g. Where appropriate, does it treat women and minority groups in a way that highlights their problems and their contributions?

h. Is the content clearly outlined in the table of contents?

   - Is the pagination definite and clear?

   - Are chapter titles and subtitles clearly outlined?

i. Is appended material useful?

j. Are pupil aids to learning provided?

   - Is there a glossary?

   - Are aids to pronunciation and meaning provided?

   - Are summaries and reviews provided where appropriate?

   - Are exercises and activities appropriate and provocative?

   - Are various related materials listed?

k. Is the index adequate for pupils at the level for which the book is intended?

l. Do the visual aids (e.g., pictures, maps, graphs, charts) contribute to the development of the text?

   - Are they attractive?

   - Are they placed for greatest usefulness?

   - Are they adequate in number?

   - Where appropriate, are the illustrations multiethnic and free from stereotype?

m. Is the copyright date a significant factor in evaluating usefulness of content?

6. Technical quality.

   a. Is the size of the book appropriate for use at the interest level?

   b. Is the binding durable and strong?

   c. Is the binding sewn?

   d. Is the cover attractive?

e. Is the paper durable and opaque?

f. Is the typography clear and easy to read?

g. Is the type size appropriate for the level intended?

h. Are the page layouts well-designed?

i. Is the space between the lines appropriate for the level intended?

j. Illustrations:

- Is the art or photographic quality acceptable (sharpness, composition, distortion, color)?

- Is there a good balance between artistic technique and educational need?

- Are the captions readable?

- Are the illustrations and captions suitable for teaching and learning purposes?

- Are illustrations located properly for greatest usefulness?

- Are the illustrations adequate in number?

7. Supporting opinion.

a. Does it appear on one or more reputable book lists or selection aids?

b. Has it been favorably reviewed by experts in the field?

8. Supplementary information for textbooks.

a. Are teacher's aids provided?

b. Are teaching suggestions practical and provocative?

c. Does teacher's guide strengthen presentation of textual material?

d. Is a useful bibliography provided for teachers?

e. Are evaluation programs provided?

CHARTS

1. Is the content of this material well-organized and well-balanced?

a. Is the material presented logically and clearly?

b. Does the material achieve its stated purpose?

c. Does the chart aid conceptualization of subject matter?

   d. Is the content presented as clearly and simply as possible for the level intended?

   e. Is material arranged in logical sequence?

   f. Are charts presented in a series?

   g. Is the scale or size such that comparisons can be made between or among charts?

   h. Are symbolizations adequately explained?

2. Is the technical quality of this material acceptable?

   a. Is printed material sharply and clearly defined?

   b. Is the media used durable and opaque?

   c. Is some provision made for display?

- Are the charts provided with wall attachments?

- Are the charts mounted on a tripod or other floor display holder?

- Is the holder easy to manipulate?

- Does the holder take only a reasonable amount of space?

FILMS, FILMSTRIPS, CARTRIDGE FILMS, SLIDES, AND TRANSPARENCIES

1. Is the content of this material well-organized and well-balanced?

   a. Have the principles of learning (e.g., reinforcement, transfer) been followed in developing the material?

   b. Is the material presented logically and clearly?

   c. Is the sequence developed adequately?

   d. Is data sufficiently comprehensive to be useful?

   e. Is the content appropriate for this type of presentation?

   f. Is the material imaginative when imagination is really needed?

   g. Is the quality of the script or commentary satisfactory?

   h. Is the music or background satisfactory?

   i. Are the titles, labels, or captions appropriate?

   j. Is there extraneous or unnecessary material?

2. Is the technical quality of this material acceptable?

   a. Is the visual image satisfactory?

     • Is the photography clear and artistic?

     • Does it have enough close-ups?

     • Are printed items adequate in size?

   b. Is the quality of sound clear and intelligible?

   c. Is color used effectively?

   d. Are sound and visual image synchronized?

GLOBES

1. Is the content of this material well-organized and well-balanced?

   a. Is the material presented logically and clearly?

   b. Does the material achieve its stated purpose?

   c. Are latitude and longitude lines or indicators provided?

   d. Are color symbolizations pleasing but distinctive in quality?

   e. If raised-relief techniques are used, is vertical exaggeration excessive?

2. Is the technical quality of this material acceptable?

   a. Will materials used in the construction of the globe resist denting and breakage?

   b. Are jointures on globes smooth and relatively unnoticeable?

     • Are map segments well-registered?

     • Are places where parts of a globe are jointed in construction prominent?

   c. Is the base firm and heavy enough to resist tipping in use?

   d. Will connections of movable parts deteriorate or become separated through use?

   e. Is there an axis provided for the globe?

   f. Is a place provided for the storage of an axis pin if it is removable?

   g. Is the surface soil-resistant and cleanable?

   h. Is the surface made to be marked upon?

MAPS

1. Is the content of this material well-organized and well-balanced?

    a. Is the material presented logically and clearly?

    b. Does the material achieve its stated purpose?

    c. Is the projection suitable for use at the level intended?

    d. Is the projection suitable for the content to be shown?

    e. Is the map scale suitable for the purpose intended?

    f. Is the map area adequate for the purpose intended?

    g. Is the legend adequately and clearly presented?

    h. Are color symbolizations pleasing but distinctive in quality?

    i. If raised-relief technique is used, is vertical exaggeration excessive?

    j. Are latitude and longitude clearly delineated?

    k. Are contents dated when this is a significant factor in their utilization?

    l. Are the contents developed on a comparable basis if the map is part of a series?

    m. Is there too much detail?

2. Is the technical quality of this material acceptable?

    a. Is the durability of the material upon which the map is reproduced adequate for the purposes intended?

    • Will it curl along the edges?

    • Will it crack, split, or tear easily?

    b. Are printed materials acceptable in terms of legibility and placement?

    c. Is the mounting device durable?

    d. Is the mounting device appropriate for the intended use?

    e. Is the surface washable?

    f. Is the surface as nonreflecting as possible?

    g. Can marking devices be used on the surface?

PROGRAMED MATERIALS

1. Is the content of this material well-organized and well-balanced?

   a. Have the principles of learning (e.g., reinforcement, transfer) been followed in developing the material?

   b. Is the material presented logically and clearly?

   c. Does the material achieve its stated purpose?

   d. Is the program consistent with the behavioral objectives which are desired?

   e. Does the program emphasize the major objectives of the course content?

   f. Does the program offer the type of response (e.g., multiple choice, constructed response) that is desired?

   g. Does the program orient the student to a problem and prepare him for new information?

   h. Does the program use interesting and novel cues?

   i. Are those cueing techniques being used most appropriate for the kind of behavioral outcomes desired?

   j. Is the program overcued?

   k. Does the program raise questions for discussion at different intervals in order to further learning?

   l. Can the teacher develop problems from the programed activities to be performed as follow-up activities in the program?

   m. Is there an efficient way to refer to specific content?

2. Is the technical quality of this material acceptable?

   a. Does the program provide a record of the performance of the participant which can aid in diagnosis of individual learning problems?

   b. Does the program require a separate answer sheet?

   c. Does the learner participate actively at each step of the program?

   d. Does the program reinforce after each student's answer by telling him immediately whether he has responded correctly or not?

   e. Does the program provide too many responses within a frame before correction or reinforcement?

   f. Does each frame provide too much reading?

g. Is the program easy to handle physically?

h. Is the size of type appropriate for the grade level?

TAPE AND PHONOGRAPH RECORDS

1. Is the content of this material well-organized and well-balanced?

   a. Have the principles of learning (e.g., reinforcement, transfer) been followed in developing the material?

   b. Is the material presented logically and clearly?

   c. Does the material achieve its stated purpose?

   d. Is the content appropriate for presentation in recorded form?

   e. Does the material complement printed and visual teaching resources in the same subject area?

   f. Is the quality of the script or commentary satisfactory?

2. Is the technical quality of this material acceptable?

   a. Is the recording clearly labeled (title, number indicating playing sequence, and speed)?

   b. Is the type of material used for the record or tape durable?

   c. Is the quality of sound satisfactory?

      • Are the speakers' or actors' voices clear and understandable?

      • Is the music free from distortion?

FLAT PICTURES AND STUDY PRINTS

1. Is the content of this material well-organized and well-balanced?

   a. Is the material presented logically and clearly?

   b. Does the material achieve its stated purpose?

   c. Do the colors used (including black and white) contribute to learning?

   d. Is the size commensurate with the purpose for which it is intended?

   e. Has the composition been planned to illustrate or emphasize the intended purpose?

   f. Is explanatory material provided?

g. Do captions distract the reader from reading and interpreting material visualized in pictures?

h. Is there a recognizable sequence if the picture is a part of a series?

i. Will the material be outdated quickly by the style shown?

2. Is the technical quality of this material acceptable?

a. Is the definition sharp and clear?

b. Are the color reproductions accurately registered?

c. Is the base material durable and opaque?

d. Is the surface highly reflective?

e. Will material curl, split, or tear easily?

OTHER TYPES OF INSTRUCTIONAL MATERIALS: WORKBOOKS, ANSWER SHEETS, DITTO MASTERS, PUZZLES, GAMES

1. Is the content of this material well-organized and well-balanced?

a. Have the principles of learning (e.g., reinforcement, transfer) been followed in developing the material?

b. Is the material presented logically and clearly?

c. Does the material achieve its stated purpose?

d. Is the content developed for use with a specific text?

e. Is the content adaptable to basic courses of study in the designated field?

f. Does the content provide drill in basic skills?

g. Can the teacher develop problems from the programed activities to be performed as follow-up activities?

h. If examples or directions are needed, are they stated clearly?

i. Are visual aids to learning provided when appropriate?

j. Is there an efficient way to refer to specific content?

2. Is the technical quality of this material acceptable?

a. Is the size of the material appropriate for use at the intended level?

b. Is the material attractive?

c. Is the material durable?

d. Is the typography clear and easy to read?

e. Is the type size appropriate for the level intended?

f. Are the layouts well-designed?

STANDARDS FOR EVALUATION OF INSTRUCTIONAL EQUIPMENT

Evaluations of any instructional equipment should include the judgment of those who are to use them and should be group evaluations whenever possible. Evaluations are improved when they are based upon actual classroom use of the equipment.

Specifications relating to basic construction and safety features of specific types of equipment will be verified by personnel in the Department of Educational Media and Technology and the Division of Procurement. This will be done before such instructional equipment is submitted for formal evaluation for school use.

Evaluation procedures for instructional equipment shall include appropriate criteria from the following list:

1. Demonstrations of competitive equipment under identical conditions.

2. Demonstrations of specific equipment under varying light and sound conditions.

3. Actual tryout of equipment for an extended period of time.

4. Application of directions given in the manual to determine clarity of directions, ease of operation, and simplicity of maintenance.

5. Continuous operation of equipment for a few hours to check temperature and any other critical operating characteristics.

6. Actual practice in cleaning, adjusting, dismantling, and reassembling equipment where professional maintenance is not required.

Because of the great variety of equipment in the areas of music, physical education, industrial arts, and home economics, it will be necessary to develop specific criteria for each item of equipment. Until such time as these specific criteria are formulated and approved, only the record of evaluation need be submitted to the Department of Educational Media and Technology.

AUDIO, VISUAL, AND AUDIOVISUAL

(Amplifier, Listening Station, Record Player, Tape Recorder, Camera, Microscopes, Projectors, Televisions, and Office Practice Machines)

1. Is the equipment portable?

    a. Is it reasonably light in weight in comparison with others?

    b. Is it compact?

2. Is the equipment sturdy and attractive?

    a. Does the material of which the equipment is constructed appear durable?

    • Is the equipment well-constructed?

    • Is the material of which the equipment is constructed easily damaged or broken?

    b. Are the control features durable and reliable?

3. Is the equipment easy to operate?

    a. Are the controls accessible and plainly marked?

    b. Are there a minimum number of operating controls?

4. Does this equipment consistently meet desirable performance standards in terms of its specific function?

    a. Is tonal quality true?

    b. Is volume range adequate and well-defined?

    c. Is image sharply defined?

    d. Is light supply adequate?

    e. Is magnification of projection adequate?

    f. Are sound and visual image synchronized?

5. Are adaptations easy to perform?

    a. Are adaptors included within the equipment or its container?

    b. Is the equipment compatible for use with other types of equipment?

6. Is the equipment easy to maintain and repair?

    a. Can minor adjustments be made simply and quickly when needed?

    b. Is it easy to remove parts likely to need repairs?

    c. Are the parts standard and easily available for replacement?

7. Is the distributor dependable?

    a. Does the distributor have a proper credit rating?

    b. Are the distributor and manufacturer faithful to their agreements?

    c. Are repair and emergency service facilities readily available?

    d. Are adequate stocks of spare parts maintained locally?

8. In comparison with the cost of similar equipment, is the price reasonable?

FLANNEL BOARDS, MAGNETIC BOARDS, AND OTHER SIMILAR BOARDS

1. Is the board portable?

    a. Is it reasonably light in weight in comparison with others?

    b. Is it compact?

2. Is the equipment sturdy and attractive?

    a. Does the material of which the equipment is constructed appear durable?

       • Is the board well-constructed?

       • Is the material of which the board is constructed easily damaged, broken, or torn?

    b. Does the board have an attractive appearance?

3. Is the board easy to use?

4. Does this board consistently meet desirable performance standards in terms of its specific function?

5. Is the board versatile?

6. Is the board easy to maintain and repair?

    a. Can minor adjustments be made simply and quickly when needed?

    b. Is it easy to remove parts likely to need repairs?

    c. Are the parts standard and easily available for replacement?

7. Is the distributor dependable?

    a. Does the distributor have a proper credit rating?

    b. Are the distributor and manufacturer faithful to their agreements?

c. Are repair and emergency service facilities readily available?

d. Are adequate stocks of spare parts maintained locally?

8. In comparison with the cost of similar equipment, is the price reasonable?

POWER TOOLS

1. Is the equipment portable?

    a. Is it reasonably light in weight in comparison with others?

    b. Is it compact?

2. Is the equipment sturdy and attractive?

    a. Does the material of which the equipment is constructed appear durable?

    b. Does the equipment have an attractive appearance?

    c. Are the control features durable and reliable?

3. Is operation of the equipment easy to learn?

    a. Are the controls accessible and plainly marked?

    b. Are there a minimum number of operating controls?

4. Does this equipment consistently meet desirable performance standards?

    a. Is the power adequate?

    b. Are adequate safety devices provided?

    c. Can speed be controlled for efficiency and accuracy?

    d. Does the tool meet the specific tolerance for its operation?

5. Are adaptations easy to perform?

    a. Are adaptors included within the equipment or its container?

    b. Is the equipment compatible for use with other types of equipment?

6. Is the equipment easy to maintain and repair?

    a. Can minor adjustments be made simply and quickly when needed?

    b. Is it easy to remove parts likely to need repairs?

    c. Are the parts standard and easily available for replacement?

7. Is the distributor dependable?

    a. Does the distributor have a proper credit rating?

    b. Are the distributor and manufacturer faithful to their agreements?

    c. Are repair and emergency service facilities readily available?

    d. Are adequate stocks of spare parts maintained locally?

8. In comparison with the cost of similar equipment, is the price reasonable?

SCREENS

1. Is the screen portable?

    a. Is it reasonably light in weight in comparison with others?

    b. Is it compact?

2. Is the equipment sturdy and attractive?

    a. Does the material of which the equipment is constructed appear durable?

      • Is the equipment well-constructed?

      • Is the material of which the equipment is constructed easily damaged or torn?

      • Is the reflective surface long-lasting?

3. Is the screen easy to use?

4. Does this equipment consistently meet desirable performance standards in terms of its specific function?

    a. Is the reflective quality adequate?

    b. Is there a minimum of distortion?

    c. Is size adequate for purpose?

5. Is this screen versatile?

6. Is the equipment easy to maintain and repair?

7. Is the distributor dependable?

    a. Does the distributor have a proper credit rating?

    b. Are the distributor and manufacturer faithful to their agreements?

    c. Are repair and emergency service facilities readily available?

d. Are adequate stocks of spare parts maintained locally?

8. In comparison with the cost of similar equipment, is the price reasonable?

TEACHING MACHINES

1. Is the equipment portable?

    a. Is it reasonably light in weight in comparison with others?

    b. Is it compact?

2. Is the equipment sturdy and attractive?

    a. Does the material of which the equipment is constructed appear durable?

    b. Does the equipment have an attractive appearance?

    c. Are the control features durable and reliable?

3. Is the operation of the equipment easy to learn?

    a. Are the controls accessible and plainly marked?

    b. Is there a minimum number of operating controls?

4. Does this equipment consistently meet desirable performance standards in terms of its specific function?

    a. Does the device effectively present the kind of subject matter material that the teacher chooses to present?

    b. Does the learning device allow the response required by the program?

    c. Does the operation of the device offer any motivation in itself?

    d. Does the machine focus the attention of the student on one frame at a time in the proper order?

    e. Does the machine have a simple operation of advancing frames with ease?

    f. Is the tonal quality true?

    g. Is the volume range adequate and well-defined?

    h. Is the image sharply defined?

    i. Is the light supply adequate?

    j. Is the magnification of projection adequate?

5. Are adaptations easy to perform?

   a. Are adaptors included within the equipment or its container?

   b. Is the equipment comparable for use with other types of equipment?

6. Is the equipment easy to maintain and repair?

   a. Can minor adjustments be made simply and quickly when needed?

   b. Is it easy to remove parts likely to need repairs?

   c. Are the parts standard and easily available for replacement?

7. Is the distributor dependable?

   a. Does the distributor have a proper credit rating?

   b. Are the distributor and manufacturer faithful to their agreements?

   c. Are repair and emergency service facilities readily available?

   d. Are adequate stocks of spare parts maintained locally?

8. In comparison with the cost of similar equipment, is the price reasonable?

Interlibrary Loan

Coffeyville Unified School District

Each of the USD 445 school libraries is an integral component of the total district library program and is not an entity in and of itself.

Budget funds are allocated on the basis of a district program of uniform excellence and the individual library's role in that program.

Each library collection is considered a segment of the total district library collection. All materials are shared; all materials are made available upon request to any school library in the district. All requests for interlibrary loan are to be made via telephone to the education center. The library supervisor locates the requested materials and, if available, ships the materials directly to the librarian making the request.

Teachers, librarians and students are free to borrow materials from the Southeast Kansas Library System. USD 445 schools are free to loan materials to Southeast Kansas Library System members.

Weeding

Greenwich Public Schools

The selection process begins with the evaluation of materials before purchase and is completed with the evaluation of materials before discarding them. Weeding out of the school media center collection materials that are factually inaccurate or instructionally useless is as important as keeping them out initially. How rigorously and how often a collection is weeded depends on considerations of space, budget, curriculum requirements, and user needs unique to each media center. Both print and nonprint materials should be reviewed at regular intervals.

Some suggested criteria for weeding out undesirable materials are as follows:

1. *Record of use*—If the item has not circulated in 3 years.

2. *Currency*—If the subject matter is out-of-date, factually inaccurate, or no longer relevant to the educational program; if illustrations are outmoded or perpetuate sexual, racial, or cultural stereotypes.

3. *Technical quality*—In nonprint materials, if visuals are poor, faded, or off-color; if sound reproductions are faulty or inferior.

4. *Dispensability*—If it is a duplicate copy or duplicates materials no longer needed in the collection.

5. *Physical condition*—If it is worn, torn, soiled; if pages or parts are missing.

Here are some reasons for not discarding materials, even if they meet the above listed criteria:

1. If it is a work of historical significance in the field of children's literature.

2. If it has unusual illustrations or illustrations done by a well-known artist.

3. If it is a work by a local author, illustrator, or editor.

4. If it describes local history or personalities.

5. If it is a memorial gift.

Before discarding books, remove cards from the card catalog and shelflist. Remove book pocket, circulation card, and all marks of ownership. For books to be destroyed, tear out the title page and, if possible, remove book covers. Do not give discarded books to students or teachers, or donate them to book drives or rummage sales where they are likely to surface again as public property. If books are in good condition and, although eligible for discarding, have a potential usefulness in a prison or other needy institutional library, they may be donated to the Darien Book Aid Plan, which distributes books to such libraries. All ownership markings should be removed first. The address is: Darien Book Aid Plan, 1976 Post Road, Darien, CT 06820.

Jackson Local School District

1. *Objectives of discard.*

   a. The systematic removal from the collection of educational materials no longer useful is essential to maintaining the purposes and quality of the resources. The discarding of materials should average at least 5 percent of the total collection annually and requires the same degree of attention and careful study as the initial selection.

   b. All discarding decisions should be handled by the professional in charge of the media center.

2. *Print and audiovisual software.*

   a. Cause for discard:

   - Materials are out-of-date because their content has become obsolete, inaccurate, and/or misleading.

   - Materials are out-of-step with the interests, customs, or dress of the present generation (other than those on periods of time, costumes, etc.) and therefore are taking up shelf space instead of being read.

   - Materials are worn out and falling apart. (Some books can be rebound but, at current prices, it is often less expensive to buy a new copy.)

   b. Discarding procedure:

   - Pockets should be torn out.

- School stamp must be blackened out wherever it appears.
- Books should be stamped or marked (using magic marker) DISCARDED.

c. Salable print items:

- Should be marked properly for discard.
- Should be placed in a "Book Sale" (price depending on item and condition) and receipts used for purchase of replacement materials by the professional in charge of the library.

d. Usable nonprint items:

- Should be made available for teacher and/or student projects. (For example, individual frames of filmstrips can be used for slides for a student project.)
- Should be turned in to vendors when credit can be obtained toward purchase of new software.

e. Nonsalable and nonusable items:

- Should be burnt.
- Should be thrown out if not burnable.

3. Audiovisual hardware:

a. Cause for discard:

- Equipment would cost more to repair and keep in repair than to replace.
- Equipment is old, worn-out, or no longer reparable.

b. Method of discard:

- Should be traded in on purchases of new equipment when possible.
- Parts sold to general public if possible.
- Parts may be donated to the high school vocational department.
- Should be thrown out when no trade-in or sale possible.

Challenged Materials

Boulder Valley Schools

PROCEDURES FOR HANDLING COMPLAINTS

The Board of Education of the Boulder Valley Public Schools recognizes the right of individuals and groups to present complaints concerning instructional materials and educational activities in the schools. Despite all efforts to safeguard the rights of all concerned and to enhance the academic freedom so necessary to a quality educational program, occasional errors of omission, commission, indiscretion, poor judgment, or misinterpretation are bound to occur. The board recognizes this fact and urges any complainant to exercise the same principles of integrity, rationality, and objectivity explicit in the statements of this policy and clearly implicit in its spirit.

In the interest of handling all legitimate complaints fairly and expeditiously, the following guidelines will be used:

1. Most difficulties can and should be resolved at the building level. Isolated misunderstanding, often the result of faulty communication or misinformation, can usually be resolved through informal inquiry and discussion with principals and teachers.

2. Should an issue of substance remain unresolved, the complainant should be requested to make the complaint in writing. The building principal should then within 10 days hold a meeting of the parties named in the complaint.

3. If the complaint is resolved at this meeting, the only additional action necessary would be to send a copy of the complaint with resolution reached, attested to by the parties, to the appropriate executive director or assistant superintendent.

4. If the complaint is not resolved to the satisfaction of all parties involved, the complaint will be sent to the chairperson of the Issues Commission.

5. The Issues Commission shall consist of the following members: 4 classroom teachers, one building principal, one instructional services person, one media specialist (librarian), and 4 lay citizens.

6. The Issues Commission members will be selected by the superintendent in June of each year prior to the ending of the school year, to serve during the following school year. Teachers selected to serve on the Issues Commission will be drawn from 2 lists of names made up of persons selected from each building by the teachers of that building. One list of names will be made up exclusively of elementary teachers and the other list will be made up exclusively of secondary teachers. The building principal will be selected from among principals and assistant principals. The instructional services person will be selected from among the categories of certificated personnel listed as "instructional" in the district directory, excluding the assistant superintendent and executive directors. The media specialist (librarian) will be selected from among the media specialists wherever assigned in the district. The lay citizens will be selected from Citizen Advisory Councils.

7. It is hereby stipulated that no person's name may be included on any of the aforementioned lists without his/her written consent. Such written consent will be taken to mean that s/he will serve if selected. It is further stipulated that any member of the Issues Commission is automatically disqualified from serving if the issue involves him/her.

8. The Issues Commission will select its own chairperson who will serve for the entire year, except as the automatic disqualification stipulation may obtain, in which case the remaining members of the commission will select a temporary chairperson.

9. The Issues Commission would sit at fact-finding hearings requesting the presence of all parties of interest and would make written recommendations to the appropriate administrative level for any action indicated by the hearing. (The recommendations would be advisory in nature and could be overruled by the Board of Education.)

The hearings of the Issues Commission shall result in one of the following recommendations:

1. The material, issue, or practice is compatible with the criteria and guidelines of this policy statement and should not be restricted.

2. The material, issue, or practice is not compatible with the criteria and guidelines of this policy statement and should be discontinued.

3. The material, issue, or practice should be limited to the conditions specified by the Issues Commission.

The recommendations of the Issues Commission are subject to review by the Board of Education and, upon review, patrons of the district shall have the right to present their position directly to the Board of Education.

PROCEDURES DETAILED

In accordance with board policy, efforts should be made to resolve complaints as close to their point of origin as possible.

If, after informal discussions with the teacher and principal, the concern is still unresolved, the complainant should be requested to make the complaint in writing by letter or completion of a form. Information needed includes the topic or material to which the complainant objects, including the title, author, and publisher; the name and address of the complainant; specific objection to the topic or material (cite pages, passages, references, etc.); the reason for the objection; how much of the material was read, viewed, heard; if not the entire material, what parts were read, viewed, and heard; and any recommendation concerning the material/topic and suggested materials or topics to be used in its place.

1. The building principal should (within 10 days) hold a meeting of all parties named in the complaint.

2. If the issue is resolved at this meeting, the building principal will notify the appropriate level director in writing of the disposition of the complaint.

3. If the issue is not resolved to the satisfaction of all parties involved, the complaint will be sent by the building principal (within 5 days) to the chairperson of the Issues Commission.

4. The Issues Commission will sit at fact-finding hearings requesting the presence of all parties of interest and will make recommendations to the assistant superintendent of educational services any action indicated by the hearing. The chairperson of the Issues Commission will call the hearing within 10 days of receipt of the complaint and the Issues Commission will make its recommendations as outlined in board policy.

The recommendations of the Issues Commission are subject to review by the Board of Education and, upon review, patrons of the district shall have the right to present their position directly to the Board of Education. The superintendent or assistant superintendent of educational services will assist any complainant in bringing any unresolved concerns to the attention of the Board of Education.

The complainant may write a letter, attaching a copy of the written disposition of the complaint, directly to the president of the Board of Education. The letter should set forth the reasons why the complainant believes such disposition to be unsatisfactory. Upon receipt of such a written complaint, the president of the Board of Education shall bring the matter to the board for review and evaluation. Such review may include but is not limited to the securing of documentary evidence, personal interviews, a group meeting, a hearing, or any combination thereof. However, the board may also decline to consider the complaint further.

Following review of the matter, the president of the Board of Education shall advise the complainant in writing of the decision of the board. The decision of the Board of Education shall be final.

Coleman High School

A standardized procedure for handling complaints will avoid misunderstanding and rumors and will assure a courteous and efficient approach to the problem. Freedom of inquiry is essential; those within the school must have a chance to be heard, and any person outside the school should feel that his/her opinion will be considered and that his/her interest is welcomed.

PROCEDURE

1. Any oral or written criticism of media center material should first of all be directed to the building principal and librarian coordinator, whether the criticism is received by a member of the Board of Education, an administrator, or a teacher.

2. When the principal and library coordinator feel they cannot resolve the problem in discussion with the complainant, they will ask that a signed complaint be presented in writing, to assure him/her of a courteous and fair hearing.

3. When the written complaint is received, the principal and the coordinator will call the library advisory committee together for reevaluation of the material in question.

4. The committee will consider the material, and after a meeting together, report of its findings to the superintendent and the Board of Education.

5. The decision of the Board of Education based upon the committee's recommendation shall be sent in writing to the complainant.

Hood River County School District 1

This procedure recognizes the right of staff and patrons to request a review of materials which appear not to meet the criteria of selection listed in the selection statement. These criteria apply to materials used in the classroom as well as in the library and this review procedure applies to both areas. The intent of the procedure is to provide a fair and orderly basis for considering criticisms, complaints, requests for banning, and challenges of instructional materials. In this procedural statement, all such allegations are referred to as ''challenges.''

1. Challenges, written or verbal, shall be directed to the school principal, who shall officially acknowledge them.

2. The school principal will immediately notify the staff member/members directly involved of the challenge.

3. The school principal and staff member/members shall arrange a meeting with the complainant in an attempt to solve the objection.

4. Any complainant not satisfied after conferring with the principal and staff should be invited to file his/her challenge in writing and should be given a district form, *Request for Reconsideration of Instructional Materials*. [See Part III for a similar sample form.]

5. The materials in question shall continue to be used until the school board takes final action.

6. The district will take no formal action on any citizens' objection to instructional materials until the *Request for Reconsideration of Instructional Materials* form has been submitted to the superintendent of the district.

7. Upon receipt of the form, *Request for Reconsideration of Instructional Materials*, the superintendent shall activate the District Instructional Materials Review Committee. The person submitting the challenge may withdraw the request at any time, thereby negating the necessity of further action.

REVIEW COMMITTEE

A District Instructional Materials Review Committee shall consist of 9 members: one board member appointed by the chairperson of the Board of Directors; 2 lay persons appointed by the Board of Directors; and the following appointed by the superintendent of schools: 3 staff members from the appropriate grade level and subject area who are not affected by the challenge, an administrator, a librarian.and the media supervisor. The Review Committee shall designate a chairperson and a secretary.

1. Committee members will receive copies of the challenge.

2. Representatives from the school involved and the complainant have the privilege of being heard in person.

3. The committee will review the material in question and recommend to dismiss or sustain the challenge.

4. The committee will weigh values and faults and form opinions based on the material as a whole and not on passages or excerpts pulled out of context.

5. The committee will check general acceptance of the materials by reading reviews.

6. The committee may call consultants to review materials in particular subject areas.

7. The committee will prepare a report of recommendations for the superintendent.

8. The committee will notify complainant and involved school principal of its action and recommendations, and the date, time, and place of the next scheduled board meeting when final action will be taken.

BOARD ACTION

1. The superintendent will submit the committee's report to the school board for final consideration.

2. The superintendent will communicate, by letter, the school board's decision to the complainant and all concerned school personnel.

Mount Pleasant Community Schools

OBJECTION

1. Any resident of the school district may raise objection to instructional materials used in the district's educational program despite the fact that the individuals selecting such material were duly qualified to make the

selection, followed the proper procedure, and observed the criteria for selecting such material.

 a. The school official or staff member receiving a complaint regarding instructional materials shall try to resolve the issue informally. The materials shall remain in use, unless removed temporarily.

 b. The school official or staff member initially receiving a complaint shall explain to the complainant the school's selection procedure, criteria, and qualifications of those persons selecting the material.

 c. The school official or staff member initially receiving a complaint shall explain to the best of his/her ability the particular place the material occupies in the educational program, its intended educational usefulness, and additional information regarding its use, or refer the complaining party to someone who can identify and explain the use of the material.

2. In the event that the person making an objection to material is not satisfied with the initial explanation, s/he should be referred to someone designated by the principal or person in charge of the attendance center to handle such complaints or to the media specialist for that attendance center. If, after private counseling, the complainant desires to file a formal complaint, the person to whom the complainant has been referred will assist in filling out a *Reconsideration Request Form* in full. [See Part III for a similar sample form.]

3. The individual receiving the initial complaint shall advise the principal or person in charge of the attendance center where the challenged material is being used of the initial contact no later than the end of the following school day, whether or not the complainant has apparently been satisfied by the initial contact. A written record of the contact shall be maintained by the principal or other person in charge of the attendance center.

4. The principal or his designee shall make copies available in each attendance center of the selection and objection rules.

REQUEST FOR RECONSIDERATION

1. Any resident or employee of the school district may formally challenge instructional materials used in the district's educational program on the basis of appropriateness. This procedure is for the purpose of considering the opinions of those persons in the schools and the community who are not directly involved in the selection process.

2. Each attendance center and the school district's central office will keep on hand and make available *Reconsideration Request Forms*. All formal objections to instructional materials must be made on this form.

3. The *Reconsideration Request Form* shall be signed by the complainant and filed with the superintendent or someone so designated by the superintendent.

4. Within 5 business days of the filing of the form, the superintendent or person so designated by the superintendent shall file the material in question with the Reconsideration Committee for reevaluation. The committee shall recommend disposition to the office of the superintendent.

5. Generally, access to challenged material shall not be restricted during the reconsideration process. However, in unusual circumstances, the material may be removed temporarily.

6. The Reconsideration Committee:

   a. The Reconsideration Committee shall be made up of 9 members.

      • One teacher designated annually by the superintendent.

      • One school media specialist designated annually by the superintendent.

      • One member of the central administrative staff designated annually by the superintendent. (This position will normally be filled by the supervisor or person responsible for the district's media services.)

      • Five members from the community appointed annually from the school advisory committees.

      • One high school student, selected annually from and by the high school Student Council.

   b. The chairperson of the committee shall not be an employee or officer of the district. The secretary shall be an employee or officer of the district.

   c. The committee shall first meet each year during the third week in September at a time and place designated by the superintendent and made known to the members of the committee at least 3 school days in advance.

   d. A calendar of subsequent regular meetings for the year shall be established and a chairperson and secretary selected at the first meeting.

e. Special meetings may be called by the superintendent to consider temporary removal of materials in unusual circumstances. Temporary removal shall require a three-fourths vote of the committee.

f. The calendar of regular meetings and notice of special meetings shall be made public through appropriate student publications and other communications methods.

g. The committee shall receive all *Reconsideration Request Forms* from the superintendent or person designated by the superintendent.

h. The procedure for the first meeting following receipt of a *Reconsideration Request Form* is as follows:

   • Distribute copies of written request form.

   • Give complainant or a group spokesperson an opportunity to talk about and expand on the request form.

   • Distribute reputable, professionally prepared reviews of the material when available.

   • Distribute copies of challenged material as available.

i. At a subsequent meeting, interested persons, including the complainant, may have the opportunity to share their views. The committee may request that individuals with special knowledge be present to give information to the committee.

j. The complainant shall be kept informed by the secretary concerning the status of his/her complaint throughout the committee's reconsideration process. The complainant and known interested parties shall be given appropriate notice of such meetings.

k. At the second or a subsequent meeting, as desired, the committee shall make its decision in either open or closed session. The committee's final decision will be: (1) to take no removal action, (2) to remove all or part of the challenged material from the total school environment, or (3) to limit the educational use of the challenged material. The sole criteria for the final decision is the appropriateness of the material for its intended educational use. The vote on the decision shall be by secret ballot. The written decision and its justification shall be forwarded to the superintendent for appropriate action, the complainant, and the appropriate attendance centers.

l. A decision to sustain a challenge shall not be interpreted as a judgment of irresponsibility on the part of the professionals involved in the original selection or use of the material.

m. Requests to reconsider materials which have previously been before the committee must receive approval of a majority of the committee members before the materials will again be reconsidered. Every *Reconsideration Request Form* shall be acted upon by the committee.

n. In the event of a severe overload of challenges, the committee may appoint a subcommittee of members or nonmembers to consolidate challenges and to make recommendations to the full committee. The composition of this subcommittee shall approximate the representation on the full Committee.

o. Committee members directly associated with the selection, use, or challenge of the challenged material shall be excused from the committee during the deliberation on such materials. The superintendent may appoint a temporary replacement for the excused committee member, but such replacement shall be of the same general qualifications of that person excused.

p. If the complainant is not satisfied with the decision, s/he may request that the matter be placed on the agenda of the next regularly scheduled meeting of the board.

q. Any person dissatisfied with the decision of the board may appeal to the State Board of Public Instruction pursuant to state law.

INSTRUCTIONS TO THE RECONSIDERATION COMMITTEE

The policy of this school district related to selection of learning materials states that any resident of the district may formally challenge instructional materials used in the district's educational program. This policy allows those persons in the school and the community who are not directly involved in the selection of materials to make their opinions known. The task of the Reconsideration Committee is to provide an open forum for discussion of challenged materials and to make an informed decision on the challenge.

The most critical component of the reconsideration process is the establishment and maintenance of the committee's credibility in the community. For this purpose, the committee is composed primarily of community members. The community should not therefore infer that the committee is biased or is obligated to uphold prior professional decisions. For this same reason, a community member will be selected to chair the committee.

The presence on the committee of the school media specialist and the administrative staff member will assure continuity from year to year as well as lend professional knowledge of the selection process. Student members are essential since they are the closest to the student body and will be immediately affected by the decision of the committee.

The reconsideration process, the task of this Committee, is just one part of the selection continuum. Material is purchased to meet a need. It is reviewed and examined, if possible, prior to purchase; it is periodically reevaluated through updating, discarding, or reexamination. The committee must be ready to acknowledge that an error in selection may have been made despite this process. Librarians and school personnel regularly use a great number of reviews in the selection process, and occasional errors are possible.

In reconsidering challenged materials, the role of the committee, and particularly the chairperson, is to produce a climate for disagreement. However, the committee should begin by finding items of agreement, keeping in mind that the larger the group participating, the greater the amount of information available and, therefore, the greater the number of possible approaches to the problem.

If the complainant chooses, s/he may make an oral presentation to the committee to expand and elaborate on the complaint. The committee will listen to the complainant, to those with special knowledge, and to any other interested persons. In these discussions, the committee should be aware of relevant social pressures which are affecting the situation. Individuals who may try to dominate or impose a decision must not be allowed to do so. Minority viewpoints expressed by groups or individuals must be heard, and observers must be made to feel welcome. It is important that the committee create a calm, nonvolatile environment in which to deal with a potentially volatile situation. To this end, the complainant will be kept continuously informed of the progress of his/her complaint.

The committee will listen to the views of all interested persons before reaching a decision. In deliberating its decision, the committee should remember that the school system must be responsive to the needs, tastes, and opinions of the community it serves. Therefore, the committee must distinguish between broad community sentiment and attempts to impose personal standards. The deliberations should concentrate on the appropriateness of the material. The question to be answered by the committee is: "Is the material appropriate for its designated audience at this time?"

The committee's final decision will be: (1) to remove the challenged material from the total school environment, (2) to take no removal action, or (3) to agree on a limitation of the educational use of the materials. The decision will be reached through secret ballot.

The committee chairperson will instruct the secretary to convey the committee's decision to the office of the superintendent. The decision should detail the rationale on which it was based. A letter will be sent to the complainant outlining the committee's final decision.

New Prague Public Schools

PROCEDURES FOR HANDLING QUESTIONED MATERIALS

1. Upon receiving a complaint, the building principal shall meet informally with the parties involved, including the complainant and the teachers and/or media personnel.

2. If the issue has not been resolved after the informal consultation, the complainant should then complete a *Request for Reconsideration of Instructional Material* form. [A similar sample form is in Part III.]

3. The questioned material shall immediately be read and evaluated by a reviewing committee. This committee shall consist of:

   a. One school board member designated by the chairperson of the Board of Education.

   b. Two parents appointed by the committee chairperson.

   c. One teacher at the level of the problem, designated by the teachers' local education association.

   d. Two students, where appropriate, selected by the student council.

   e. One media generalist, designated by the media staff.

   f. One principal from the appropriate building.

   g. The superintendent of schools who shall serve as committee chairperson.

   When necessary, the reviewing committee may consult with persons who are specially competent in the area involved.

4. Material being objected to will not be withdrawn until a final decision from the reviewing committee has been reached.

5. If the complainant is present at the meeting, s/he shall be welcome to present his/her views but shall not vote on the disposition of the material under consideration.

6. The committee's decision (which shall be reached by simple majority) shall be given to the appropriate director who will see that implementation of the decision takes place.

7. Material which has undergone a challenge may not be rechallenged until one calendar year after the recommendation of the review committee.

PART III
PROCEDURES

Ordering and Processing—
Two Partial Policies

Greenwich Public Schools

BOOKS

Book orders originate in the schools. They should be entered on multiple order slips, covered by a purchase order, showing list price and net price after discount, if possible. An adding maching tape for the books requested should accompany the purchase order. The purchase order should have attached to it a Town of Greenwich standard invoice. The purchase order must be signed by the principal and forwarded to the coordinator of school media services. Original copies of the multiple order slips are submitted with and firmly attached to the purchase order. They are forwarded to the accounting office for processing and sent to the vendor.

In the secondary schools, orders are entered into the computer before being submitted to the coordinator.

Second copies of the multiple order slips are retained for filing in the media center's outstanding order file. Third copies are kept intact as a record of the order sent. The buff copy is used for filing in the public card catalog pending arrival of the books. A specification sheet should accompany Baker and Taylor orders.

LETTER OF INTENT

By means of a letter of intent, the media specialist may order books from Baker and Taylor between May 1 and July 1, prior to the beginning of a new fiscal year, which begins on July 1. This enables the book supplier to process book orders during the summer and deliver books prior to the opening of school in September. A letter of intent is used only for Baker and Taylor orders and must be signed by the coordinator of media services.

Greenwich Public Schools, Greenwich, CT 06830

CHECKING IN ORDERS

Books, unlike other merchandise ordered for the school system, are checked in by media personnel in the schools. They should be checked in promptly, if possible within 24 hours, and blue receiving reports forwarded to the business office for payment.

The checking-in process includes verifying titles against the shipping slip, against the invoice, and against the outstanding order file. Pull cards from the outstanding order file. Make sure the books received are the books ordered. Verify the processing to see that catalog cards and titles agree and that book pockets and spine labels are accurate. Verify the suitability of Dewey numbers and subject headings. From the catalog cards, select shelflist, main entry, title, and subjects cards that are appropriate for the media center. Examine books, at this time, for their possible use in subject bibliographies and new book lists.

PAYMENT OF ORDERS

When an order is complete, sign and forward to the business office the blue copy of the purchase order, attaching the original copy of the invoice. If there are errors in the order, notify the vendor promptly and request a mailing label for returning the books in question. Cross off missing titles from the invoice and pay the amount due, minus their cost. If there are price or discount errors, write the vendor promptly and wait for a reply before processing the blue receiving report. Keep records of all transactions and correspondence.

PARTIAL PAYMENTS

An order may be shipped to a media center in two or more parts. When a partial shipment is received and has been verified for accuracy, a partial payment may be authorized on a partial payment blue receiving report. This form is similar to a purchase order but authorizes the accounting office to pay only a portion of the total sum encumbered by the order. Attach to it the Baker and Taylor invoice and the Town of Greenwich invoice and forward these to the accounting office. When the final portion of the order arrives, the blue copy of the original purchase order is forwarded to the accounting office, authorizing final payment.

PROCESSING OF BOOKS

After checking the order for errors and authorizing payment, stamp the accession number on title page, book pocket, book card, shelflist card, and on a preselected page in the text. Write the book price on the shelflist card and circulation card. On the title page, along the binding interface, pencil in the price, vendor, and date purchased.

AUDIOVISUAL MATERIALS

Since audiovisual materials are not regularly or exhaustively reviewed in professional journals, it is advisable to purchase them only after firsthand examination and evaluation. This can be done in several ways:

1. They may be ordered directly from a vendor by purchase order clearly marked "For preview with intent to purchase." If they meet selection requirements, authorize payment; if not, return merchandise promptly within the preview period specified by the vendor. Be sure to send a copy of the evaluation form to the media services center office.

2. The media specialist may ask the media service center to request an item for preview. Use the film booking form for this purpose. When received, it will be forwarded to the requestor for preview and subsequently to other reviewers in the system. If satisfactory, the item should be purchased by usual purchasing procedures.

NONPRINT MATERIALS

Where possible, nonprint items (films, tapes, filmstrips, recordings, transparencies, video tapes, slides, realia, study prints, etc.) should be integrated into the total collection in terms of access through the catalog and on the shelves.

Most nonprint items may be ordered with preprocessing; the checking-in procedure is essentially identical to that used in checking-in book orders. Shelflist card, main entry, title cards, and subject access cards appropriate for the individual media center should be prepared and filed. Dewey numbers should be assigned, if applicable. Make a duplicate cassette recording before allowing sound filmstrip kits to circulate; study prints, maps, flash cards, etc., should be laminated to increase durability and life span of the materials.

When nonprint materials arrive without preprocessing, the cataloger of these materials may find the following handbooks useful:

Canadian Library Association. *Nonbook Materials: The Organization of Integrated Collections*. 1st ed. Ottawa, Canada: Canadian Library Association, 1973. 107 pp.

Tillin, Alma M., and Quinly, William J. *Standards for Cataloging Nonprint Materials: An Interpretation and Practical Application*. 4th ed. Washington, DC: Association for Educational Communications and Technology, 1976. 230 pp.

MAGAZINES

Periodicals are ordered through the central business office and placed with a magazine jobber for a subscription year beginning on July 1. Instructions for ordering are sent to each media center in the spring. A list of periodicals requested for the following year must be returned to the business office by April 1. Not only periodicals to be used in the library but professional and classroom periodicals may be entered on the annual magazine requisition.

Media specialists should consult the teaching staff on periodicals to be ordered, and when the list is complete, submit it to the principal for signature and forward it to the media services coordinator. Periodicals ordered for curriculum programs should be typed separately for each department and corresponding program code numbers assigned to them.

It is the responsibility of the school media center to check in all periodicals received in the school, to report missing issues on forms provided, and to clear invoices for payment when the periodicals are being regularly received.

A useful guide in the selection of periodicals for school libraries is the American Library Association's *Periodicals for School Libraries*.

Readers' Guide to Periodical Literature, Current Biography, and other Wilson or Bowker publications must be ordered directly from the publishers and should not be included in the annual magazine requisition. The magazine supplier may recommend other periodicals that should be ordered direct, as well.

Fort Bend Independent School District

ACQUISITIONS

Acquisitions is the term used to apply to all the processes involved in the securing of media for the library media center. The center has an established, accepted procedure for securing the best possible media for the library media center collection.

Preparing and placing an order

1. *Consideration file.*

   a. Remove from the consideration file cards for all media which are to be included on the order to be prepared.

Fort Bend Independent School District, Stafford, TX 77477

2. *Steps in placing an order.*

   a. Prepare the order cards.

- Use the consideration file card as an order/work card, or prepare an order/work card and discard the consideration file card. (Cards used may be a 3x5 card of your own design, or you may invest in order cards from a library supply company. Keep the card as simple as possible to meet your need.)

   b. Check *Books in Print.* (Currently our junior and senior high libraries purchase *Books in Print* annually.)

- Bibliographic information.

- Price (usually trade edition listed).

   c. Add number of copies needed.

   d. To be sure this is not an unwanted duplication, check against:

- Card catalog.

- Books-on-order file.

   e. If it is a desired duplicate, indicate so on order/work card.

   f. Main entry for each title being ordered may be established at this time.

   g. Check availability of catalog cards, and indicate suggested call number on order card.

   h. Check for complete information.

- Bibliographic.

- Binding desired.

- Who requested (curriculum area).

   i. Arrange order cards in preparation for typing order (as jobber desires).

   j. Type media order (double-spaced, in columns).

   k. Prepare proper requisition forms and attach to media order, usually prepared in triplicate, as follows:

- One copy for media center files.

- One copy for principal's files.

- One copy to be sent to administration building.

   l. At top of media order and on requisition form, indicate terms of the order, including:

- Cut-off amount for order.
- Number of shipments to be allowed.
- Number of days allowed for shipment.
- Instructions as to type of bindings desired.
- Desire for commercial processing or catalog cards.
- Request for packing invoice.

m. Submit to principal for review and signature of approval.

n. Order is then sent to administration building where purchase order is prepared.

o. Place order/work cards in media-on-order file, usually alphabetically under name of supplier.

3. *Receiving media into the library media center.*

a. Secure copy of invoice before unpacking (usually packed in the box).

b. Carefully unpack and arrange in order as listed on packing invoice.

c. Check media against the invoice.

d. Pull cards from media-on-order file.

- Place cards for out-of-print books into proper file (or discard).

- Place cards for out-of-stock media into proper file (or indicate "out-of-stock" with date and return to consideration file).

- Place each card for media received with the media it matches after verifying the price.

e. Date and sign invoice and duplicate purchase order when completely checked.

f. Make proper notation on the duplicate requisition in your file and on your budget record sheet.

g. Place available catalog cards with proper media.

h. Separate any imperfect books or errors in filling order so that they can be returned to suppliers.

- Keep this material in separate place with proper notation until the other media have been double-checked.

- Write note explaining error and send to business office along with media to be returned.

i. Media are now ready for classifying, cataloging, and processing.

Selection Aids

BOOKS

Adventuring with Books: A Book List for Pre-School to Grade 8. 2d ed. Urbana, IL: Compiled by National Council of Teachers of English, 1973.

Best Books for Children. Ed. by John T. Gillespie and Christine Gilbert. New York: R. R. Bowker. Annual.

Brown, Lucy Gregor. *Core Media Collections for Secondary Schools.* New York: R. R. Bowker, 1975.

Carlsen, G. Robert. *Books and the Teen Age Reader.* Rev. ed. New York: Harper and Row, 1972.

Children's Catalog. 13th ed. New York: H. W. Wilson, 1976 and supplements.

Gaver, Mary, ed. *The Elementary School Library Collection.* 11th ed. Williamsport, PA: Brodart, 1977 and supplements.

High Interest—Easy Reading for Junior and Senior High School Students. Urbana, IL: Compiled by a committee of the National Council of Teachers of English, 1972.

Junior High School Library Catalog. 3rd ed. New York: H. W. Wilson, 1975 and supplements.

Senior High School Library Catalog. 11th ed. New York: H. W. Wilson, 1977 and supplements.

Wynar, Christine L. *Guide to Reference Books for School Media Centers.* Littleton, CO: Libraries Unlimited, Inc., 1973 and 1976. (1974-75 supplement.)

PERIODICALS

Audio-Visual Instruction. Washington, DC: Association for Educational Communications & Technology. Monthly, September through May, with one June/July issue.

Booklist. Chicago: American Library Association. Semimonthly, except August.

Bulletin of the Center for Children's Books. Chicago: University of Chicago Press. Monthly, except August.

Horn Book Magazine. Boston, MA: Horn Book, Inc. Bimonthly.

Instructor. Dansville, NY: Instructor Publications, Inc. Nine times yearly, with May/June and August/September issues.

Learning. Palo Alto, CA: Education Today Co., Inc. Monthly, September through May.

Library Journal. New York: R. R. Bowker. Monthly, July/August; semimonthly, September through June.

Media and Methods. Philadelphia, PA: North American Publishing Co. Nine times annually, September through May/June.

New York Times Book Review. New York: The New York Times. Weekly.

Previews. New York: R. R. Bowker. Monthly, September through May.

Reading Teacher. Newark, DE: International Reading Association, Inc. Monthly, October through May.

School Library Journal. New York: R. R. Bowker. Monthly, September through May.

School Media Quarterly. Chicago: American Library Association. Quarterly.

Teacher. Greenwich, CT: Macmillan Professional Magazines, Inc. Nine times annually, September through May/June.

Top of the News. Chicago: American Library Association. Quarterly.

Wilson Library Bulletin. New York: H. W. Wilson. Monthly, September through June.

Book Jobbers

Baker & Taylor Co.
1515 Broadway
New York, NY 10036

    Gladiola Ave.
    Momence, IL 60954

    380 Edison Way
    Reno, NV 89564

    50 Kirby Ave.,
    Somerville, NJ 08876

    P.O. Box 458
    Commerce, GA 30529

Bound to Stay Bound Books, Inc.
W. Morton Rd.
Jacksonville, IL 62650

Brodart, Inc.
500 Arch St.
Williamsport, PA 17701

Follett Library Book Co.
4506 NW Highway
Crystal Lake, IL 60014

Mook & Blanchard
546 S. Hofgaarden St.
La Puente, CA 91744

Western Library Service
7262 Beverly Blvd.
Los Angeles, CA 90036

Magazine Subscription Agencies

American Companies, Inc.
914 Jefferson
Topeka, KS 66607

Ancorp National Services, Inc.
131 Varick St.
New York, NY 10013

Black Magazine Agency
Box 342
Logansport, IN 46947

W. T. Cox Subscription Agency
Rt. 6
411 Marcia Drive
Goldsboro, NC 27530

Demco, Inc.
P.O. Box 7488
Madison, WI 53707

    Box 7767
    5683 Fountain Way
    Fresno, CA 93727

EBSCO Subscription Service
(Div. of EBSCO Industries, Inc.)
P.O. Box 1943
Birmingham, AL 35201

F. W. Faxon, Co., Inc.
15 Southwest Park
Westwood, MA 02090

Reginald F. Fennell Subscription
    Service
508 W. Michigan Ave.
Jackson, MD 49202

McGregory Magazine Agency
Mount Morris, IL 61054

Magazine Supply House, Inc.
30 Washington Square
P.O. Box 606
Worcester, MA 01613

Mid-South Magazine Agency
P.O. Box 4585
Jackson, MS 39216

Moore/Cottrell Subscription
    Agencies, Inc.
North Cohocton, NY 14868

Walter Peck Magazine Agency
3331 Bank of Galesburg Building
Galesburg, IL 61401

Popular Subscription Service
P.O. Box 1566
Terre Haute, IN 47808

Rayner Agency Magazine Sub-
    scriptions
100 E. Chicago St.
Elgin, IL 60120

Solle's Inc.
304 WCCO Radio Building
Minneapolis, MN 55402

Turner Subscription Agency, Inc.
235 Park Ave. South
New York, NY 10003

Sources for Printed Catalog Cards

Associated Libraries, Inc.,
229-33 N. 63rd St.
Philadelphia, PA 19139

Brodart
500 Arch Street
Williamsport, PA 17701

Catalog Card Corp.
1300 E. 115th St.
Burnsville, MN 55337

Demco, Inc.
Box 7488
Madison, WI 53707

Box 7767
5683 Fountain Way
Fresno, CA 93727

Metro Litho Co.
900 N. Franklin St.
Chicago, IL 60610

3M Library Systems
3M Center
St. Paul, MN 55101

Forms—Samples

PURCHASE REQUISITION

Date:_____

Recommended source:

Name _____

Address _____

City _____

Fund	Func- tion	Class/ Object	Sub Obj.	Organi- zation

QUANTITY	DESCRIPTION & PART OR CATALOG NO.	UNIT PRICE	TOTAL AMOUNT

Prepared by: _____ Approved by: _____

P.O. No. _____Dated_____ Authorized for P.O. by: _____

McAllen Independent School District, McAllen, TX 78501

MATERIALS ORDER FORM

_____ School

Please use a separate sheet for each publisher.

QUAN-TITY	NAME OF BOOK (in alphabetical order)	AUTHOR	PUB-LISHER	UNIT PRICE	TOTAL

McAllen Independent School District, McAllen, TX 78501

PERIODICAL ORDER FORM

_____ School

19___-19___

Please arrange in alphabetical order by title.

NAME OF MAGAZINE	NEW	RENEWAL	COST

McAllen Independent School District, McAllen, TX 78501

ANNUAL INVENTORY

_____ School

19__ -19 __

Period of time covered in this report:

From: _____

Month   Day   Year

To: _____

Month   Day   Year

1. Number of books at the beginning of the school
   year . . . . Titles___Volumes_____

2. Number of books lost and paid for . . . . _____

3. Total number of books lost . . . . _____

4. Number of books withdrawn . . . . _____

5. Total number of books removed from inventory
   (Lines 3 & 4) . . . . _____

6. Number of books added this year . . . . Titles___Volumes_____

7. Number of books in collection at time of this
   report . . . . Titles_____ Volumes__

Signed_____
(Principal)

Signed _____
(Librarian)

McAllen Independent School District, McAllen, TX 78501

BOOK COLLECTION INVENTORY

_____ School

19___-19___

CLASS	PREVIOUS INVENTORY		NEW BOOKS ADDED		WITHDRAWN BOOKS		ANNUAL INVENTORY	
	TITLES	VOL-UMES	TITLES	VOL-UMES	TITLES	VOL-UMES	TITLES	VOL-UMES
Reference								
000								
100								
200								
300								
400								
500								
600								
700								
800								
900								
920								
Biography								
Fiction/Story Collections								
Easy								
Total								

Paperbacks

No. P.B. processed . . . . ._____

No. P.B. not processed . . . . ._____

No. P.B. (sets) not counted in inventory . . . . ._____

No. magazine subscriptions (titles) . . . . ._____

No. newspapers made available . . . . ._____

McAllen Independent School District, McAllen, TX 78501

INVENTORY OF ENCYCLOPEDIAS IN
LEARNING RESOURCE CENTER

_____School

19__ -19__

NAME OF SET	DATE OF PUBLICATION	CONDITION OF SET

McAllen Independent School District, McAllen, TX 78501

AUDIOVISUAL INVENTORY

_____ School

Charts

19__ -19 __

Class	Last Inventory	Added	With-drawn	Annual Inventory
Reference				
000				
100				
200				
300				
400				
500				
600				
700				
800				
900				
920				
Biography				
Fiction/Story Collections				
Easy				
Total				

Filmstrips

Class	Last Inventory	Added	With-drawn	Annual Inventory
Reference				
000				
100				
200				
300				
400				
500				
600				
700				
800				
900				
920				
Biography				
Fiction/Story Collections				
Easy				
Total				

McAllen Independent School District, McAllen, TX 78501

AUDIOVISUAL INVENTORY

_____ School

19___-19 ___

Flashcards

Class	Last Inventory	Added	With-drawn	Annual Inventory
Reference				
000				
100				
200				
300				
400				
500				
600				
700				
800				
900				
920				
Biography				
Fiction/Story Collections				
Easy				
Total				

Games

Class	Last Inventory	Added	With-drawn	Annual Inventory
Reference				
000				
100				
200				
300				
400				
500				
600				
700				
800				
900				
920				
Biography				
Fiction/Story Collections				
Easy				
Total				

McAllen Independent School District, McAllen, TX 78501

AUDIOVISUAL INVENTORY

_____ School

Motion Pictures

19___-19 ___

Class	Last Inventory	Added	With-drawn	Annual Inventory
Reference				
000				
100				
200				
300				
400				
500				
600				
700				
800				
900				
920				
Biography				
Fiction/Story Collections				
Easy				
Total				

Realia

Class	Last Inventory	Added	With-drawn	Annual Inventory
Reference				
000				
100				
200				
300				
400				
500				
600				
700				
800				
900				
920				
Biography				
Fiction/Story Collections				
Easy				
Total				

McAllen Independent School District, McAllen, TX 78501

AUDIOVISUAL INVENTORY

_____ School

19__-19__

Rec-Cassette

Class	Last Inventory	Added	Withdrawn	Annual Inventory
Reference				
000				
100				
200				
300				
400				
500				
600				
700				
800				
900				
920				
Biography				
Fiction/Story Collections				
Easy				
Total				

Rec-Disc

Class	Last Inventory	Added	Withdrawn	Annual Inventory
Reference				
000				
100				
200				
300				
400				
500				
600				
700				
800				
900				
920				
Biography				
Fiction/Story Collections				
Easy				
Total				

McAllen Independent School District, McAllen, TX 78501

AUDIOVISUAL INVENTORY

_____ School

Rec-Reel to Reel   19___-19 ___

Class	Last Inventory	Added	With-drawn	Annual Inventory
Reference				
000				
100				
200				
300				
400				
500				
600				
700				
800				
900				
920				
Biography				
Fiction/Story Collections				
Easy				
Total				

Slides

Class	Last Inventory	Added	With-drawn	Annual Inventory
Reference				
000				
100				
200				
300				
400				
500				
600				
700				
800				
900				
920				
Biography				
Fiction/Story Collections				
Easy				
Total				

McAllen Independent School District, McAllen, TX 78501

AUDIOVISUAL INVENTORY

_____ School

19___-19___

Study Prints

Class	Last Inventory	Added	With-drawn	Annual Inventory
Reference				
000				
100				
200				
300				
400				
500				
600				
700				
800				
900				
920				
Biography				
Fiction/Story Collections				
Easy				
Total				

Other

Class	Last Inventory	Added	With-drawn	Annual Inventory
Reference				
000				
100				
200				
300				
400				
500				
600				
700				
800				
900				
920				
Biography				
Fiction/Story Collections				
Easy				
Total				

McAllen Independent School District, McAllen, TX 78501

CIRCULATION STATISTICS

_____ School

19__-19__

	SEP.	OCT.	NOV.	DEC.	JAN.	FEB.	MAR.	APR.	MAY	TOTAL
Total books										
Av. per student										
No. of classes										
Models										
Charts										
Games										
Film										
Flash cards										
Globes										
Kits										
Maps										
Rec-disc										
Rec-cassette										
Rec-reel to reel										
Slides										
Pictures										
Motion pictures										
Total nonbook										

McAllen Independent School District, McAllen, TX 78501

WITHDRAWN ITEMS

CLASS NO.	AUTHOR	TITLE	PUBLISHER OR PROD.

_____ School

19__-19__

Fund: _____

McAllen Independent School District, McAllen, TX 78501

LOST ITEMS

_____ School

19___ -19___ .

Fund: _____

CLASS NO.	AUTHOR	TITLE	PUBLISHER OR PROD.	PRICE	AMOUNT PAID

McAllen Independent School District, McAllen, TX 78501

RECORD OF EVALUATION OF INSTRUCTIONAL MATERIALS

Identification—Title _____ Author _____
　　Publisher/source _____
　　Date of publication _____
　　(Check) Book ____ Guide____ Film____ Film Strip____ Other ____
　　Description (length, size, format, packaging, or other pertinent data)

　　_____

　　_____

Usage—Subject and grade level _____
　　Unique qualities (if any) _____
　　Additional possibilities for usage (gifted, remedial, resource, etc.)

　　_____

　　_____

Assessment
　　Assessor_____ Date assessed _____
　　　　　　(Chairperson)　　　　　　Poor　　　　Excellent

	Poor				Excellent
Authenticity and scholarship	1	2	3	4	5
Comments (if any) _____					
Appropriateness	1	2	3	4	5
Comments (if any) _____					
Content	1	2	3	4	5
Comments (if any) _____					
Motivational qualities	1	2	3	4	5
Comments (if any) _____					
Technical qualities	1	2	3	4	5
Comments (if any) _____					

Total—Composite assessment
Final recommendation　_____

_____

_____

_____

_____

_____

_____

Authorized for use by Selection Committee—Date _____
Refused for use by Selection Committee—Date _____
Signature _____
　　　　　(Assistant superintendent for instruction)

Laredo Independent School District, Laredo, TX 78040

REQUEST FOR DISPOSAL OF BOOKS CLASSIFIED AS OBSOLETE, WORN, OR DISCARD

| _____ | _____ | _____ |
| School | Principal | Date |

Instructions:

1. Complete this form in duplicate.
2. Securely box, bundle, or package all books to be disposed of. List title and quantity on package or box.
3. Send both copies of this form to the Educational Materials Building administrator.
4. Educational Materials Building administrator will initiate work order to pick up books and return one copy of completed form to principal.

| | | | STATUS OF BK.-CK.ONE | | |
TITLE	PUBLISHER	EDITION	WORN DIS-CARD	OBSO-LETE	QUANTITY TO BE DIS-POSED OF

Date on which material will be ready for pick-up_____
Principal's signature_____
Educational Materials Building use only—Pickup and disposal authorized_____
Work order no. _____ Date issued_____

cc: Originating school

Torrance Unified School District, Torrance, CA 90509

PERIODICAL EVALUATION FORM

(*Items to be completed prior to evaluation.)
*1. Title:_____ Price:_____
*2. Publisher:_____Issues per year:_____
*3. Publisher's address:_____
4. If there is advertising, is it objectionable? (Circle) Yes No
5. Circle appropriate rating: E - Excellent, S - Satisfactory,
   U - Unsatisfactory

Content:	-accurate, current information	E S U
	-authenticity	E S U
	-interest	E S U
	-handling of controversial issues	E S U
	-style	E S U
Vocabulary appropriate for intended use		E S U

Format (photos, illustrations, maps, print, etc.)	E S U
Educational objectives sound	E S U
Relevancy to course or to curriculum	E S U
Concepts presented clearly	E S U

6. Are other similar periodicals available on the current MASTER PERIODICAL LIST? *YES NO*
7. If "Yes," what are the periodicals?_____
8. What other periodicals are available that present a different point of view?_____

9. Recommended utilization: (Circle) K 1 2 3 4 5 6 7 8 9 10 11 12 Teacher
*10. Specific curriculum area or course for which intended:
_____
*11. Intended use of periodical:_____
12. Possible additional uses of periodical:_____
13. If you feel this periodical might be considered "controversial" or reflect adversely upon persons because of their race, color, creed, national origin, ancestry, sex, or occupation, please use the reverse side of this form and state why you recommend acceptance or rejection.

See reverse: ☐
(Check)

14. Check your recommendation:
_____ I do not recommend this periodical be added to the Master List of Approved Periodicals.
_____ I recommend this periodical for teacher and student use.
_____ I recommend this periodical for teacher use only.

Name:_____ School:_____ Position:_____ Date:_____

Torrance Unified School District, Torrance, CA 90509

PERIODICALS EVALUATION—TABULATION SUMMARY SHEET

Date: _____

Periodical: _____ School _____

School recommendation: _____

Tabulation:

___ Do not recommend this periodical.

___ Recommend for teacher and student use.

___ Recommend for teacher use only.

Sufficient number of evaluations should be obtained to allow each school and/or department to make a specific recommendation regarding each periodical considered.

Summary of positive-negative comments (or attach formal recommendation from a specific department concerning one or several periodicals):

Attach individual periodical evaluation forms to this sheet.

Torrance Unified School District, Torrance, CA 90509

EQUIPMENT EVALUATION FORM

Type of equipment___ Manufacturer_____ Model_____

Popular model name_____ No. in use_____

   1-4. Is equipment suitable for uses in

     1. Large Group? _____
     2. Classroom? _____
     3. Small Group? _____
     4. Individual? _____

     5. Has evaluator used this equipment in
        actual instructional application?   5. Yes__No __

Check only those categories and items which are appropriate:

A. *Ease of operation.*
    6-7. Were the instructions readily available?   6. Yes__No __
        Were the instructions complete and
        understandable?   7. Yes__No __
    8-9. Were the controls adequate and func-
        tional?   8. Yes__No __
        Were the controls accessible?   9. Yes__No __
     10. Was machine threading or loading rel-
        atively easy?   10. Yes__No __
     11. Would clearer instructions have sim-
        plified threading or loading?   11. Yes__No __

B. *Sound characteristics.*
     12. Was volume adequate?   12. Yes__No __
     13. Was sound clear?   13. Yes__No __
     14. Was tone quality and control adequate?   14. Yes__No __

EQUIPMENT EVALUATION FORM (CONT'D)

C. *Projection characteristics.*

15. Was the projected image sharp and clear?   15. Yes__No __

16. Was the focus easy to adjust?   16. Yes__No __

17. Was the focusing range adequate?   17. Yes__No __

18. Was the elevation adjustment adequate?   18. Yes__No __

19. Was the elevation adjustment easily operated?   19. Yes__No __

20. Would lamps be changed easily?   20. Yes__No __

21. Were lamp(s) of standard type(s) having ASA code(s)?   21. Yes__No __

D. *Special characteristics.*

22. Was rewinding rapid and easy?   22. Yes__No __

23. Was fast-forward operation easily achieved?   23. Yes__No __

24. Were interlock provisions ("record" mode; still picture; etc.) adequate and functional?   24. Yes__No __

25. Was the machine easy to set up and put away in comparison to other similar machines?   25. Yes__No __

26. Was cord storage practical and adequate?   26. Yes__No __

27-28. Was the equipment suitable for use by children?   27. Elem. Age __

                                                                     28. Jr. Hi. Age __

EQUIPMENT EVALUATION FORM (CONT'D)

E. *Comments*.

29. Were there any features about the product that you particularly liked, as compared to similar units you may have used?

_____

_____

_____

_____

_____

30. Were there any features about the product that you particularly dis liked, as compared to similar units you may have used?

_____

_____

_____

_____

_____

31. Describe any problems you encountered with this equipment.

_____

_____

_____

_____

_____

32. Suggest improvements you would appreciate.

_____

_____

_____

_____

_____

33-36. Overall rating: Excellent___Good___Fair___Poor___

Evaluator: _____ School:_____Date:_____

Jefferson County School District 509-J, Madras. OR 97741 (Form developed by Oregon Department of Education, Instructional Technology Division.)

INSTRUCTIONAL EQUIPMENT EVALUATION FORM

	Check Appropriate Column		
	Fair	Good	Excel.
1. Is the equipment portable?			
a. Is it reasonably light in weight in comparison with others?	___	___	___
b. Is it compact?	___	___	___
2. Is the equipment sturdy?			
a. Does the material of which the equipment is constructed appear durable?	___	___	___
b. Does the equipment have an attractive appearance?	___	___	___
3. Is operation of the equipment easy to learn?			
a. Are the controls accessible and plainly marked?	___	___	___
b. Are there a minimum number of operating controls?	___	___	___
4. Does this equipment consistently meet desirable performance standards in terms of its specific function?			
a. Is tonal quality true?	___	___	___
b. Is volume range adequate and well defined?	___	___	___
c. Is image sharply defined?	___	___	___
d. Is light supply adequate?	___	___	___
5. Are adaptations easy to perform?			
a. Are adaptors included within the equipment or its container?	___	___	___

Comments:

_____

_____

_____

6. Is the equipment easy to maintain and repair?			
a. Can minor adjustments be made simply and quickly when needed?	___	___	___
b. Is it easy to remove parts likely to need repairs?	___	___	___
c. Are the parts standard and easily available for replacement?	___	___	___

INSTRUCTIONAL EQUIPMENT EVALUATION FORM (CONT'D)

7. Is the distributor dependable?
   a. Does the distributor have a proper credit rating? ____ ____ ____
   b. Are the distributor and manufacturer faithful to their agreements? ____ ____ ____
   c. Are repair and emergency service facilities readily available? ____ ____ ____
   d. Are adequate stocks of spare parts maintained locally? ____ ____ ____

8. In comparison with the cost of similar equipment, is the price reasonable? ____ ____ ____

Appraisal

(Circle appropriate rating)   1 - highest or best   3 - lowest or poorest

Portability   1 2 3 Comments:
Durability   1 2 3 Comments:
Ease of operation   1 2 3 Comments:
Performance   1 2 3 Comments:
Dependability of distributor 1 2 3 Comments:
Cost   1 2 3 Comments:

Final Recommendation

____ Purchase: high priority   _____ Do not purchase

_____   _____   _____
(Evaluator)   (Office)   (Position)

Equipment: _____ Distributor: _____
Make: _____ Price: _____
Model: _____

Montgomery County Public Schools, Rockville, MD 20850

MEDIA EVALUATION FORM

Title _____ Series _____
Producer _____ Distributor _____
                                (if different) _____
Address _____ Price _____ Length _____
_____ Date _____ Color _____ B&W ___

Type of Material (Indicate quantities)

16MM____8MM _____
F/S____W. CASSETTES _____
SLIDES____W. CASSETTES __
MULTI MEDIA KITS _____
CASSETTES _____
TRANSPARENCIES _____
VIDEO CASSETTES ½"__¾" __
OTHER _____

Grade Level(s)

PRIMARY _____
INTERMEDIATE _____
JR. HIGH _____
SR. HIGH _____
TEACHER _____

	POOR	FAIR	AVERAGE	GOOD	VERY GOOD	EXCELLENT	DOESN'T APPLY	Subject Area(s)
SOUND QUALITY (audibility, voice music, effects)								
PHOTOGRAPHY (clarity, composition, color)								
UP-TO-DATE								
AUTHENTICITY & ACCURACY								
CONTENT COVERAGE								
CURRICULAR USEFULNESS								
TYPE OF MEDIA APPROPRIATE TO CONTENT								
TREATMENT OF MINORITIES								
TREATMENT OF SEX ROLES								
TREATMENT OF HANDICAPPED								
STUDENT REACTION								
OVERALL RATING								

PERSONAL REACTION OR COMMENTS:

In terms of the needs of the curriculum and media/films already in the WCISD collection, do you recommend purchase?   Yes   No

Evaluated by _____ District _____

Subject area/grade _____ Date _____

Wayne County Intermediate School District, Wayne, MI 48184

APPLICATION FOR USE OF FREE OR INEXPENSIVE MATERIALS

Originator's name:_____ School: _____ Date:_____

Submit examination copy. If several items are in a packet from one distributor, list all titles and give brief description of contents on back of this sheet. Identify type of media: pamphlet__poster__film__other__. Do not include material from more than one distributor on one application.

Title:_____ Publisher or advertiser:_____

Address of publisher: _____ Cost:_____

Evaluation of content:

Accurate, current	E S U	Format (photos, illus.,		
Authentic	E S U	maps, prints, etc.)	E S U	
Interest	E S U	Educational objectives		
Handling of controversial		sound	E S U	
issues	E S U	Relevance to course or		
Style	E S U	curriculum	E S U	
Vocabulary appropriate		Clarity of concepts	E S U	
for intended use	E S U			

How will this material be used and in what class? Be specific: _____

_____

_____

_____

_____

_____

_____

_____

_____

Does this material meet the following criteria:

Does this material reflect adversely upon persons because of their race, sex, color, creed, national origin, or ancestry?   Yes__No__

Is there objectionable repetition of the name of the manufacturer or undue pressure on the student to purchase the product?   Yes__No__

APPLICATION FOR USE OF FREE OR INEXPENSIVE MATERIALS (CONT'D)

Is this material "slanted" or biased to an objectionable degree?   Yes__No __

Is the use of this material apt to result in a "public relations" problem? Are parents likely to object to its use?   Yes__No __

Has this material been previously disapproved by the governing board?   Yes__No __

Does this material constitute instruction in religious principles or aid any religious sect, church, creed, or sectarian purpose?   Yes__No __

In view of the answers to the above questions, I request that this material be authorized for use in the classroom.

Teacher's signature:_____ Date:_____

I recommend that this material be authorized by the board of education for use in _____ classes of my school.

Principal's signature: _____

School: _____ Date: _____

Recommended for authorization:_____

Signature: Supervisor of instr. media   Date _____

Torrance Unified School District, Torrance, CA 90509

CITIZEN'S REQUEST FOR RECONSIDERATION OF MATERIALS

Author_____ Hardcover ( ) Paperback ( ) A/V ( )
Title_____ Copyright date_____
Publisher (if known) _____
                    (films, filmstrips, records, etc.)

A/V material: Kind of media_____

Other material _____
                    (magazines, pamphlets, etc.)
Request initiated by_____
Telephone no. _____ Street address_____
City and state_____ Zip code_____

Complainant represents
Self____ Organization or group _____
                                (name)
School
1. To what in this material do you object? Please be specific; cite
   pages, passages, etc. _____
   _____

2. What do you feel might result from use of this material?_____

3. For what age group would you recommend this material?_____

4. Is there anything good about this material?_____
   _____

5. Did you read the entire book or view the A/V material?_____
   What parts? _____

6. What reviews of this material have you read?_____

7. What do you believe is the theme of this book or A/V material?_____

8. What action do you recommend that the school take on this material?__

9. In its place, what material do you recommend that would
   provide adequate information on the subject? _____
   _____

                    _____
                    (Signature of complainant)

National Council of Teachers of English, Urbania, IL 61801 [Many school districts use or adapt for use this form.]

REQUEST FOR REVIEW OF EDUCATIONAL MATERIALS OR PROCEDURES

1. Request initiated by: Name_____ School_____
   Address_____City_____ Phone____
2. Representing (individual or name of organization or group): _____
3. Request submitted to: _____
4. Brief statement explaining the request: _____
5. If this request is for the review of material (textbook, library book, or film), give author, title, publisher, and copyright date:_____
   _____
6. If a material is being questioned, have you read (or viewed) the entire material? Yes ☐ No ☐. If not, what parts have you read (or viewed)? __
   _____
7. Specify the portion of the subject, material, or procedure which you question: _____
   _____
8. What do you think is the effect of this subject, material, or procedure on students?_____
   _____
   _____
9. In its place, what material or procedure would you recommend?_____
   _____
   _____
10. What is there of educational value in this subject, material, or procedure? _____
    _____
11. To your knowledge, what has been the judgment of qualified professional persons regarding this matter? (State and/or District Adoption Committees, book reviews, court decisions, etc.)_____
    _____
    _____
    _____
12. What action would you like your school district to take regarding this matter?_____
    _____

Date submitted:_____ Signature: _____
NOTE: Please feel free to attach additional material, references, or any other pertinent information.

Clark County School District, Las Vegas, NV 89121 [A variation of frequently used form of National Council of Teachers of English.]

CHALLENGED INSTRUCTIONAL MATERIALS—INFORMATION FORM

Please fill in all of the following blanks.

1. Author of book/media: _____
2. Title of book/media: _____
3. Publisher/producer of book/media: _____
4. Page number or portion of each item to which objection is being made:

_____
_____
_____
_____

5. Reasons for objections: _____

_____
_____
_____

Use additional sheets if necessary.
6. Have you reviewed the entire book/media?   ☐ Yes ☐ No
7. Complainant's signature: _____
8. Complainant's home address: Street _____
                                 City _____
9. Complainant's home telephone number: _____
10. Group complainant represents (if any): _____
11. School district location which has the challenged materials: _____

_____
_____

Present or send completed form to the school principal.

Routing:
   Principal
   Administrator, Instructional Media
   Deputy Superintendent, Instruction
   Instructional Materials Advisory Committee
   Superintendent
   Board of Education

Orange Unified School District, Orange, CA 92666

SIMPLE COMPLAINT CARD

When there is cause for concern by a member or members of the public, a written request should be made for an informal discussion with the building principal and classroom teacher concerning textbooks, or the building principal and the librarian/media specialist concerning any library/media materials. (Use *Simple Complaint Card—*Form #1.)

After the informal meeting with the concerned person(s), the principal and/or librarian/media specialist should write a letter to the person(s), recapitulating the meeting and its outcome, keeping a copy of the letter on file.

If the complainant(s) is not satisfied after this meeting, a request in writing may be made for a formal *Request for Reconsideration* form (Form 2) within reasonable time.

Simple Complaint Card

Date: _____
Material challenged: _____

Name: _____
Address: _____
Telephone: _____
Complainant represents: _____
  Himself/Herself _____
  Organization _____
Reason for complaint: _____

_____

_____

Took Form 2 (*Request for
Reconsideration*)   Yes __ No ___
Date form returned: _____
Signature: _____

Disposition of complaint: _____

_____

_____

Harrisburg Community Unit School District 3, Harrisburg, IL 62946

RESPONSE TO REQUEST FOR RECONSIDERATION

Dear_____ :

    Thank you for your letter (call) of_____ in which you have questioned the use of_____ in our schools. We appreciate your concern and wish to assure you that we will certainly give the matter serious consideration.

    I am sure you understand the complexity of providing materials suitable to the maturity, needs, interest, and abilities of all students on all grade levels. This is a continuous task of reevaluation, and an important responsibility that often requires direction and guidance from the parents of our students.

    In order that we may fully understand your position on the material in question, we ask you to read the Board of Directors policy and to fill out and return the enclosed form. I assure you we will give it immediate consideration and be in touch with you in the very near future.

            Sincerely,

_____
            Principal

cc: Board members _____
    Lay persons_____
    Department head_____
    Media specialist_____
    Teacher_____
    Superintendent_____

Crosby-Ironton Public Schools, District 182, Crosby, MN 56441

APPENDIX I:
STATEMENTS ON
LIBRARY POLICIES

The Students' Right to Read

The right to read, like all rights guaranteed or implied within our constitutional tradition, can be used wisely or foolishly. In many ways, education is an effort to improve the quality of choices open to man. But to deny the freedom of choice in fear that it may be unwisely used is to destroy the freedom itself. For this reason, we respect the right of individuals to be selective in their own reading. But for the same reason, we oppose efforts of individuals or groups to limit the freedom of choice of others or to impose their own standards or tastes upon the community at large.

The right of any individual not just to read but to read whatever he wants to read is basic to a democratic society. This right is based on an assumption that the educated and reading man possesses judgment and understanding and can be trusted with the determination of his own actions. In effect, the reading man is freed from the burden of discovering all things and all facts and all truths through his own direct experiences for his reading allows him to meet people, debate philosophies, and experience events far beyond the narrow confines of his own existence.

In selecting books for reading by young people, English teachers consider the contribution which each work may make to the education of the reader, its aesthetic value, its honesty, its readability for a particular group of students, and its appeal to adolescents. English teachers, however, may use different works for different purposes. The criteria for choosing a work to be read by an entire class are somewhat different from the criteria for choosing works to be read by small groups. For example, a teacher might select John Knowles' *A Separate Peace* for reading by an entire class, partly because the book has received wide critical recognition, partly because it is relatively short and will keep the attention of many slow readers, and partly because it has proved popular with many students of widely differing abilities. The same teacher, faced with the responsibility of choosing or recommending books for several small groups of students, might select or recommend books as different as Nathaniel Hawthorne's

Reprinted by permission of National Council of Teachers, Urbana, IL 61801.

The Scarlet Letter, Jack Schaefer's *Shane*, Alexander Solzhenitsyn's *One Day in the Life of Ivan Denisovitch*, Pierre Boulle's *The Bridge over the River Kwai*, Charles Dickens' *Great Expectations*, or Paul Zindel's *The Pigman*, depending upon the abilities and interests of the students in each group. And the criteria for suggesting books to individuals or for recommending something worth reading for a student who casually stops by after class are different from selecting material for a class or group. But the teacher selects books; he does not censor them. Selection implies that a teacher is free to choose this or that work, depending upon the purpose to be achieved and the student or class in question, but a book selected this year may be ignored next year, and the reverse. Censorship implies that certain works are not open to selection, this year or any year.

Many works contain isolated elements to which some individuals or groups may object. The literary artist seeks truth, as he is able to see and feel it. As a seeker of truth, he must necessarily challenge at times the common beliefs or values of a society; he must analyze and comment on people's actions and values and the frequent discrepancy between what they purport to live by and what they do live by. In seeking to discover meaning behind reality, the artist strives to achieve a work which is honest. Moreover, the value and impact of any literary work must be examined as a whole and not in part—the impact of the entire work being more important than the words, phrases, or incidents out of which it is made.

Wallace Stevens once wrote, "Literature is the better part of life. To this it seems inevitably necessary to add, provided life is the better part of literature." Students and parents have the right to demand that education today keep students in touch with the reality of the world outside the classroom. Much of classic literature asks questions as valid and significant today as when the literature first appeared, questions like "What is the nature of humanity?" "Why do people praise individuality and practice conformity?" "What do people need for a good life?" and "What is the nature of the good person?" But youth is the age of revolt, and the times today show much of the world in revolt. To pretend otherwise is to ignore a reality made clear to young people and adults alike on television and radio, in newspapers and magazines. English teachers must be free to employ books, classic or contemporary, which do not lie to the young about one perilous but wondrous times we live in, books which talk of the fears, hopes, joys, and frustrations people experience, books about people not only as they are but as they can be. English teachers forced through the pressures of censorship to use only safe or antiseptic works are placed in the morally and intellectually untenable position of lying to their students about the nature and condition of mankind.

The teacher must exercise care to select or recommend works for class reading and group discussion which will not embarrass students in discussions with their peers. One of the most important responsibilities of the English teacher is developing rapport and respect among students. Respect for the uniqueness and potential of the individual, an important facet of the study of literature, should be emphasized in the English class. For students to develop a respect for each individual, no matter what his race or creed or values may be, multiethnic materials must become a part of the literature program in all schools, regardless of the ethnic composition of the school population. It is time that literature classes reflect the cultural contributions of many minority groups in the United States, just as they should acquaint students with contributions from the peoples of Asia, Africa, and Latin America.

What a young reader gets from any book depends both on the selection and on the reader himself. A teacher should choose books with an awareness of the student's interests, his reading ability, his mental and emotional maturity, and the values he may derive from the reading. A wide knowledge of many works, common sense, and professional dedication to students and to literature will guide the teacher in making his selections. The community that entrusts students to the care of an English teacher should also trust that teacher to exercise professional judgment in selecting or recommending books.

THE THREAT TO EDUCATION

Censorship leaves students with an inadequate and distorted picture of the ideals, values, and problems of their culture. Writers may often be the spokesmen of their culture, or they may stand to the side attempting to describe and evaluate that culture. Yet, partly because of censorship or the fear of censorship, many writers are ignored or inadequately represented in the public schools, and many are represented in anthologies not by their best work but by their "safest" or "least offensive" work.

The censorship pressures receiving the greatest publicity are those of small groups who protest the use of a limited number of books with some "objectionable" realistic elements, such as *Brave New World, Lord of the Flies, Catcher in the Rye, The Stranger, Johnny Got His Gun, The Assistant, Catch-22, Soul on Ice,* or *Stranger in a Strange Land.* The most obvious and immediate victims are often found among our best and most creative English teachers, those who have ventured outside the narrow boundaries of conventional texts. Ultimately, however, the real victims are the students, denied the freedom to explore ideas and pursue truth wherever and however they wish.

Great damage may be done by book committees appointed by national or local organizations to pore over anthologies, texts, library books, and paperbacks to find sentences which advocate, or seem to advocate, causes or concepts or practices these organizations condemn. As a result, some publishers, sensitive to possible objections, carefully exclude sentences or selections that might conceivably offend some group somehow, sometime, somewhere.

Many well-meaning people wish to restrict reading materials in schools to books that do not mention certain aspects of life they find offensive: drugs, profanity, Black Power, antiwar marches, smoking, sex, racial unrest, rock music, politics, pregnancy, school dropouts, peace rallies, drinking, Chicano protests, or divorce. Although he may personally abhor one or more of these facets of modern life, the English teacher has the responsibility to encourage students to read about and reflect on many aspects, good and bad, of their own society and of other cultures.

THE ENGLISH TEACHER'S PURPOSES AND RESPONSIBILITIES

The purpose of education remains what it has always been in a free society: to develop a free and reasoning human being who can think for himself, who understands his own and, to some extent, other cultures, who lives compassionately and cooperatively with his fellow man, who respects both himself and others, who has developed self-discipline and self-motivation and exercises both, who can laugh at a world which often seems mad, and who can successfully develop survival strategies for existence in that world.

The English teacher knows that literature is a significant part of the education of man, for literature raises problems and questions and dilemmas that have perplexed and intrigued and frustrated man since the dawn of time. Literature presents some solutions to complex problems and some answers to abiding questions, perhaps incomplete but the best we have found. Even more important, literature continues to raise questions man can never wholly answer: What is the relationship between power and moral responsibility? Why does the good man sometimes suffer and the evil man sometimes go untouched by adversity? How can man reconcile the conflict of duty between what he owes society and what he owes his own conscience? The continued search for answers, tentative as they must prove, is a necessary part of the educated man's life, and the search for answers may in part be found through reading.

Aware of the vital role of literature in the education of mankind, the English teacher has unique responsibilities to his students and to adults in the community. To his students, he is responsible for knowing many books from many cultures, for demonstrating a personal commitment to the search for truth through wide reading and continual critical questioning of his own values and beliefs, for respecting the unique qualities and potential of each student, for studying many cultures and societies and their values, and for exhibiting the qualities of the educated man. To adults, he is responsible for communicating information about his literature program; for explaining, not defending, what books he uses with what students, for what reasons, and with what results; and for communicating the necessity of free inquiry and the search for truth in a democratic society and the dangers of censorship and repression.

THE COMMUNITY'S RESPONSIBILITY

American citizens who care about the improvement of education are urged to join students, teachers, librarians, administrators, boards of education, and professional and scholarly organizations in support of the students' right to read. Only widespread and informed support in every community can assure that:

1. Enough citizens are interested in the development and maintenance of a superior school system to guarantee its achievement.

2. Malicious gossip, ignorant rumors, and deceptive letters to the editor will not be circulated without challenge and correction.

3. Newspapers will be convinced that the public sincerely desires objective school news reporting, free from slanting or editorial comment which destroys confidence in and support for schools.

4. The community will not permit its resources and energies to be dissipated in conflicts created by special interest groups striving to advance their ideologies or biases.

5. Faith in democratic traditions and processes will be maintained.

National Council of Teachers of English, Urbana, IL 61820.

American Association of School Librarians' Statement on *Library Bill of Rights* *

The American Association of School Librarians endorses the *Library Bill of Rights* of the American Library Association:

The American Library Association affirms that all libraries are forums for information and ideas and that the following basic policies should guide their services:

1. Books and other library resources should be provided for the interest, information, and enlightenment of all people of the community the library serves. Materials should not be excluded because of the origin, background, or views of those contributing to their creation.

2. Libraries should provide materials and information presenting all points of view on current and historical issues. Materials should not be proscribed or removed because of partisan or doctrinal disapproval.

3. Libraries should challenge censorship in the fulfillment of their responsibility to provide information and enlightenment.

4. Libraries should cooperate with all persons and groups concerned with resisting abridgment of free expression and free access to ideas.

5. A person's right to use a library should not be denied or abridged because of origin, age, background, or views.

---

*Reprinted by permission of the American Library Association. The Intellectual Freedom Committee is presently reviewing all interpretations of the *Library Bill of Rights*, which also follow here and are reprinted by permission. It is anticipated that these revisions will be completed in February 1981. For further information, school LMC specialists should communicate with the Office for Intellectual Freedom, American Library Association, 50 E. Huron St., Chicago, IL 60611.

6. Libraries which make exhibit spaces and meeting rooms available to the public they serve should make such facilities available on an equitable basis, regardless of the beliefs or affiliations of individuals or groups requesting their use.

Adopted June 18, 1948; amended February 2, 1969, June 27, 1967, and January 23, 1980, by the American Library Association Council.

These rights are fundamental to the philosophy of school library media center programs as stated in *Media Programs: District and School.* (Chicago: American Library Association and American Association of School Librarians and Washington, DC: Association for Educational Communications nd Technology, 1975.)

Freedom to Read

The freedom to read is essential to our democracy. It is under attack. Private groups and public authorities in various parts of the country are working to remove books from sale, to censor textbooks, to label "controversial" books, to distribute lists of "objectionable" books or authors, and to purge libraries. These actions apparently rise from a view that our national tradition of free expression is no longer valid; that censorship and suppression are needed to avoid the subversion of politics and the corruption of morals. We, as citizens devoted to the use of books and as librarians and publishers responsible for disseminating them, wish to assert the public interest in the preservation of the freedom to read.

We are deeply concerned about these attempts at suppression. Most such attempts rest on a denial of the fundamental premise of democracy: that the ordinary citizen, by exercising his critical judgment, will accept the good and reject the bad. The censors, public and private, assume that they should determine what is good and what is bad for their fellow citizens.

We trust Americans to recognize propaganda, and to reject obscenity. We do not believe they need the help of censors to assist them in this task. We do not believe they are prepared to sacrifice their heritage of a free press in order to be "protected" against what others think may be bad for them. We believe they still favor free enterprise in ideas and expression.

We are aware, of course, that books are not alone in being subjected to efforts at suppression. We are aware that these efforts are related to a larger pattern of pressures being brought against education, the press, films, radio, and television. The problem is not only one of actual censorship. The shadow of fear cast by these pressures leads, we suspect, to an even larger voluntary curtailment of expression by those who seek to avoid controversy.

Such pressure toward conformity is perhaps natural to a time of uneasy change and pervading fear. Especially when so many of our apprehensions are directed against an ideology, the expression of a dissident idea becomes a thing feared in itself, and we tend to move against it as against a hostile deed, with suppression.

And yet suppression is never more dangerous than in such a time of social tension. Freedom has given the United States the elasticity to endure strain. Freedom keeps open the path of novel and creative solutions, and enables change to come by choice. Every silencing of a heresy, every enforcement of an orthodoxy, diminishes the toughness and resilience of our society and leaves it the less able to deal with stress.

Now as always in our history, books are among our greatest instruments of freedom. They are almost the only means for making generally available ideas or manners of expression that can initially command only a small audience. They are the natural medium for the new idea and the untried voice from which come the original contributions to social growth. They are essential to the extended discussion which serious thought requires and to the accumulation of knowledge and ideas into organized collections.

We believe that free communication is essential to the preservation of a free society and a creative culture. We believe that these pressures towards conformity present the danger of limiting the range and variety of inquiry and expression on which our democracy and our culture depend. We believe that every American community must jealously guard the freedom to publish and to circulate, in order to preserve its own freedom to read. We believe that publishers and librarians have a profound responsibility to give validity to that freedom to read by making it possible for the readers to choose freely from a variety of offerings.

The freedom to read is guaranteed by the Constitution. Those with faith in free men will stand firm on these constitutional guarantees of essential rights and will exercise the responsibilities that accompany these rights.

We therefore affirm these propositions:

1. *It is in the public interest for publishers and librarians to make available the widest diversity of views and expressions, including those which are unorthodox or unpopular with the majority.*

   Creative thought is by definition new, and what is new is different. The bearer of every new thought is a rebel until his idea is refined and tested. Totalitarian systems attempt to maintain themselves in power by the ruthless suppression of any concept which challenges the established orthodoxy. The power of a democratic system to adapt to change is vastly strengthened by the freedom of its citizens to choose widely from among conflicting opinions offered freely to them. To stifle every nonconformist idea at birth would mark the end of the democratic process. Furthermore, only through the constant activity of weighing and selecting can the democratic mind attain the strength demanded by times like these. We need to know not only what we believe but why we

2. *Publishers and librarians do not need to endorse every idea or presentation contained in the books they make available. It would conflict with the public interest for them to establish their own political, moral or aesthetic views as the sole standard for determining what books should be published or circulated.*

Publishers and librarians serve the educational process by helping to make available knowledge and ideas required for the growth of the mind and the increase of learning. They do not foster education by imposing as mentors the patterns of their own thought. The people should have the freedom to read and consider a broader range of ideas than those that may be held by any single librarian or publisher or government or church. It is wrong that what one man can read should be confined to what another thinks proper.

3. *It is contrary to the public interest for publishers or librarians to determine the acceptability of a book solely on the basis of the personal history or political affiliations of the author.*

A book should be judged as a book. No art or literature can flourish if it is to be measured by the political views or private lives of its creators. No society of free men can flourish which draws up lists of writers to whom it will not listen, whatever they may have to say.

4. *The present laws dealing with obscenity should be vigorously enforced. Beyond that, there is no place in our society for extralegal efforts to coerce the taste of others, to confine adults to the reading matter deemed suitable for adolescents, or to inhibit the efforts of writers to achieve artistic expression.*

To some, much of modern literature is shocking. But is not much of life itself shocking? We cut off literature at the source if we prevent serious artists from dealing with the stuff of life. Parents and teachers have a responsibility to prepare the young to meet the diversity of experiences in life to which they will be exposed, as they have a responsibility to help them learn to think critically for themselves. These are affirmative responsibilities, not to be discharged simply by preventing them from reading works for which they are not yet prepared. In these matters taste differs, and taste cannot be legislated; nor can machinery be devised which will suit the demands of one group without limiting the freedom of others. We deplore the catering to the immature, the retarded or the maladjusted taste. But those concerned with freedom have the responsibility of seeing to it that each individual book or publication, whatever its contents, price or method of distribution, is dealt with in accordance with due process of law.

5. *It is not in the public interest to force a reader to accept with any book the prejudgment of a label characterizing the book or author as subversive or dangerous.*

The idea of labeling presupposes the existence of individuals or groups with wisdom to determine by authority what is good or bad for the citizen. It presupposes that each individual must be directed in making up his mind about the ideas he examines. But Americans do not need others to do their thinking for them.

6. *It is the responsibility of publishers and librarians, as guardians of the people's freedom to read, to contest encroachments upon that freedom by individuals or groups seeking to impose their own standards or tastes upon the community at large.*

It is inevitable in the give and take of the democratic process that the political, the moral, or the aesthetic concepts of an individual or group will occasionally collide with those of another individual or group. In a free society each individual is free to determine for himself what he wishes to read, and each group is free to determine what it will recommend to its freely associated members. But no group has the right to take the law into its own hands, and to impose its own concept of politics or morality upon other members of a democratic society. Freedom is no freedom if it is accorded only to the accepted and the inoffensive.

7. *It is the responsibility of publishers and librarians to give full meaning to the freedom to read by providing books that enrich the quality of thought and expression. By the exercise of this affirmative responsibility, bookmen can demonstrate that the answer to a bad book is a good one, the answer to a bad idea is a good one.*

The freedom to read is of little consequence when expended on the trivial; it is frustrated when the reader cannot obtain matter fit for his purpose. What is needed is not only the absence of restraint, but the positive provision of opportunity for the people to read the best that has been thought and said. Books are the major channel by which the intellectual inheritance is handed down, and the principal means of its testing and growth. The defense of their freedom and integrity, and the enlargement of their service to society, requires of all bookmen the utmost of their faculties, and deserves of all citizens the fullest of their support.

We state these propositions neither lightly nor as easy generalizations. We here stake out a lofty claim for the value of books. We do so because we believe that they are good, possessed of enormous variety and usefulness, worthy of cherishing and keeping free. We realize that the application of these propositions may mean the dissemination of ideas and manners of expression that are repugnant to many persons. We do not state these propositions in the comfortable belief that what people read is unimportant. We believe rather that what people read is deeply important; that ideas can be dangerous; but that the suppression of ideas is fatal to a democratic society. Freedom itself is a dangerous way of life, but it is ours.

Adopted June 25, 1953, by the American Library Association Council. Endorsed by American Library Association Council, June 25, 1953; American Book Publishers Council Board of Directors, June 18, 1953. Subsequently endorsed by American Booksellers Association Board of Directors, Book Manufacturers' Institute Board of Directors, National Education Association Commission for the Defense of Democracy through Education.

How Libraries Can Resist Censorship: An Interpretation of the *Library Bill of Rights*

Libraries of all sizes and types continue to be targets of pressure from groups and individuals who wish to use the library as an instrument of their own tastes and views. The problem differs somewhat between the public library, with a responsibility to present as wide a spectrum of materials as its budget can afford, and the school or academic library, whose collection is designed to support the educational objectives of the institution. Both, however, involve the freedom of the library to meet its professional responsibilities to the whole community.

To combat censorship efforts from groups and individuals, every library should take certain measures to clarify policies and establish community relations. While these steps should be taken regardless of any attack or prospect of attack, they will provide a firm and clearly defined position if selection policies *are* challenged. As normal operating procedure, each library should:

1. Maintain a definite materials selection policy. It should be in written form and approved by the appropriate regents or other governing authority. It should apply to all library materials equally.

2. Maintain a clearly defined method for handling complaints. Basic requirements should be that the complaint be filed in writing and the complainant be properly identified before his request is considered. Action should be deferred until full consideration by appropriate administrative authority. [Upon request, the Office for Intellectual Freedom will provide a sample complaint form adapted from one recommended by the National Council of Teachers of English.]

3. Maintain lines of communication with civic, religious, educational and political bodies of the community. Participation in local civic organizations and in community affairs is desirable. Because the library and the

school are key centers of the community, the librarian should be known publicly as a community leader.

4. Maintain a vigorous public relations program on behalf of intellectual freedom. Newspapers, radio and television should be informed of policies governing materials selection and use and of any special activities pertaining to intellectual freedom.

Adherence to the practices listed above will not preclude confrontations with pressure groups or individuals but may provide a base from which to counter efforts to place restraints on the library. If a confrontation does occur, librarians should remember the following:

1. Remain calm. Don't confuse noise with substance. Require the deliberate handling of the complaint under previously established rules. Treat the group or individual who complains with dignity, courtesy, and good humor. Given the facts, most citizens will support the responsible exercise of professional freedom by teachers and librarians and will insist on protecting their own freedom to read.

2. Take immediate steps to assure that the full facts surrounding a complaint are known to the administration and the governing authority. The school librarian should go through the principal to the superintendent and the school board; the public librarian, to the board of trustees or to the appropriate governing authority of the community; the college or university librarian, to the president and through him to the board of trustees. Present full, written information giving the nature of the complaint and identifying the source.

3. Seek the support of the local press when appropriate. The freedom to read and freedom of the press go hand in hand.

4. Inform local civic organizations of the facts and enlist their support when appropriate. Meet negative pressure with positive pressure.

5. In most cases, defend the *principle* of the freedom to read and the professional responsibility of teachers and librarians. Only rarely is it necessary to defend the individual item. Laws governing obscenity, subversive material, and other questionable matter are subject to interpretation by courts. Responsibility for removal of any library material from public access rests with this established process.

6. Inform the American Library Association Office for Intellectual Freedom and other appropriate national and state organizations concerned with intellectual freedom of the nature of this problem. Even though censorship must be fought at the local level, there is value in the support and assistance of agencies outside the area which have no personal

involvement. They can often cite parallel cases and suggest methods of meeting an attack.

The principles and procedures discussed above apply to all kinds of censorship attacks and are supported by groups such as the National Education Association, the American Civil Liberties Union and the National Council of Teachers of English, as well as the American Library Association. While the practices provide positive means for preparing for and meeting pressure group complaints, they serve the more general purpose of supporting the *Library Bill of Rights*, particularly Article III which states that: "Censorship should be challenged by libraries in the maintenance of their responsibility to provide public information and enlightenment." Adherence to this principle is especially necessary when under pressure.

Adopted February 1, 1962; amended January 28, 1972 by the American Library Association Council.

Intellectual Freedom Statement:
An Interpretation of the
Library Bill of Rights

The heritage of free men is ours. In the Bill of Rights to the United States Constitution, the founders of our nation proclaimed certain fundamental freedoms to be essential to our form of government. Primary among these is the freedom of expression, specifically the right to publish diverse opinions and the right to unrestricted access to those opinions. As citizens committed to the full and free use of all communications media and as professional persons responsible for making the content of those media accessible to all without prejudice, we, the undersigned, wish to assert the public interest in the preservation of freedom of expression.

Through continuing judicial interpretations of the First Amendment to the United States Constitution, freedom of expression has been guaranteed. Every American who aspires to the success of our experiment in democracy—who has faith in the political and social integrity of free men—must stand firm on those constitutional guarantees of essential rights. Such Americans can be expected to fulfill the responsibilities implicit in those rights.

We, therefore, affirm these propositions:

1. We will make available to everyone who needs or desires them the widest possible diversity of views and modes of expression, including those which are strange, unorthodox or unpopular.

    Creative thought is, by its nature, new. New ideas are always different and, to some people, distressing and even threatening. The creator of every new idea is likely to be regarded as unconventional—occasionally heretical—until his idea is first examined, then refined, then tested in its political, social or moral applications. The characteristic ability of our governmental system to adapt to necessary change is vastly strengthened by the option of the people to choose freely from among conflicting opinions. To stifle nonconformist ideas at their inception would be to end the democratic process. Only through continuous weighing and selection from among opposing views can free individuals obtain the strength needed for intelligent, constructive decisions and actions. In short, we need to understand not only what we believe, but why we believe as we do.

2. We need not endorse every idea contained in the materials we produce and make available.

We serve the educational process by disseminating the knowledge and wisdom required for the growth of the mind and the expansion of learning. For us to employ our own political, moral, or esthetic views as standards for determining what materials are published or circulated conflicts with the public interest. We cannot foster true education by imposing on others the structure and content of our own opinions. We must preserve and enhance the people's right to a broader range of ideas than those held by any librarian or publisher or church or government. We hold that it is wrong to limit any person to those ideas and that information another believes to be true, good, and proper.

3. We regard as irrelevant to the acceptance and distribution of any creative work the personal history or political affiliations of the author or others responsible for it or its publication.

A work of art must be judged solely on its own merits. Creativity cannot flourish if its appraisal and acceptance by the community is influenced by the political views or private lives of the artists of the creators. A society that allows blacklists to be compiled and used to silence writers and artists cannot exist as a free society.

4. With every available legal means, we will challenge laws or governmental action restricting or prohibiting the publication of certain materials or limiting free access to such materials.

Our society has no place for legislative efforts to coerce the taste of its members, to restrict adults to reading matter deemed suitable only for children, or to inhibit the efforts of creative persons in their attempts to achieve artistic perfection. When we prevent serious artists from dealing with truth as they see it, we stifle creative endeavor at its source. Those who direct and control the intellectual development of our children—parents, teachers, religious leaders, scientists, philosophers, statesmen—must assume the responsibility for preparing young people to cope with life as it is and to face the diversity of experience to which they will be exposed as they mature. This is an affirmative responsibility that cannot be discharged easily, certainly not with the added burden of curtailing one's access to art, literature, and opinion. Tastes differ. Taste, like morality, cannot be controlled by government, for governmental action, devised to suit the demands of one group, thereby limits the freedom of all others.

5. We oppose labeling any work of literature or art, or any persons responsible for its creation, as subversive, dangerous, or otherwise undesirable.

   Labeling attempts to predispose users of the various media of communication, and to ultimately close off a path to knowledge. Labeling rests on the assumption that persons exist who have a special wisdom, and who, therefore, can be permitted to determine what will have good and bad effects on other people. But freedom of expression rests on the premise of ideas vying in the open marketplace for acceptance, change, or rejection by individuals. Free men choose this path.

6. We, as guardians of intellectual freedom, oppose and will resist every encroachment upon that freedom by individuals or groups, private or official.

   It is inevitable in the give-and-take of the democratic process that the political, moral and esthetic preferences of a person or group will conflict occasionally with those of others. A fundamental premise of our free society is that each citizen is privileged to decide those opinions to which he will adhere or which he will recommend to the members of a privately organized group or association. But no private group may usurp the law and impose its own political or moral concepts upon the general public. Freedom cannot be accorded only to selected groups for it is then transmuted into privilege and unwarranted license.

7. Both as citizens and professionals, we will strive by all legitimate means open to us to be relieved of the threat of personal, economic, and legal reprisals resulting from our support and defense of the principles of intellectual freedom.

   Those who refuse to compromise their ideals in support of intellectual freedom have often suffered dismissals from employment, forced resignations, boycotts of products and establishments, and other invidious forms of punishment. We perceive the admirable, often lonely, refusal to succumb to threats of punitive action as the highest form of true professionalism: dedication to the cause of intellectual freedom and the preservation of vital human and civil liberties.

   In our various capacities, we will actively resist incursions against the full exercise of our professional responsibility for creating and maintaining an intellectual environment which fosters unrestrained creative endeavor and true freedom of choice and access for all members of the community.

We state these propositions with conviction, not as easy generalizations. We advance a noble claim for the value of ideas, freely expressed, as embodied in books and other kinds of communication. We do this in our belief that a free intellectual climate fosters creative endeavors capable of enormous variety, beauty, and usefulness, and thus worthy of support and preservation. We recognize that application of these propositions may encourage the dissemination of ideas and forms of expression that will be frightening or abhorrent to some. We believe that what people read, view, and hear is a critically important issue. We recognize, too, that ideas can be dangerous. It may be, however, that they are effectually dangerous only when opposing ideas are suppressed. Freedom, in its many facets, is a precarious course. We espouse it heartily.

Adopted by the American Library Association Council, June 25, 1971.

Sexism, Racism, and Other -Isms in Library Materials: An Interpretation of the *Library Bill of Rights*

Traditional aims of censorship efforts have been to suppress political, sexual, or religious expressions. The same three subjects have also been the source of most complaints about materials in library collections. Another basis for complaints, however, has become more and more frequent. Due, perhaps, to increased awareness of the rights of minorities and increased efforts to secure those rights, libraries are being asked to remove, restrict or reconsider some materials which are allegedly derogatory to specific minorities or which supposedly perpetuate stereotypes and false images of minorities. Among the several recurring "isms" used to describe the contents of materials objected to are "racism" and "sexism."

Complaints that library materials convey a derogatory or false image of a minority strike the personal social consciousness and sense of responsibility of some librarians who—accordingly—comply with the requests to remove such materials. While such efforts to counteract injustices are understandable, and perhaps even commendable as reflections of deep personal commitments to the ideal of equality for all people, they are—nonetheless—in conflict with the professional responsibility of librarians to guard against encroachments upon intellectual freedom.

This responsibility has been espoused and reaffirmed by the American Library Association in many of its basic documents on intellectual freedom over the past thirty years. The most concise statement of the Association's position appears in Article II of the *Library Bill of Rights* which states that "libraries should provide books and materials presenting all points of view concerning the problems and issues of our times; no library materials should be proscribed or removed because of partisan or doctrinal disapproval."

While the application of this philosophy may seem simple when dealing with political, religious or even sexual expressions, its full implications become somewhat difficult when dealing with ideas, such as racism or sexism, which many find abhorrent, repugnant and inhumane. But, as stated in the statement of *Freedom to Read:*

> It is inevitable in the give and take of the democratic process that the political, the moral, or the aesthetic concepts of an individual or group will occasionally collide with those of another individual or group. In a free society, each individual is free to determine for himself what he wishes to read, and each group is free to determine what it will recommend to its freely associated members. But no group has the right to take the law into its own hands, and to impose its own concept of politics or morality upon other members of a democratic society. Freedom is no freedom if it is accorded only to the accepted and the inoffensive. . . . We realize that application of these propositions may mean the dissemination of ideas and manners of expression that are repugnant to many persons. We do not state these propositions in the comfortable belief that what people read is unimportant. We believe rather that what people read is deeply important; that ideas can be dangerous; but that the suppression of ideas is fatal to a democratic society. Freedom itself is a dangerous way of life, but it is ours.

Some find this creed acceptable when dealing with materials for adults but cannot extend its application to materials for children. Such reluctance is generally based on the belief that children are more susceptible to being permanently influenced—even damaged—by objectionable materials than are adults. The *Library Bill of Rights*, however, makes no distinction between materials and services for children and adults. Its principles of free access to all materials available apply to every person, as stated in Article V: "The Rights of an individual to the use of a library should not be denied or abridged because of his age, race, religion, national origins, or social or political views."

Some librarians deal with the problem of objectionable materials by labeling them or listing them as "racist" or "sexist." This kind of action, too, has long been opposed by the American Library Association in its *Statement on Labeling*, which says:

> If materials are labeled to pacify one group, there is no excuse for refusing to label any item in the library's collection. Because authoritarians tend to suppress ideas and attempt to coerce individuals to conform to a specific ideology, the American Library Association opposes such efforts which aim at closing any path to knowledge.

Others deal with the problem of objectionable materials by instituting restrictive circulation or relegating materials to closed or restricted collections. This practice, too, is in violation of the *Library Bill of Rights* as explained in "Restricted Access to Library Materials," which says:

> Too often only "controversial" materials are the subject of such segregation, leading to the conclusion that factors other than theft and mutilation were the true considerations. The distinction is extremely difficult to make, both for the librarian and the patron. Unrestrictive

selection policies, developed with care for the principles of intellectual freedom and the *Library Bill of Rights*, should not be vitiated by administrative practices such as restricted circulation.

The American Library Association has made clear its position concerning the removal of library materials because of partisan or doctrinal disapproval, or because of pressures from interest groups, in yet another policy statement, the "Resolution on Challenged Materials":

> The American Library Association declares as a matter of firm principle that no challenged material should be removed from any library under any legal or extralegal pressure, save after an independent determination by a judicial officer in a court of competent jurisdiction and only after an adversary hearing, in accordance with well-established principles of law.

Intellectual freedom, in its purest sense, promotes no causes, furthers no movements, and favors no viewpoints. It only provides for free access to all ideas through which any and all sides of causes and movements may be exposed, discussed, and argued. The librarian cannot let his own preferences limit his degree of tolerance, for freedom is indivisible. Toleration is meaningless without toleration for the detestable.

Adopted February 2, 1973 by the American Library Association Council.

APPENDIX II:
LIST OF
STATE EDUCATION
AGENCIES

Education Agencies—By State

Chief Specialist, Library Media
Services
State Department of Education
501 Dexter Ave.
Montgomery, AL 36130

Director, Division of Libraries and
Museums
State Department of Education
Alaska Office Building, Pouch F
Juneau, AK 99811

Superintendent's Office
Arizona Department of Education
1535 W. Jefferson St.
Phoenix, AZ 85007

State Department of Education
Little Rock, AR 72201

State Librarian, Division of
Libraries
State Department of Education
721 Capitol Mall
Sacramento, CA 95814

State Commissioner's Office
State Office Building
201 E. Colfax St.
Denver, CO 80203

Connecticut State Department of
Education
Box 2219
Hartford, CT 06115

State Department of Public
Instruction
John Townsend Building
P.O. Box 1402
Dover, DE 19901

Administrator, Library Media
Services
State Superintendent's Office
Knott Education Building
Tallahassee, FL 32304

State Superintendent's Office
State Department of Education
242 State Office Building
Atlanta, GA 30304

State Department of Education
1390 Miller St.
Honolulu, HI 96813

State Department of Education
Len B. Jordan Office Building
Boise, ID 83720

State Superintendent's Office
100 N. First St.
Springfield, IL 62777

Director, Division of Instructional
Media
State Superintendent's Office
Department of Public Instruction
Indianapolis, IN 46206

Chief of Educational Media
State Superintendent's Office
State Department of Education
State Office Building
Des Moines, IA 50319

State Department of Public
Instruction
120 E. 10th St.
Topeka, KS 66612

State Superintendent's Office
State Department of Education
Frankfort, KY 40601

State Superintendent's Office
State Education Building
P.O. Box 44064
Baton Rouge, LA 70804

State Department of Education
Education Building
Augusta, ME 04333

Division of Library Development
Superintendent's Office
State Department of Education
P.O. Box 8717
Baltimore-Washington
    International Airport
Baltimore, MD 21240

State Department of Education
182 Tremont St.
Boston, MA 02111

State Librarian
State Superintendent's Office
State Department of Education
P.O. Box 30008
Lansing, MI 48909

State Department of Education
Capitol Square Building
St. Paul, MN 55101

State Superintendent's Office
Siller's State Office Building
P.O. Box 771
Jackson, MS 39205

State Department of Education
Jefferson Building
P.O. Box 480
Jefferson City, MO 65102

State Department of Public
    Instruction
State Capitol, Room 106
Helena, MT 59601

State Department of Education
P.O. Box 94987
Lincoln, NE 68509

State Superintendent's Office
State Department of Education
400 W. King St.
Carson City, NV 89710

New Hampshire State
    Commissioner's Office
State House Annex
Concord, NH 03301

New Jersey State Department of
    Education
225 West State St.
Trenton, NJ 08625

State Superintendent's Office
State Department of Education
Santa Fe, NM 87503

Library Development
State Education Department
State Education Building
31 Washington Ave.
Albany, NY 12234

Director, Educational Media
State Department of Education
Raleigh, NC 27611

Coordinator of Library Services
North Dakota State Department of
    Public Instruction
Bismarck, ND 58505

State Superintendent's Office
State Department of Education
Columbus, OH 43215

Oklahoma State Superintendent's
    Office
Oliver Hodge Memorial Education
    Building
Oklahoma City, OK 73105

Oregon State Superintendent's
    Office
Salem, OR 97310

Chief, Educational Media
State Department of Education
P.O. Box 911
Harrisburg, PA 17126

Office of Commissioner of
    Education
199 Promenade St.
Providence, RI 02908

Consultant, Library Services
State Superintendent's Office
State Department of Education
Columbia, SC 29201

State Superintendent's Office
State Department of Education
Pierre, SD 57501

State Commissioner's Office
State Department of Education
100A Cordell Hull Building
Nashville, TN 37219

Director of Instructional
    Resources
Texas Education Agency
201 E. 11th St.
Austin, TX 78701

State Superintendent's Office
State Board of Education
250 E. 5th South
Salt Lake City, UT 84111

State Department of Education
Montpelier, VT 05602

Supervisor, School Libraries and
    Textbooks
State Superintendent's Office
State Department of Education
Richmond, VA 23216

State Superintendent's Office
Old Capitol Building
Olympia, WA 98504

State Department of Education
1900 Washington St., East
Charleston, WV 25305

Assistant Superintendent,
    Division for Library Services
Wisconsin Department of Public
    Instruction
Wisconsin Hall, 126 Langdon St.
Madison, WI 53702

State Superintendent's Office
State Department of Education
Hathaway Building
Cheyenne, WY 82002

Index

Compiled by Susan Stein